From
BROMSGROVE
TO ASTON FIELDS

A Story of Victorian Expansion

By the same author:

Victorian Greenhill, Burcot to Blackwell: The Development
of a Worcestershire Lane, Coombe Cottage Books, 2000

John Cotton: The Life of a Midlands Architect 1844-1834,
Coombe Cottage Books, 2002

For Graham and Heather

From BROMSGROVE TO ASTON FIELDS

A Story of Victorian Expansion

Jennie McGregor-Smith

BREWIN BOOKS

First published by
Brewin Books Ltd, 56 Alcester Road,
Studley, Warwickshire B80 7LG in 2008
www.brewinbooks.com

Reprinted February 2009
Reprinted August 2016

ISBN: 978-1-85858-439-3

A Cataloguing in Publication Record
for this title is available from the British Library.

Typeset in Baskerville
Printed in Great Britain by
4edge Ltd.

Contents

Preface

Frequently friends have asked me why I have been writing this book. The answer is in the word 'why'. Having lived in the area for just over forty years I found, as I drove around Aston Fields and up New Road to the town, that I wanted to know why the station is so far from the High Street, why Aston Fields is a Victorian village, why Stoney Hill has so many differently designed small houses, why does College Road have that name - the town's college is away to the north; why are Station Street and Old Station Road so called – had there been an earlier, long lost railway? Other books on Bromsgrove answered some of the questions, but no-one had written about the expansion of Bromsgrove during Queen Victoria's reign.

When I was working on my book about John Cotton, the Bromsgrove architect, I found out some of the answers, but the more I learned the more I wanted to delve further. *The Bromsgrove Messengers* of the period are a wonderful resource, for the Editor of the time reported on town meetings almost word for word. The people who appear in this book became much more real because of this, and I hope that you too will enjoy reading about some of the men who made this side of Bromsgrove and the houses they left behind.

Jennie McGregor-Smith
August 2008

Acknowledgements

The three most important sources of information for this book were film of *The Bromsgrove Messenger* from 1860 onwards, kept in Bromsgrove Library; the Cotton Collection, John and W.A. Cotton's extraordinary hoard of cuttings, Sale prospectuses and images that John Cotton presented to Birmingham Library before his death; and Tim Brotherton's large collection of photographs, Sale prospectuses and other material looked after by Bob Richardson in Bromsgrove. The crediting of sources of information has been kept to a minimum, for otherwise each page would be scattered with notes. It should be assumed that uncredited information comes from one of the above.

Many people have given their time to pass on information, particularly by letting me see early deeds of their properties or loaning photographs and postcards. The list here is long, but if I have forgotten someone please accept my apologies. Particularly generous with their time and knowledge have been Neville Billington, Ron Swift and John Weston, and as ever, Bob and Sylvia Richardson.

Richard Alton, Philip Amphlett, Tim Ayling, David Banner, Judy Bennett, Neville Billington, Birmingham City Archives, Paddy Blacker, Adrian Booth, Jeremy Bourne, Roger Brazier, Bromsgrove Library, Malcolm Brooks, Mrs Cole, Andy Cooke, Margaret Cooper, Jenny Deighton, Sir Michael Drury, Joyce Egremont, Paul & Margaret Evans, Gillian Ford, Michael Ford, Miss Goode, Mrs Griffin, Jo Halfpenny, Ann Heath, Janet and Brian Henderson, Stuart E. Hopkins, Miss Jackson, Samantha Kay, Pete Lammas, Mary Lawrance, Tony Libetta, Caroline Lynch, Margaret Macpherson, Mrs McGhie, Michele Meller, Alan Morris, Bob Moule, Jim Page, Christopher Pancheri, Miss Parker, Monica Parker, Mrs Pask-Hughes, Judy Pearce, Mrs V. Porter, David Pryke, Mary and Graham Reddie, Sylvia and Bob Richardson, Dorry Russell, Clemence Schilizzi, Severn Trent Water Ltd., Andrew Smith, Chris Steel, Harold Taylor, Joy & Nick Taylor, Philip Veale, Andy Weston, John Weston, Mary White, Jean Whittles, Diane Williams, Worcestershire Record Office, Janet Young.

Tom & Sonia French, Zoe and Gordon Long and Kate and Robin Shaw have very kindly read the manuscript, but of course remaining mistakes are my own.

Changes happen all the time, and even in the last few weeks before the printing of this book decisions have been made by Councils, developers and home owners that caused hurried alterations to the text. Thus when the author refers to present day it should be remembered that the book records what existed in July 2008.

Illustrations

Reproduction of old postcards and the author's own images have not been credited. Many postcards have been generously lent by collectors and others, particularly by Jo Halfpenny, Miss Jackson and Janet Young, to whom I am most grateful. Sections from Ordnance Survey maps are © Crown Copyright and are reproduced with permission.

Images from the following have been indicated by initials as shown below:
BR   Bob Richardson, Bromsgrove
BC   Brotherton Collection, Bromsgrove
BM   *The Bromsgrove Messenger*
CC   Cotton Collection, Birmingham City Archives
HC   Hughes Collection, Bromsgrove
OS   Ordnance Survey
RS   R.C. Swift, Bromsgrove
WRO   Worcestershire Record Office

In some cases it has not been possible to find out who owns copyright, for which I apologise.

Earnings in the Nineteenth Century

In 1830 workmen earned 11s-15s per week; the cost of building a workman's house was £70-£80. The rent was 2s to 4s per week, about a fifth of the average wage. In 1850 the average weekly wage for skilled men was approximately £1.5s and for agricultural labourers was 9s 3½d. In 1881 skilled men earned £1.10s p.w.

Bromsgrove

There is a road from north to south
 That runs through Worcestershire
And on it the old market town
 Of Bromsgrove doth appear.

It is a calm, well ordered place
 With shops and houses neat
Arranged – as an old writer says –
 In the form of one long street.

A rippling brook runs through the town
 Whose waters, bright and clean,
Flow downward from the Lickey Hills
 That to the north are seen.

In bygone times by cottagers
 Much nailmaking was done,
But other modes now supersede
 And gain what handcraft won.

Few tinkling hammers now are heard,
 Few bellows wheeze and drone,
Machine production elsewhere does
 What hands once made alone.

In days of yore what busy sights
 Of carts and gigs and wains
Were to be seen upon the roads
 Before the age of trains!

But change is active everywhere,
 Things go and leave no trace,
Town aspects alter to the view
 Like features of a face.

But still the grand old Church remains
    With tower uplifted high.
Supporting its tall tapering spire
    That points up to the sky.

A Hospital, a School of Art
    And Institute are there,
To cure men's ills or injuries
    And give their minds good fare.

There may be places in our land
    Of greater grace and worth
But I view Bromsgrove lovingly,
    For in it I had birth.

Long may it prosper and remain
    A pattern to the Shire
For quiet charm, goodwill, and all
    That worthy men admire.

John Cotton, *The Bromsgrove Messenger*, October 1931
Several verses not printed here.

Introduction

When considering New Road, Bromsgrove today it is hard to believe it was ever new. But the name in part tells its story – it was indeed *the new road to the station*, built in 1865 after many years of wrangling within the Bromsgrove corridors of power – and also within the Shoulder of Mutton [now The Wishing Well] and the Golden Cross, the Institute and the columns of *The Bromsgrove Messenger*.

Many people reading this only know New Road as it is today, but some of us remember when there was no Bromsgrove by-pass, when Fordhouse Farm still existed, and when football and cricket were played on Three Cornered Meadow before Harwood Park was but a dream in the developer's eye. There were public buildings some of us remember: the Victorian Gothic Methodist Church with its turret, on the corner of the Crescent, the Institute and School of Art where some of us were educated and which was for many years the Public Library, and especially the much loved Cottage Hospital where numberless children had their scraped legs and broken arms dealt with by nurses in smart white aprons and starched frilly caps.

There may perhaps still be a few people around who remember when in 1927 the Aston Fields council house estate was begun on the fields that were part of the Dragoon Farm. Many who remember Banner's shop in the old pub, and even more who remember the Wagon Works beyond the station, once one of the biggest employers in Bromsgrove.

So what was there before the new road? Nothing but fields and a couple of farms. The fields had names such as Nine Acres Pasture, Wheelers Close, Badgers Garden Field, and the First, Second and Third Aston Fields. In the early nineteenth century they were mainly pasture land, though there were also cherry and apple orchards. Towards the town there were 'garden grounds' – what we would know today as allotments – and even a brickyard or two.

This book aims to tell the story of the development of New Road and the eastern side of Bromsgrove, but first we must set the scene and describe the area from the time before the coming of the railway changed everything.

Let us start in the late 1830s.

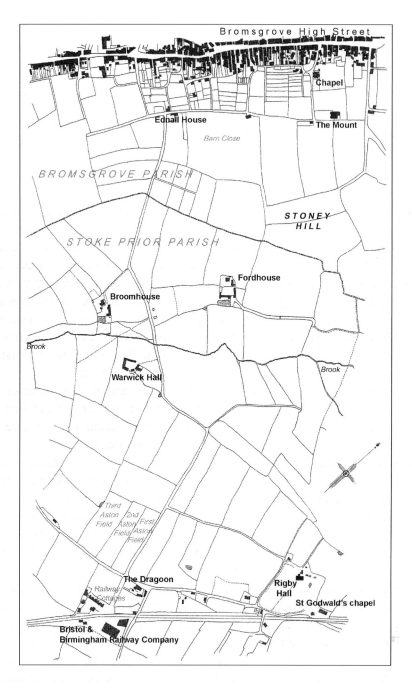

Part of the Bromsgrove tithe map of 1840, joined at the boundary to part of the Stoke Prior parish tithe map of 1846.

Chapter One

Before the Railway

Before we start we must sort out the names of Finstall and Aston Fields.

In the Domesday Book Estone (Aston) is listed, an outlying part of Stoke (Prior) in Came Hundred; the name Finstall does not appear. In the 1830s, however, there was no place known by locals as Aston – Stoke Chapel was the official name of the immediate area and sometimes it was known as Little Finstall. Finstall was at the eastern end of Stoke Prior parish and stretched widely to include the Oakalls and Slideslow farms, Finstall village and The Cross Inn, Grimley Hall and part of the canal down to the Queen's Head, Charford corn and worsted mill, Warwick Hall and Fordhouse Farms. It was not until the beginning of the nineteenth century that Aston Fields was given a separate identity, but the confusions continue, for Finstall school and Finstall church are in Aston Fields. Today the division between communities is taken to be the railway skew bridge by the graveyard.

However, in the 1830s there were three fields, part of the Dragoon Farm, called the First, Second and Third Aston Fields [where Carlyle and Middlefield Roads were built], and adjoining them on their northern border were First, Second and Top Aston Fields, part of the Warwick Hall farmland.

At this time Finstall was a large area with a small population, which was in the main engaged in working the land or servicing the needs of the farmer – cordwainers, wheelwrights, carpenters – plus a few canal workers. There were two small brickworks, one on present day St Godwald's Road and the other off Old Station Road [now under the by-pass]. Surprisingly there was no nailing in Finstall. There were also no shops so all provisions needed to be purchased in Bromsgrove on market days. The itinerant pedlar must have been very welcome.

When the railway arrived Aston Fields was tiny. The only real road was that coming from Droitwich and Stoke Prior (Stoke Road), leading up to Finstall. Little lanes or tracks led to the bigger houses and local farms – Finstall House, Rigby Hall, Finch End Farm, Upper Gambolds, Broom House and Warwick Hall. To get to Bromsgrove on market days meant following the lane that wound its way from the Dragoon to Warwick Hall Farm, then along the present Old Station Road and Ednall Lane, and down the steep hill which later became Station Street. The lane was described by George Bradfield[1]:

'There must be very few now who can remember as I do the Old Station Road, with all its country loveliness, and ornamented by its beautiful row of poplar trees, as it existed nearly 70 years ago. The poplars were swept down in one night by a violent storm, to the regret of everybody. Except for a handful of cottages at the town end it was purely a country lane leading to Finstall and the railway station.'

The centre of the hamlet in the 1830s was the Dragoon, where the tenant farmer Mr Henry Griffin served ale to passers-by and provided a useful staging post for wagons and carriages. The only other dwellings immediately nearby were three or four cottages down the road towards Rigby Hall and Stoke Chapel. This was the one

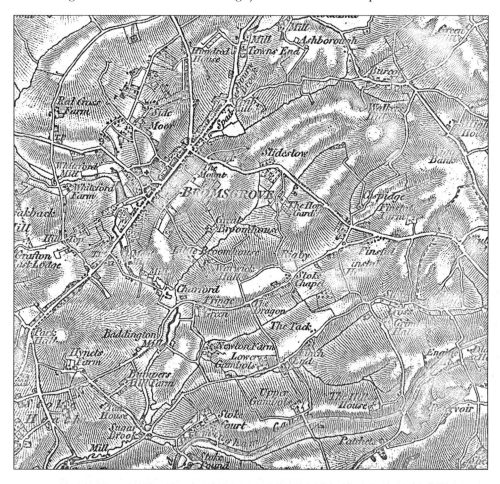

1836 map surveyed before the railway was built. For Great Broomhouse read Fordhouse Farm, The Dragon read Dragoon (now The Ladybird), Baddington Mill read Bant Mill. OS.

public building, a chapel of ease[2] belonging to Stoke Prior church, where people from Finstall and the surrounding area came to worship on a Sunday by way of the numerous footpaths that led to it. Today hardly anything of the chapel remains, which was and still is surrounded by the burial ground for the village.

This chapel, dedicated to St Godwald, was a small, plain rectangular building with simple Gothic windows and a tiny bell turret, built in 1772 on the foundations of an earlier chapel that dated back to the thirteenth century. It was Richard Brettell Esquire of Finstall House who lavished money on the little building, for which he commissioned a gallery for a choir, and seating for 130 people – probably more than enough for the inhabitants of Finstall – and a vault for his family tombs beneath the chancel. After the new St Godwald's church was built (see Chapter Ten) the chapel was used for occasional services – even weddings until the late 1960s, then for safety reasons it was demolished in 1970.

Finstall House – previously Finstall Farm – was nearby, the largest estate in the locality. It was a sandstone house built in the late 18th century, and over the years enlarged by several occupants. The Brettells, living there from 1770, were wealthy folk, who farmed their several hundred acres of land that included Caspidge and

Stoke Chapel, rebuilt in 1772 on 13th century foundations by Richard Brettell Esq. of Finstall House. There is a small bell turret on the roof. The chapel was demolished in 1970.
C.R. Sayer, 1887.

Slideslow farms.[3] Richard Brettell, a Stourbridge solicitor, became squire to the neighbourhood, higher up the social tree than George Ellins, Nailmaster, who, retreating from the smoke and nailers' slums of Bromsgrove, in 1838 built his elegant home on land purchased from Brettell.

By 1836 rumours were flying around that a new railway line was to be built in the neighbourhood, following the incorporation of The Birmingham & Gloucester Railway Company by a Parliamentary Act of 22 April 1836. Captain W.S. Moorsom was employed as surveyor and engineer to build the line. There were disagreements about the route; the great engineers Brunel and Stephenson proposed taking the line a longer, more circuitous way. However, it being cheaper to build, the B&G money-men insisted on a scheme to cut straight over the Lickey Hills to Birmingham. Thus it was the benefits to investors that determined that the new line did not go through Bromsgrove – nor Droitwich, nor Pershore, nor Tewkesbury.

Cheaper in the building it may have been, but cheaper in the running it was not, for all the expensive problems were to come when the trains ran. Land was purchased in 1839 – Messrs Brettell and Rufford, owner of the Dragoon Farm, must have done very nicely out of that – and work started. The first stretch was from Bromsgrove to Cheltenham, completed on 24 June, Midsummer's Day, 1840. Then work began on what has become one of the best known railway lines in England, the incline to the top of the Lickey Hills, 2½ miles long at a gradient of 1 in 37·7.

An engineer responsible for two of the bridges on the line, Finstall and Defford, was young Herbert Spencer, a trainee engineer who later became a famous philosopher, firmly believing in evolution before Darwin, and author of the phrase 'survival of the fittest'. There was already a small pedestrian bridge over the new railway line, to allow parishioners to reach the now isolated chapel.

Herbert Spencer's Finstall bridge of August 1840 was a replacement for another 1839 shoddily built skew bridge passing under the railway near Rigby Hall, part of the ancient roadway between Stoke and Finstall. The 19½ year old Spencer left a description of his workings:[4]

> I am engaged in superintending the pulling-down and re-erection of a large bridge under the inclined plane at Bromsgrove. It is to be completed within three weeks and four days from the commencement ... I have had to make out the drawings, estimate, etc, and to see to the details of the work during its progress. ... The contract is between one and two thousand pounds. ... [The construction was] entirely after my own designs (Capt. Moorsom not interfering in any way);

Describing the design of the bridge he said:

Finstall skew bridge built under the railway in 1840 by Herbert Spencer with 'strong timber balks'
to support the too-short girders, completed in three weeks and four days. The wall on the left (being
repaired) is against Finstall House land; Rigby Hall's white rendered garden wall is behind the
bridge; the fence on the right is against Rigby Hall orchard. C.R. Sayer 1889, WRO.

The time allowed was so small that there was no possibility of designing fit girders and having them cast. Such girders as had been designed for other purposes, and could be obtained forthwith, were consequently used. These were, however, too short to span the width of the road obliquely; and the result was a framework, partly of these girders and partly of strong timber balks, had to be made. I was a little nervous about it, but it proved strong enough.

The bridge was indeed strong enough, and lasted for fifty-four years, though as will be seen in Chapter Thirteen, it was replaced in 1894.

It is said that a thousand navvies were brought in to work on making cuttings through the sandstone, building the sandstone bridges, blasting through the hillsides and creating long embankments that towered over the surrounding fields. They certainly had to be fit to survive. All the heavy earth and stone had to be dug out with pick-axes and moved in horse-

Herbert Spencer aged 19, the
age he was when he built the
first skew bridge at Finstall.
Later he became one of
England's greatest philosophers.
Drawing by Field Talfourd.
Life & Letters of HS, David
Duncan 1908.

drawn tip-up wagons. They were a rough lot, camping by the workshops at what was to be Bromsgrove Station. In 1839 an engineer with the London & Birmingham Railway wrote:[5]

> '[Having] all the daring recklessness of the Smuggler, without any of his redeeming qualities, their ferocious behaviour can only be equalled by the brutality of their language. It may truly be said, their hand is against every man, and before they have been long located, every man's hand is against them.'

While another more charitable viewpoint comes from a Congregational minister who, maybe wearing rose coloured spectacles, wrote:

> 'The navvies, bare-throated, their massive torsos covered but by the shirt, their strong, lissom loins lightly girt, and the muscles showing out on their shapely legs through the tight, short breeches, and ribbed stockings that surmount the ankle-jacks, are the perfection of animal vigour.'

Mothers of young girls must have quaked!

But the drunken, riotous men were here for a surprisingly short time; only three months later the line was open to Cofton Farm, and by mid December 1840 it reached the Birmingham Camp Hill terminus, and the railway was really open. Aston Fields was then to become a very different place.

Chapter Two

The First Years of the Railway

There were three sets of buildings at Bromsgrove Station: the usual public booking office and waiting room, a ladies' waiting room and even an earth closet; there was a row of neat workmen's dwellings known as Railway Cottages, and across the line were the engine sheds and wagon repair workshops.

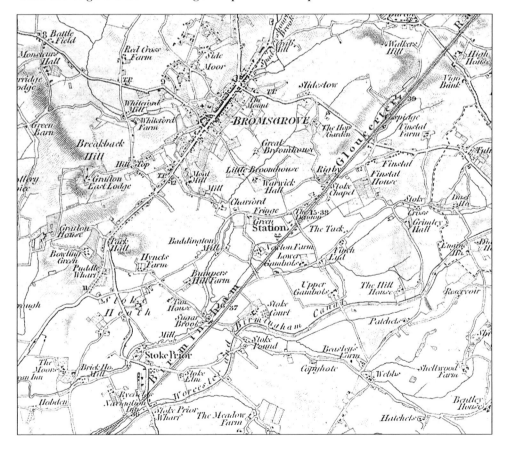

The railway was added in 1840 to this map originally surveyed in 1832, engraved and published at the Ordnance Map Office at the Tower of London. For Great Broomhouse read Fordhouse Farm.

Waiting for the train on Bromsgrove Station c.1880 showing the footbridge.

It was with much excitement that the first trains were seen puffing along the flat from Cheltenham, halting until a banker was in place and then beginning their slow progress up the Lickey Incline. That all sounds very easy, but in reality it was not, and it was a very dangerous process.[6] A bank engine is a locomotive that if pulling is temporarily attached to the train, but usually is pushing, unattached, from behind. The incline was very steep. A passenger train might take only about seven minutes from bottom to top at Blackwell, but the freight trains, being so much heavier, sometimes needed as many as three bankers which had, of course, to return to the station to be prepared for another trip. This caused difficult logistical problems on what was a mainly double track line, and the operations needed much manpower.

One day in 1840, before her marriage, the young Queen Victoria 'passed through Bromsgrove Station, going to Birmingham,' Dr Fletcher wrote,[7]

'and the train was halted to fasten on the extra so-called "bank" engine, which pulled trains up to Blackwell. Mr Scroxton took his camera and hoped to obtain a photograph. But alas! His only result was a picture of a lot of smoke and the top of a first-class railway carriage door.'

At Bromsgrove there was a siding where the bankers waited, with coal store and water laid on. When an Up train arrived the policeman on duty rang his bell and one of the big American Norris engines moved along the centre line in the station to the Up line, waiting under the bridge to be coupled to the front of the coming train. On whistled signals from both drivers they would set off up the incline. After the laborious drive the banker would go over the summit until the tail of the train was over the top. The bank engine then had to be uncoupled *with one hand* by the fireman who had to climb from his cab, over his tender, to the buffers, and then the engine had to turn off to a siding – when the pointsman had to change back the points to the main line. All this with the train still running behind them, albeit slowing down. Fortunately in 1842 James McConnell invented a slip coupling so that firemen could uncouple by pressing a foot lever. Once there were three or four of the Norris bankers at the top they were coupled together for their descent back to Aston Fields.

Even more dangerous was the down journey. Here coal-laden wagons were such a weight that they could have ended up hurtling down the incline – and occasionally did, overshooting the station. Trains from Birmingham had to halt and shut off steam at the Linthurst (Blackwell) bridge, stopping dead by a white marker post. Two brakesmen operated the brakes on every third or fourth wagon, then travelled with the train and were in charge on its journey downhill. After the cautious descent, with a 20 mph speed limit for passenger trains and 10 mph for goods trains, all totally reliant on the brakes, the train went into a siding and waited until the brakes were released.

A goods train passing over upper Finstall bridge c.1901, climbing the incline towards Blackwell.

It was an obligation for railway companies to provide housing for their workers, and the row of a dozen cottages built near to the station buildings was very necessary. Six months after the railway opened there were 21 workers, some with their families, living in these cottages. The youth of the men is notable – most of them were between 25 and 30 years, earning their wages in this new exciting world mainly as engine fitters, engine drivers, engineers, with a book keeper, a brazier, and the station Inspector. The brakesmen lived in a smaller row of cottages at the top of the incline by Blackwell station. Later in their history the Bromsgrove railway cottages became known as Bug Row, but at the beginning of their life the cottages were of

The Stationmaster's house high above Station Approach, a well appointed house with splendid stone gateposts, appropriate to the Stationmaster's position. RS.

Bug Row, as the Railway Cottages were known in their latter years; they were condemned in 1970. Built for the first railwaymen in 1840 they would have been cheaply built, yet at the time served an important role in providing homes for the workers in a hamlet with very few houses. This view is of the backs, which faced the railway; entrance was from the bottom of Station Approach. The station bell is on the post. RS.

reasonable standard, probably better than the agricultural labourers' cottages on local farms. They were demolished in the 1960s.

Also living in Railway Cottages was Hannah Rutherford, aged 30, with her two children aged 4 and 2. The 1841 census was taken a few months after the dreadful explosion of the tank-engine Surprise that killed her husband Joseph, the Works Foreman. Memorial stones to him and to Thomas Scaife, killed in the same accident, can be seen in Bromsgrove Parish church graveyard. I wonder how long Hannah was allowed to live in Railway Cottages, whether she received compensation, or if the little family were turned out onto the streets.

The same year Superintendent William Creuze, when very drunk, was scalded to death by steam spray from a botched repair; his grave is in St Godwald's chapel graveyard.

These three accidents were the most publicised of many that happened on the railway, which were partially caused by the long hours expected of the railwaymen. *The Messenger's* reports of nasty accidents to the Bromsgrove men were unpleasantly regular – almost every month there was an 'incident' which would have crippled a man. As late as 1880 a guard on another railway was asked by a Royal Commission what compensation was paid by his Company to widows – his reply was 'I believe the compensation they receive is a nice coffin'.[8]

The third group of buildings, and the most important to Bromsgrove, was the locomotive works, then known as the Engine House. Captain Moorsom decided that the obvious place for the repair yard and engine factory would be at the lowest point of the Lickey Incline. His plans were unfortunately reduced in scale and content by the Company money-men, and so when the Cheltenham-Bromsgrove line opened there were minimal facilities and little equipment. The disasters leading to the deaths of Rutherford, Scaife and Superintendent Creuze were all an indirect result of cheeseparing and poor safety practice; but the bad publicity from these accidents pushed the Company into employing a 26 year old Irish engineer called James McConnell. It was the energetic Superintendent McConnell who rescued the Company.

Under McConnell's leadership the engine stock was greatly improved, notably by his design for a powerful locomotive named *Great Britain*. He also designed a pair of goods engines, *Bristol* and *Hercules*, which lasted for some fifty years. Apart from new rolling stock McConnell also persuaded the Company to build him a house, set almost under the bridge on St Godwald's Road.

McConnell's house played a part in the forming of a new institution for mechanical engineers. Although railway engineers belonged to the Institute of Civil Engineers they found it held too broad a brief and did not give them opportunity to circulate new ideas and theories amongst themselves. One day in 1846 McConnell and other engineers, including it is said, George Stephenson, were watching engine trials on the incline; a shower of rain sent them into a platelayer's hut, where the idea of forming their own institution was mooted. On returning to McConnell's house plans were made, and the following January the Institution of Mechanical Engineers held its inaugural meeting in the Queen's Hotel in Birmingham, electing Stephenson as its first President and McConnell as Chairman. In 1997, 150 years later, the President of the Mechanicals placed a commemorative plaque on the wall nearest to the site of the house.

Although a Listed building, the Chief Engineer's house was demolished in the late 1980s. The wrought iron balcony, upon which it is said George Stephenson stood to survey the incline, can now be seen fixed to the frontage of Bromsgrove Museum[9] at Davenal House, Birmingham Road, saved by Dennis Norton when the house was demolished. The demolition was necessary to allow a new bridge to be built to replace the narrow St. Godwald's Road bridge, strong enough to carry the heavy vehicles needed to clear the Wagon Works site, in readiness for building the new housing estate. The demolition of the old bridge on the night of 3 July 1988 was an event that drew a large audience to watch the explosion.

Water supply became a problem in the 1850s; the wells on site were found to be impure and were furring up the engines, so McConnell ingeniously piped purer water from Pikes Pool, half way up the incline. Shortly afterwards he built a stone reservoir on the opposite side of the tracks which provided enough water. He also built a gas works on the wagon works site, and in 1846 laid a pipe to Blackwell to serve the station; not only that, he sold the remaining surplus to the Bromsgrove Gas Company.

After a few bad months when lack of money meant the workshops were closed, the Birmingham & Gloucester in 1847 amalgamated with the Midland Railway who reopened the works. This then became one of its most important carriage and wagon sites, and for the next twenty years the business thrived, known now to all as the Wagon Works. The same year McConnell left Bromsgrove to further his career at the LNWR at Bletchley. He is remembered not only as a great inventor and engineer, but also as a humanitarian determined to improve safety on the railways.

The house built for Chief Engineer James McConnell, showing the small balcony on which it is said George Stephenson stood to survey the Lickey Incline on the day the Institution of Mechanical Engineers was conceived. RS.

Chapter Three

A New Road?

When the railway arrived habits and customs of Bromsgrove people changed. Previously all traffic depended on roads – Bromsgrove has no navigable river, and the canal, four miles away, though used for some carrying, was not convenient for general household or small commercial travel. The most important turnpike road, later becoming the A38, passed along Bromsgrove High Street leading to Birmingham and the Black Country in the north and Worcester in the south. The other turnpike roads were to Alcester, Kidderminster and Stourbridge; all others were small local lanes that wended their way round fields to outlying farms and cottages.

Carriers took people and goods to and from Birmingham, Worcester and local towns, working from the Coach and Horses by the Alcester Road [now Stratford Road] and the Crown [near where Woolworths is today]. Stage coaches transporting travellers passed through the town daily, and there was a carriage for hire at the Crown, while those who could afford it kept their own horses and small carriages. However the prime means of transport for most people was their own two feet. It was quite normal for people to walk from Tardebigge, for instance, to come to Bromsgrove Market – though doubtless hitching a lift if they could from a passing wagon. Employees of the railway who lived in Bromsgrove and Sidemoor daily tramped along lanes or footpaths through the fields to reach their employment.

When the station opened there was a new opportunity for carriers, and soon there was a service from the Golden Cross to the station, leaving 20 minutes before each train was due to arrive. The charge in 1854 was fourpence, while first and second class passengers to Birmingham who were carried to and from the station were charged nothing. In the 1850s there was a one-horse omnibus; Dr Fletcher remembered:[10]

> 'The railway omnibus ran backwards and forwards to the railway station to meet most of the trains at the station a long mile off. A bell with a rope attached was hung at the entrance to the yard, outside the coffee room window. It was vigorously rung five minutes before the omnibus started to meet the trains, and woe betide the boy who for mischief pulled that 'Railway Bell' and ran away. But as all the "likely" boys were well known, his punishment was only postponed.'

A turn of the century photograph of two horse-drawn railway omnibuses waiting outside the Golden Cross in the High Street. Note the bicyclist and the gas lamp, acting as a sign-post, known as the Hallelujah Lamp because Salvation Army meetings were held beneath it. The patterns on the road were caused by the water cart, which daily sprayed the road to keep down the dust.

According to The Stroller who wrote in *Berrows Journal*, the horse bus then 'crawled along narrow and devious by-ways, a fragment of which in later days became known as Old Station Road.'

The railway service that by the 1870s ran from Bristol to Birmingham, via Gloucester and Cheltenham, provided trains thirteen times a day Bromsgrove to Birmingham, the Bromsgrove 8.17 morning train arriving in Birmingham at 9.15am, with eight stops on the way. This compares with today's similarly timed train which reaches Birmingham in 35 minutes with two stops on the way.

Not everyone was pleased about the railway. The Worcestershire writer John Noake in 1868 wrote:[11]

'It was a gloomy day for the little old town of Bromsgrove when the coaching era came to an end [which was] a high road for at least a score of coaches *per diem*. A sorry substitute for this liveliness and bustle, gossiping and tippling, money-spending and travelling accommodation, was afforded by the railway being laid at a distance of a mile or two from the town.'

Station Street with gas lighting. Note the three boulders, and the narrowness of the entrance to Worcester Street between the Wheatsheaf Inn (right) and the 'Merchant's House', which in 1964 was moved to Avoncroft Museum of Buildings. The chimney of Bolding's Brewery is on the left, behind the Dog & Pheasant in Worcester Street.

The big problem for all horse drawn wagons and carts was that the only way from Bromsgrove to the station was to go through a narrow opening – it could only have been about 8 or 9ft wide, with a very cramped access – and up the steep, slippery, cobbled 1 in 11 hill of Station Street to Ednall Lane. Dr Fletcher in 1930 remembered:[12]

> 'I am utterly unable to describe it. ... its rough, unkempt condition – very narrow and steep, the surface all uneven and bumpy, little or no footpath for the walkers, and rough in every sense of the word.'

There were regular accidents, especially after heavy rain or when frozen in winter. In February 1863 *The Bromsgrove Messenger* reported, under the heading 'The Station Road Again':

> 'An accident occasioned by the narrowness and steepness of Station-street, and which might have been attended with fatal results, occurred on Thursday morning last. One of the vehicles plying between the town and the Railway Station came into

collision with a cart, the consequence was that the two hind-wheels were knocked off, and the body of the cart fell to the ground, causing the horse to plunge violently; fortunately the occurrence took place opposite the Police Station [which was then in Station Street], so that assistance was promptly rendered and the two ladies occupying the cart were removed from their perilous position, frightened but not otherwise hurt.'

It was incidents like this that made the Local Board members begin to accept that they really should build a direct road from the town to the station. A prime agitator was Samuel Yates, the estate agent, who was largely responsible for pressing for the passing of the1846 Parliamentary Act allowing for the improvement of the town roads; but as is the way with local authorities, still nothing was done.

The Local Board met at the Town Hall [demolished in 1928] and was made up of town worthies elected by ratepayers. They were responsible for collection of rates to be used among other things for gas lighting of the town, fire engines, some planning applications and – most expensive and important of all – drainage and maintenance of roads. An early mention of the problem in *The Messenger* is an 1861 Local Board report (twenty years after the station was built) when:

> 'a plan was submitted to the meeting for widening and repairing the road above the Police Station; the subject was deferred in the hope of making, at some future period, a new street direct to the Railway Station.'

This sounds, of course, just like the usual politicians' prevarication, and it seemed to succeed for a while, but in January 1863 the Rev. Dr. Collis, headmaster of Bromsgrove Grammar School [now Bromsgrove School] and very influential personage in the town, wrote to the Local Board:

> 'calling attention to the wretched condition of the road leading from the Railway Station into the town. The advisability of making a new road was mooted, and the consideration of the subject adjourned to a future meeting.'

Rev. Dr. J.D. Collis, member of the Local Board and the Burial Board, Headmaster of Bromsgrove Grammar School 1843-1867. Holy Trinity Church, Stratford upon Avon.

This letter did have the right effect, and pretty strong opinions started flowing through the letters to *The Messenger,* some in a surprising way. In

February Messrs Scott and Horton, Solicitors brought a proposal to the Local Board 'offering to produce plans for ... a new line of railway from the station to the town, [comparing the costs with] making a turnpike road'. Cost of course being everything, the Board was now in a quandary – and the subject was dropped until the next meeting when the town railway plans were shown. These proposed a town station in Worcester Street, below the Grammar School, near the Old Malt Shovel Inn (opposite Gas Square and Factory Lane), one mile and eighty three chains from the present station. The line would run across Kiteley's field (a large meadow which later came into the possession of Bromsgrove School), and pass near to Fringe Green.

Throughout 1863 until June 1864 the arguments raged. The Rev. Dr. Collis said that 'with a good approach by a new road [from the station] they might hope to have gentlemen's houses built so that the town might become a suburb of Birmingham, ... to reside here for the benefit of the pure air, beautiful country walks, and fine views.'

Others wrote: 'At this go-ahead age it is surprising that persons can be found so blind to the welfare of the town as to bring a Highway in competition with a Railway' and 'a railway is the only thing that will fully meet the requirements of the town.'

Local Board members Mr Wm. Frances (butcher and farmer) and Mr Wm. Llewellin (grocer and maltster, whose land abutted Station Street) were sent off to Derby to try to persuade the Directors of the Midland Railway Company to put money towards a branch line; they were not successful and the proposal was rejected.

The Board therefore returned to the proposal for a road, and reported that 'in almost every case the landowners over whose property the road is destined to pass, have generously offered as much land as will be required'.

A plan for the new road was prepared for the Local Board by Mr. J. Strick, civil engineer from Aberdare, showing a line of entry to the High Street either opposite Hanover Street (rejected) or at the Hop Pole (approved), though at the end of the meeting Dr Collis, Chairman, placed in the hands of the Clerk a written protest: 'I beg to record my formal protest against the destruction of the Hop Pole Inn, as being one of the great ornaments of the town.' However, negotiations went ahead to buy and demolish the beautiful building.

The proposed width of the road worried the Board, and during a meeting their surveyor Mr Wilmot went out to measure the High Street (33 feet at the measured point), to convince the gentlemen that 35 feet (10.5m) was sufficient. Mr Strick's plan was for a road 35 feet wide, with a 10 foot (3m) wide footpath; it would be 1 mile, 14 chains and 72 links (1½ kms) long; later plans straightened and thus reduced the length. The steepest gradient would be at the point leaving the High Street, and would be 1 in 15½, and a 10 foot (3m) cutting would be made through

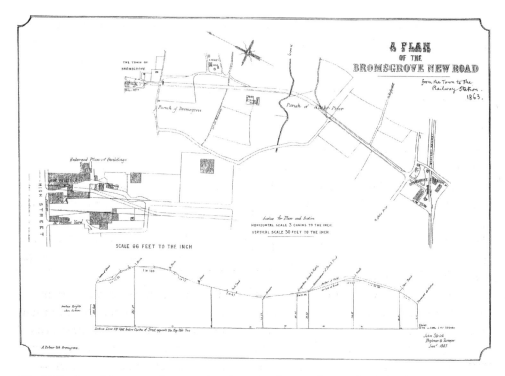

The 1863 plan of the proposed new road to the station by Mr John Strick of Aberdare. Gradients show the brook by Wellington Road at the lowest point, and proposal for a cutting where Marlborough Avenue would later meet New Road. The highest point is at the site of the barn in Barn Close belonging to Bromsgrove Grammar School. Strick has drawn the road's connection with the High Street to come through the Hop Pole Inn. The hand-written note is by John Cotton. CC.

the hillside – the reason for the still-standing blue brick walls on the southern side of the road.

'Progress' wrote to *The Messenger* in March grumbling that Mr Strick's plan had cost £30, that Mr Wilmot's services would not be gratuitous, and that 'it appears to me that the ratepayers' money is being recklessly spent, for it must be apparent to every one that the value of the old Hop Pole premises cannot be one-half so great as that of the new house occupied by Mr Stafford and Mr Frances's house, both of which it would be necessary to purchase if the entrance to the town is to be made there.'

Public meetings were held, and in April 1864 several worthies called a meeting of Ratepayers, encouraging them to vote onto the Local Board the following: Mr. T. Day, Clerk to the Board of Guardians; Mr W. Cotton, Surveyor and Auctioneer; Mr G. Willis, farmer at Charford; Mr Jas. Parry, nailmaster, and Mr W. Lamb, Innkeeper (of the White Hart, Hanover Street). The notice read:

'Ratepayers be present on the occasion, and vote only for [these] Gentlemen who, if elected, will prevent any useless expenditure of your money ... The Local Board persist in their determination to expend at least THREE THOUSAND POUNDS of your money, in making a New Road'.

The public meeting having 'condemned the course taken by the members of the Local Board', the Board asked for a Government Inquiry which took place in June 1864. Before the end of July the Secretary of State for the Home Department gave authority for a loan to the Board of £3,000 to defray costs of purchasing property and for constructing the road. The battle was won – at least the first part of it.

Not that that decision quieted the grumbles. Dr. Collis continued to insist that the Hop Pole should not be demolished, but in February 1864 the Local Board decided to sell the property in three Lots with no reserve: Lot 1 to consist of the entire front of the house; Lot 2, the remainder of the house, and Lot 3, the stablings and out-buildings, etc. in the rear.

The Hop Pole was not only a fine building but an historic one, having been erected in 1572 by Walter Brooke, whose initials were (and still are) on the centre gable. An 1836 description[13] made these comments:

'The framing of the timber is curiously decorated with scollops, flowers and leaves, and has good effect. The carving on each of the three gables is very rich, but barbarous in design, partaking very greatly of that mongrel kind of ornament, between the Gothic and Italian styles.'

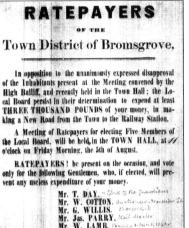

1864 poster calling a Ratepayers' Meeting to object to the costs of a New Road from the Town to the Railway Station. Notes against the names in John Cotton's hand: Mr T. Day – Clerk to the Guardians; Mr W. Cotton (John Cotton's father) – Auctioneer, Worcester Street; Mr G. Willis – Charford; Mr Jas. Parry – Nail Master; Mr W. Lamb – Farmer & Innkeeper, Hanover Street. CC.

William Cotton (1822-1874), Auctioneer, Surveyor and Estate Agent. Father of John, William Alfred and Ernest Brewster Cotton. BC.

Quoting from a paper[14] given by William A. Cotton in 1881: 'Dr Collis … had induced Mr. Hopkins of Worcester, who had had considerable experience in such matters, having lately put up the roof of the old Guesten Hall, in Worcester … to come and view the Hop Pole'. Hopkins indicated that driving the road through an archway in the Hop Pole was not sensible, but, he said the Hop Pole was 'undoubtedly the best specimen of ancient domestic architecture in the county' and should be saved. Mr Hopkins estimated that the house might be taken down and rebuilt, and the lower storey fully restored, for a sum under £1,000.

To the conservationists' relief it was found that there was just enough space in land purchased by the Board for the Hop Pole to be rebuilt on the new road at a near right

HIGH STREET, BROMSGROVE.

TO ANTIQUARIANS, BUILDERS, & OTHERS.

TO BE SOLD BY AUCTION, BY
C. STEEDMAN,

ON WEDNESDAY, the 5th day of April, 1865, at Three o'clock in the Afternoon, on the Premises, subject to conditions, all the Valuable

TIMBER, DOORS, WINDOWS,
AND
BUILDING MATERIALS,

Comprised in that Antique and Handsome Building known as the

"HOP POLE INN,"

Now in the occupation of Mr. G. Quemby, and Premises adjoining, in the occupation of Mr. G. Gunner, in the following Lots :—

Lot 1 comprises all that Antique and Handsomely TIMBERED FRONT, with WINDOWS, DOORS, &c.

Lot 2.—The whole of the Valuable TIMBER and BUILDING MATERIALS, WINDOWS, DOORS, &c., comprised in the DWELLING PART of both Houses.

Lot 3.—The whole of the TIMBER and BUILDING MATERIALS comprised in the BREWHOUSE, STABLES, OUT-OFFICES, WALLS, &c.

The Auctioneer begs to state that nearly the whole of the above Timber is Oak, of large dimensions, and sound ; and as the same must be removed to make the road to the Railway Station, the whole will be Sold without the least reserve.

Left: William Alfred Cotton (1853-1889), reluctant auctioneer and passionate local historian. Son of William Cotton, younger brother of John Cotton, step-brother of Ernest Brewster Cotton. He was Secretary of the Institute in the High Street, wrote 'Bromsgrove Church' in 1881, and bequeathed money towards the cost of the Institute in New Road. BC. Right: Bromsgrove Local Board's 1865 poster announcing the Sale of Lot 1, the frontage of the Hop Pole; Lot 2, the timber and building materials, windows, doors, etc.; and Lot 3, the timber and building materials of the brewhouse, stables, out-offices, walls, etc. Lot 1 was sold for £350 before the Sale to a sub-committee of the Board, formed to deliberate on whether the Hop Pole should be saved. The Old Houses of Bromsgrove, W.A. Cotton.

The Hop Pole Inn in its original position in the High Street. Mr Gunner the ironmonger was in the shop on the right side of the building, and the alleyway beyond was access to the rear buildings of the inn. BC.

angle to the High Street, at 'which it would form a handsome ornament'. At this point the Bromsgrove Branch of the Worcester City and County Banking Company (later Lloyds Bank) came on the scene with 'enterprising liberality', and in 1866 the façade was re-erected at a cost of about £2,000 by Richard Cook, builder of Worcester Street.

Below: The Hop Pole rebuilt in New Road as a bank, showing the 1864 new porch and ground floor windows. The upper storey shows restored detailing which has since been lost. The oriel window (left) was new as was the attached building on the right, the Bank Manager's house, which later became Parry's menswear shop and is now an estate agent's premises. BC.

The framework of the Hop Pole being rebuilt after demolition, under the eye of W.J. Hopkins, Diocesan Architect from Worcester. BC.

Saved it might have been, but, as George Bradfield wrote in 1930:[15]

'Think of the vandals who destroyed the Hop Pole. The beauty of the front of that old inn can never be replaced. No amount of argument will convince me that the building erected on the New Road (Tudor House, as it is called) can be regarded as a substitute for the old inn. The most that can be said for it is that the best was done with the materials available. I deny that the Hop Pole was reconstructed, or anything approaching it, and the photograph I have of the place before its demolition proves my assertion without controversy.'

Inevitably the carvings restored or added by Mr. W.H. Wildsmith, furniture broker of the High Street, give the building a Victorian 'look' – the porch was added, and heights adjusted so that large windows could be inserted on the ground floor. The huge oriel window was also new. Joining the 'old' building was built the bank manager's house, in similar style (currently Andrew Grant Estate Agent). One of Mr Hopkins' assistants on this project, drawing plans of the original building, was the young John Cotton (older brother of W.A. Cotton) who later became Bromsgrove's own architect.

The Hop Pole (now Tudor House) in 1928, offices of Hugh Sumner, Hedges & Luce, Auctioneers and Estate Agents. The small building alongside was built as the strong room for the previous owner, the Worcester City & County Bank. This photograph, used as an advertisement, has had all trace of adjoining High Street buildings removed.

The celebrations for the opening of the New Road in 1865 brought hundreds of people into Bromsgrove, who watched a procession of about 350 people headed by the Town Crier, members of the Local Board, the Yeomanry Band, and the Oddfellows and Foresters. The day was completed by dancing and 'kiss in the ring' in the evening. WRO.

While all this was happening the road was being built and was opened on 18 July 1865, almost exactly a year from the day the decision was made. The town celebrated. There was a procession of the Odd Fellows and the Foresters, the Town Crier, and even Robin Hood and his Merrie Men, plus some 350 people wearing holiday attire, and:

> 'the large number of visitors to Bromsgrove from the adjoining district, together with the turning out of nearly the entire population of the town ... caused a great throng in the streets. ... Many of the houses were gaily decorated with flags and banners ... the church bells rang merrily at intervals, and business and work ... seemed for a time at a standstill.
>
> The most prominent feature of the procession was no doubt a decorated chariot which contained a stuffed lioness, with attendant axe-bearer and archer, representing "Courage", and a live pet lamb, with a wreath of flowers and ribbon round its neck, attended by five little girls, dressed in white, as shepherdess and maids, representing "Innocence".'

After the formalities of speechmaking members of the Board passed over the whole length of the road in a brake drawn by four horses. *The Messenger* reported that the road was 'rather soft and rough, and consequently heavy for cattle, but the passage of every vehicle over it will help to improve it. At present it is not in a fit state to enable an impartial person to form an opinion from actual use.'

This road was not built as roads are today. Confusingly, tarmacadam was not invented by J.L. MacAdam, (1756-1836), but was a much later process named in MacAdam's memory.[16] It seems, however, that MacAdam's previous system was used for the new road, simply because of the speed at which it was built. His process was very simple – the materials for the road were laid on nearly flat land. On roads 16ft (4.9m) wide the middle of the road would only be 3 inches (7.5cm) higher than the verges. A layer of stones about 6 inches (15 cm) deep was laid and either rolled or exposed to traffic to consolidate them, and if these were clean, they would interlock as a flexible, hard-wearing surface. This achieved, a further layer was laid on top and if possible rolled. MacAdam's roadstone had to be jagged pieces between 1-1½ inches (38 mm), no heavier than 6 ounces (170 gms), which had been broken by seated men wielding small hammers. A brass ring-gauge two inches (5 cms) in diameter was used to test the size of the stones. It was an unpleasant task known as 'knapping', hated by the road gangs and used as a prison punishment at Dartmoor, though rock crushing machines had been introduced by the 1860s.

As the Editor of *The Messenger* implied, roads needed weight to weld the stones together. Horse drawn road rollers were still in their infancy and may well have been too costly for the Bromsgrove budget; steamrollers were not used in Britain

Mr Clarke, innkeeper of the Golden Cross, driving his four horse brake at the Grand Opening of the New Road on 19th July 1865. The Chairman of the Local Board, W.A. Greening, grocer, has his back to Mr Clarke; the other occupants are members of the Board with their wives.

until the end of the 1860s. Thus the new road would not be in 'a fit state' until numerous wide wheeled heavily laden carrier wagons had passed up and down for some months.

Footpaths or footways were another matter. Although there was considerable foot traffic up New Road the footpaths, such as they were, were not comfortable, as one correspondent to *The Messenger* wrote:

'the Local Board might do something in the way of improving footways in the New Road so as to render them a little more tolerable to people like me with tender feet and not rich enough to pay for a ride. I suggest a thin layer of fine gravel gas-tarred with a slight top dressing of sand or dust would answer admirably and save a good deal of individual suffering.'

By 1889 the footpaths were in a bad way, and the Board discussed asphalting them, Mr Lewis remarking that if that were done 'they would do well to have a competent man to superintend the work'. However the meeting abandoned the idea on grounds of expense.

It is probable that the macadamised new road would have lasted until the early 1900s, when the needs and problems of vehicles with pneumatic tyres (they sucked up loose stone chippings, broke the road surface and created dust clouds) would have meant repairs by the tar-macadam process.

Drainage was also simple in MacAdam's day – a gully on each side of the road, though where the water went we won't ask! However by 1868 the drainage of water from the road was helped by insertion of 6 inch (15 cms) pipes. Also at that time there was discussion about lowering the Black Hill by Marlborough Avenue, for heavy wagons pulling up from the town found it steep; this however would have cost a minimum of £400, and the discussion quickly closed.

Chapter Four

Before the Road –
Bromsgrove and Stoney Hill

'Where this New Road now comes in there was formerly a wide passage leading up a broad yard to a rustic footpath between high banks up to what we knew as the School "Barn", passing there over Mr. Skidmore's premises – a carpenter with a good business – and passing his private house recently built on the left hand side, before one came to the bowling green belonging to the Bell Inn.'[17]

(The barn belonging to Bromsgrove Grammar School [Bromsgrove School] was directly in the route of the New Road. Mr Skidmore's house was probably Oak Cottage, which is described below.)

Before looking at developments after the new road was built, comment should be made on some notable houses on the east of Bromsgrove built before 1865. There were very few houses of any size by then, probably because the land just behind the High Street and its courts full of nailmaker's cottages and workshops was gardens and orchards. Even as late as the 1880s maps show small plots which were rented out for cultivation, rather in the way that allotments work today. Until the new road most Bromsgrove businessmen with aspirations to become gentry had moved west or southwards along the turnpike roads.

The grandest of the few eastward houses was The Mount [now known as Wendron], built for the nailmaster

The Mount (now Wendron), built in the early 19C, extended and given its side Venetian window overlooking the fields of Stoney Hill by John Cotton in 1874. The home of the Green family, nail masters all, who until the early 1890s also owned fields to the east. Bromsgrove School bought the property and changed the name in 1921.

James Green in the 1840s with extensions by John Cotton in 1874 for his son, William Green. Wendron, having been a Bromsgrove School house for some years, is now owned by Worcestershire County Council. The Greens' land extended east, north of Chapel Walk to what became later the centre of College Road.

Slightly nearer the High Street, and less grand, was Windsor Cottage, built immediately south of the Independent Chapel [now the United Reformed Church] and its Schoolhouse (1852). Windsor Cottage [now Windsor Street Car Park and Windsor Gardens] was probably built and certainly lived in during the late 1850s and early '60s by the Yates family, Samuel, his wife Marianne, little Frederick (who became an architect) and his three siblings. Samuel Yates was at this stage advertising himself as a 'house and general agent and law stationer', though in 1856 was not only offering small villa residences to let but also offering loans from £50-£500. By 1860 he opened an office in St John Street as an auctioneer, appraiser and estate agent. He was an arch wheeler-dealer, as we shall see.

In 1869 Mr Yates sold the 'pleasant house and garden' with 11 cottages forming Windsor Square, and moved to The Cedars in New Road which he had built, while Mrs Catherine Horton moved in to Windsor Cottage until 1880. William Holyoake, solicitor, then moved into Windsor Cottage – now Windsor House – moving from Elmshurst [see

Windsor Cottage, later Windsor House, built near to the Congregational Chapel. Lived in first by Samuel Yates, auctioneer and surveyor. Miss Appleby of the High Street ironmonger's shop was living there in 1961 when Windsor Street was pushed through, and the house was demolished. BC.

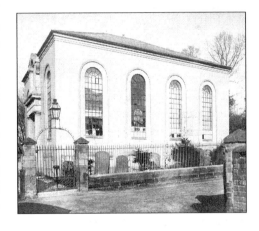

The Congregational Chapel (now United Reformed Church), built in 1832 on the site of an earlier chapel of 1693 – sandstone remnants are on the north side of the building. John Cotton added an organ chamber and renovated the chapel in 1887-8. There is a 1968 roundel window by Hardman dedicated to A.J. Davies, the stained glass artist who worked with the Bromsgrove Guild. BC.

Stoney Hill, below] for his wife Emma to run a school for half a dozen youngsters aged 7 to 14. The Holyoakes lived there until 1903 when William died, with main carriage access to their house up Chapel Lane from the High Street; after 1865 Windsor Street was taken through to the New Road, though very narrow. Windsor House was demolished in 1961 when Windsor Street was widened from New Road and pushed through to Alcester [Stratford] Road, demolishing the long row of cottages on its way. Also demolished was Scott & Horton's office building on New Road itself, which John Cotton designed in 1872 with a canted corner for wagons because the entry to Windsor Lane was so narrow.

Ednall House (later The Lion House because of an 1805 cast iron lion placed on its porch, now removed for safety) was built in its current form in the late eighteenth century. It is the last house in Ednall Lane, on the corner of Hill Lane which leads back down to Worcester Street. It started off as a fine farmhouse (at one time known as Pickering's Orchard), with deep cellars, fruit trees, duckpond, stables and pigsty. In the 20th century the then owner invested in new plasterwork ceilings made by the Bromsgrove Guild whose workshops were round the corner in Station Street.

The above three houses were built by successful Bromsgrove tradesmen, showing their status by moving from the High Street where most of their

Ednall House (by 1891 also known as The Lion House) on the corner of Ednall Lane and Hill Lane. Previously a farmhouse, it was the home of William Llewellin, maltster and grocer, from 1865 until his death in 1869, followed by his daughter Mary, married to Oswin Willcox, High Street draper, until her death in 1882.

The lion that used to sit on the porch of Ednall House, giving it a second name of The Lion House. Reputed to be of Napoleonic origin, c.1805.

peers were still living. However the first sign of a new order, ownership of property by the working class, was shown by the creation of the Stoney Hill estate.

Stoney Hill was one of the earliest developments made possible by The Bromsgrove, Stoke Prior and District Building Society. This was part of a movement found in many parts of the country, aiming 'to enable small capitalists to obtain Allotments of Land at the best possible price' on which to build their own houses.

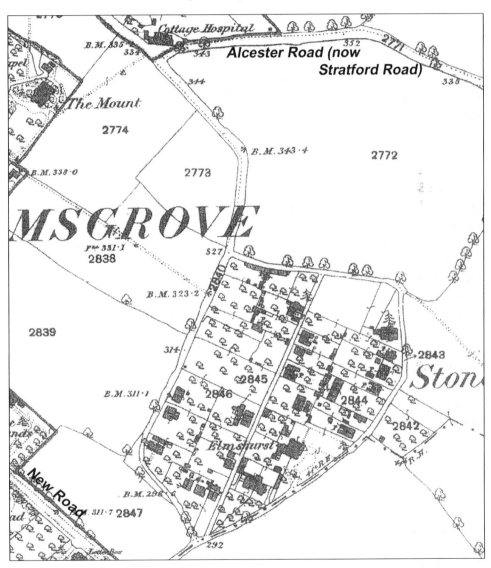

From the map surveyed in 1883. Note that all buildings are within the circle of road round Stoney Hill. The Thomas White almshouses have not yet been built, nor College Road, but the letter box, still by the Cedars Lodge, is already in place. OS.

Individual members paid 2s (10p) per share once a fortnight in cash to the Society Secretary in his office at the Literary and Scientific Institute in the High Street. When there were sufficient funds the organisation purchased building land that was then allotted (i.e. divided and pegged out into plots), and then a ballot was held and a beneficiary was granted the necessary advance to buy a property. Often the members subdivided their plots and a pair of houses was built, one to live in and one to rent out. The Building Society also aided its shareholders by advancing money on mortgages and helping with solicitors' fees. A similar system of lottery was used in the 1840s by the Chartist movement when Feargus O'Connor's Lowbands, O'Connorville, Snigs End and other Chartist estates were built – Dodford being different, for there the cottage plots were allocated to the highest bidder.

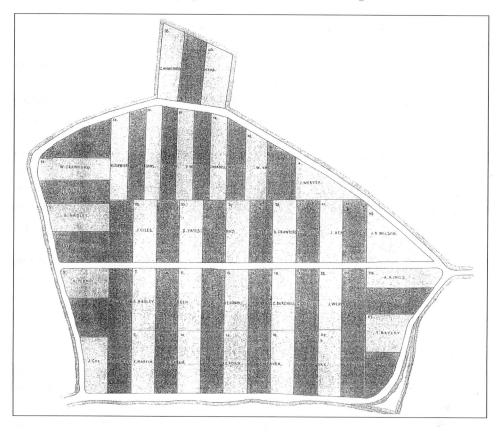

Plan of the Allotments of Stoney Hill Estate with the names of the allottees. The two fields were bought by the Bromsgrove, Stoke Prior and District Building Society and its 61 shares were apportioned on 16 January 1860. Very few of the allottees ever lived in houses built on their land; nearly all of the plots were sold on, or houses were built to rent out. WRO, BA 848.

The Bromsgrove, Stoke Prior and District Building Society bought the two Stoney Hill fields from John Topham in 1859, and the 61 apportioned shares were balloted on 16 January 1860. The individuality of the houses on the plots can be seen today (though many more recent homes have been built between the original houses). However, it would seem that the aim of providing artisans with the ability to build their own homes was not the way that many Bromsgrove men saw the scheme. Of the 34 allottees (some had more than one lot) only three took their families to live on Stoney Hill. Other allottees were clearly in the scheme for the profit, including Samuel Yates, J.B. Wilson, Sampson Weaver the innkeeper and investor in property, town clerk Thomas Day, and Enoch Hadley of the Brooklands. Many plots were sold on to builders who, as builders do, kept the land until there was a need for housing in the town. So one probably unforeseen result of the Building Society's work was that the housing and land stock became greater than the need, despite the many incomers arriving in Bromsgrove to work on the railway. Indeed, in 1883 the number of dwellings on Stoney Hill – 53 – had increased by only two houses in twenty years.

Other Building Society estates included Crabtree Lane (1862, 22 plots), Sidemoor (1862), two off Old Station Road (28 plots in 1863), two sites at Aston Fields (78 plots in 1871 and 1872), Bewell Head and Lowes Hill, Stourbridge Road and Newtown (Victoria and All Saints Roads). Thus some 350 plots over thirty years – say availability for 500 small dwellings – must have meant a superfluity of building land. Gradually this enlightened system was virtually taken over by knowing builders, estate agents (the Cotton brothers among them), surveyors, solicitors and well-breeched traders who as members purchased and resold multiple allotments. The organisation was wound up in 1890.

Stoney Hill land was a more-or-less triangular shape, determined by the two fields on which the houses were built, the roads unnamed for many years until they were not very imaginatively christened East, West and Middle or Central. Access was by a lane from the Alcester turnpike road, the lane encircling the estate with all buildings within the narrow roadway. The western side of Stoney Hill's road was not built on until after the sale of Mr George Dipple's land in 1894, which opened up College Road and offered plots for building that reached to Stoney Hill, with a promise to widen West Road to make it more accessible. The eastern border of the estate was the Bromsgrove/Stoke Prior parish boundary, which was not built upon until after World War II. That new build was on a field belonging to Fordhouse Farm, naturally considerably lower than the Terrace of early East Road, explaining why there are two levels.

Most of the dwellings on Stoney Hill were suitable for artisans or railway workers, many of them built several years after the apportionment, and there were

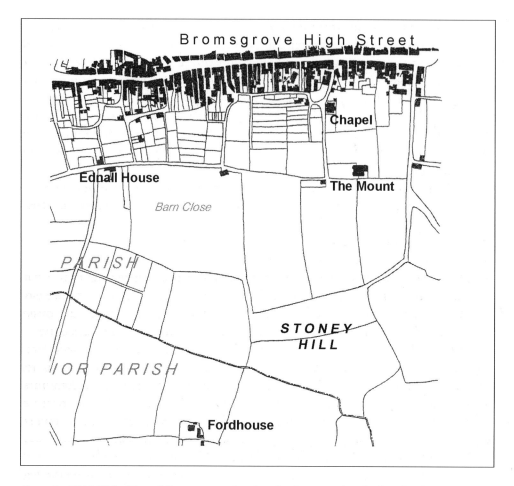

From the 1840 Tithe Map of Bromsgrove, showing the Congregational Chapel, The Mount, Ednall House and the not-quite-triangular shaped fields of Stoney Hill. The New Road to the station was to run through the barn shown in Barn Close, and to the east of Fordhouse Farm.

only seven families living on the estate in 1861, including one family of nailers – 43 year old Edwin Manning, his wife Ann, Edward aged 16, Charles aged 11, all four described as nail makers. The two youngest children were Thomas aged 7 and Pamela aged 3. There is no trace of any members of this family anywhere in England in the 1871 census.

Families living on their own plots in 1861 were those of carpenter William Sarson, carpenter Thomas Bailey and George Hanks, bricklayer. By 1871 there were 45 families, 42 of them renting, including Miss Emma Johnson, who was running a boys' school. There was then one nailing family, Hayling, and 23 families relying on the railway for their weekly wages, thirteen of them carpenters (regarded in the railway yard as superior beings). Henry Hedges, of the blacksmith family, was living here before moving up to Aston Fields.

There were four larger houses on Stoney Hill. The Landscape, on the corner of the Terrace, now East Road, and what is now North Road, was built on four plots extending back to Central Road, probably built in the late 1860s for renting out by Charles Field senior, of the milliner's and

The Landscape (No.39 East Road) on the right built in the 1860s by Charles Field Snr., Bromsgrove High Street draper; it was extended (left) and is now two dwellings.

draper's establishment in the High Street. Charles Field himself lived next door in Belle View Villa from 1866 – and a beautiful view it was, overlooking the fields towards Tardebigge church. His son, Charles Field junior, another man busily buying and selling land for development, eventually settled in The Landscape.

The second large house, Elmshurst [now Oakley House], was built by William Holyoake, where his new wife, Emma Johnson, moved her 'preparatory school for young gentlemen' for a few years before they moved to Windsor Cottage. Elmshurst was the first house planned by John Cotton and cost £1,850, built by Brazier & Weaver. When in its prime it was rather splendid, but has sadly now lost its chimneys

and had unsympathetic additions to the rear. However the 1875 date-stone with Holyoake's initials and oak leaves, the little animal heads on the porch arch dripmouldings and a winged griffin waterspout are still to be seen – typical of John Cotton's quirkiness. Elmshurst continued as a school, run by Rev. F.W. Parsons until a retired British Indian civil servant, William Hart MA, born in India, as were his four children, took the house for a few years in the early 1890s. At some point the house was bought by the Llewellin family, who were living there between 1897 and 1901, when William Llewellin died.

Carved stone dragon, a rainwater spout, funnelling water from the porch of Elmshurst (Oakley House).

After that Mrs Elizabeth Whitley and her young son Charles were in residence between 1901-1905 (see Broom House, Chapter Seven); in 1909 widow Elizabeth Llewellin unsuccessfully put the house on the market, successfully selling it in 1914. Elmshurst once again became a school, under Mr A.J. Davies. It was bought as a school house by Bromsgrove School and renamed Oakley in 1917, and in 1926 G.H. Gadd designed an extension to the rear dormitory building. During WWII, while Bromsgrove School was evacuated to Llanwyrtyd Wells, the house was taken over by the government as a hostel for evacuees. Bromsgrove School returned after the war, and used it as a preparatory school under John and Fay Webber until 1959 when Cobham was built on Broom House fields. Nowadays Oakley is divided into flats.

Architect John Cotton's drawing of Elmshurst, built in 1874 by Brazier and Weaver for William Holyoake and his wife, where she ran a preparatory school for young gentlemen until 1881. Bought then by William Llewellin, lived in by William and his son Roland until William died in 1903. Renamed Oakley House in 1920 as a Bromsgrove School house. CC.

Above: The Firs (left) and The Ferns (right) in 1910, directly behind the group of little girls. This post card shows the steep unmade road, the Terrace, that led to Elmshurst (Oakley House) and The Landscape. The road to the left is already signed West Road. In the 1950s a new road was built below the Terrace road to accommodate the new East Road houses. On the left, building is taking place of the two pairs of houses built in 1910.

Also bought by the school to be lived in by staff was The Ferns, the first on the Terrace, a semi-detached house next door to Elmshurst/Oakley. It was built in 1879, its partner being The Firs. The Ferns had a chequered career, being run as a boarding house for its first twelve years by Mrs Louisa Skidmore for young gentlemen tradesmen. For a couple of years around 1905 Mr Albert Iles, the organ builder and piano dealer, lived there and the widowed Mrs Llewellin was there in 1908. Following her came John Henry Green, who worked in cahoots with Eliza Tinsley the legendary Black Country nailmaster, while The Firs next door was the home from 1901 of William Mason, with mutton-chop whiskers and a white ear trumpet, who

Stoneleigh, East Road, one of two pairs of houses built in 1910 on land previously owned by Thomas White. The two people are Celestino Pancheri and his wife Florence, who married soon after they met at Bromsgrove Horse Fair on 24 June 1908, only a few months after Celestino arrived in Bromsgrove. Celestino was one of the most important artist craftsmen of the Bromsgrove Guild. J.Halfpenny.

was the last nail manufacturer in the town. He died in 1935 but the family warehouses in the High Street and Worcester Road were still working in 1937.[18] Many years later Bromsgrove School sold the two houses and they were demolished; a block of flats took their place.

The estate was now getting quite heavily built up – the 1881 census lists 54 households, though there was not much movement by the 1901 census, which lists 56. Many of the men worked on the railway. In 1882 problems with services came to the fore. 'The drainage!', wrote the Editor of *The Messenger*, 'It is known to every medical man in the town that practically there is no drainage at all, and that the water supply [which would have been from garden pumps] is not only defective but polluted'. The residents were naturally not pleased. The story of Bromsgrove's drainage problems ran and ran, and letters to *The Messenger* were frequent and heated, but more of that in a later chapter.

In 1889 Miss Terry, then living at Elmshurst, wrote to the Town Board complaining about the poor condition of the Stoney Hill roads. The Board huffily responded that it was not responsible for repairs because the roads were not of statutory width.

Chapter Five

A Burst of Building near the Town

The new road (still known as *the* new road, as it is even now to some older inhabitants) suddenly opened up access to land to the east of the town, an opportunity gradually taken as people realised the potential for building. There had been considerable buying and selling of plots of land for the ten years before the road was built, and once it was opened there was a burst of building, particularly by James Skidmore, a High Street carpenter builder. In 1862 he managed to purchase from William Frances and others several small parcels of land which he joined together for three properties – a pair of houses, then Oak Cottage and Sunny Lawn. These were on the east side of the road, just above the bank manager's house [now Andrew Grant's premises] and little Windsor Lane. Others involved in property deals along this stretch were John Horton, solicitor and Samuel Yates, whom we met earlier and will keep on meeting.

Oak Cottage was rented by Skidmore to young James Green the grocer, whose business premises were at the Market Place. This house, its position shown on Mr Strick's plan of the road in 1863, was the first to be built. Next in line is Sunny Lawn, rented first to James Laughton, insurance agent and nail manufacturer. Slightly later the four bedroomed semi-detached houses were built, known as Laurel Villas [now they are used by an accountancy firm]. Next to them, and on the corner of narrow little Windsor Street, Messrs Scott & Horton built new offices [demolished when Windsor Street was widened in 1961].

From the map surveyed in 1883. OS.

A photograph taken in 1961 from the School of Science & Art, showing the Hop Pole (renamed Tudor House), and next to it the shop converted from the Bank Manager's house. Next are the offices built in 1872 for Scott & Horton (taken down in 1961 when Windsor Street was opened up), then Laurel Villas, originally dwellings but now offices. The building in the foreground is the house now used by an estate agent. BR.

Renting of larger homes was much more usual than it is today, and most of the nineteenth century houses we shall be looking at were speculative building. A surveyor, estate agent, solicitor or builder would purchase land, either as an individual or in a group, build the house or houses, and then put them up for sale or to rent. Equally, a successful tradesman would realise that property was a safe investment, and once the mortgage was paid off the income from one or two houses could bring in enough to provide a pension for old age. When James Skidmore died in 1879 the sale of his New Road houses would have provided his widow with ample capital to keep her in respectable comfort.

Both Oak Cottage and Sunny Lawn still outwardly look very much as they were built. Oak Cottage is very simple with a slate roof and plain brick pilasters on each corner, four bedrooms, a bathroom, a large cellar and other conveniences. The bay windows and shutters were later additions. John R. Horton, solicitor, bought Oak Cottage at the Skidmore Sale and his mother lived there until 1893

Oak Cottage (No.13), built in 1863 by Mr James Skidmore, before the building of the New Road. BR.

when it was sold to Benjamin Sanders for £810. Dr Cameron Kidd rented the property, persuaded Sanders to build a coach house, and began the tradition of a medical house. A surgeon, he became Chairman of the hospital in 1915, a responsibility he soon gave up after the loss of his youngest son Leonard, who died in Flanders very soon after winning the Military Cross. After Dr Kidd's death in 1935 the Doctors Gaunt arrived to live in the house until the '80s when it was bought by the County Council, later selling it on for offices, as it is today.

Sunny Lawn is also of red brick, a little smaller, a three-bay house with central front door. John Cotton bought the house after the sale of Skidmore's estate in 1879, and gave it the verandah, porch, bay windows and the oriel window above the entrance. When he bought it there was no bathroom, nor did Laurel Villas have one, though they all had 'necessary outbuildings'. Sunny Lawn continued to be rented out in Cotton's ownership, and on his death in 1934 he bequeathed it to Bromsgrove Cottage Hospital across the road, hoping it would be used for a nurses' home. The Hospital decided it could not use the property, and so it was sold. It is still privately owned, and one of the few in the lower part of New Road that is lived in as a home.

Sunny Lawn (No.15), built by 1871 and rented by Mr Skidmore to Mr James Laughton, nail manufacturer and Registrar of Marriages. BR.

The next property, its garden about three metres above Sunny Lawn, and again showing on Mr Strick's 1863 road plan, was built for Samuel Yates the estate agent of Windsor Cottage, who in 1852 had cannily purchased the land, which previously was the bowling green of the High Street Bell Inn. Here as soon as the new road was opened Yates built the house and offered The Green for sale in 1866. This was a house on a grander scale than those lower down the hill, with larger grounds and there was a possibility of purchasing orcharding behind and to the side. Coincidentally Mr Samuel Saywell, running a boys' school in the High Street, wanted to expand and he seized the opportunity. Soon he had built schoolrooms and dormitories behind the house, and by the 1871 census he had fourteen boarders aged between 8 and 14. He renamed it Bromsgrove Collegiate School, later to be called The College or, unofficially, Saywell's Academy. The school thrived, with local boys as well as boarders, growing in number every year. Although Saywell himself retired from active teaching in 1908, he continued living in the big house (temporarily renamed The Elms), with the school behind, which carried on until just after his death at the end of 1914.[19]

The College house, with its beautiful view over the smoke of Bromsgrove to St John's church spire, was built with seven bedrooms, had a tiled verandah at the front and a large entrance hall, with tessellated tiled flooring. The carriage entrance was where the gateway is today, just up the entrance to what is now known as College Walk.

The College, previously known as The Green. When it became a Bromsgrove School house in 1921 it was renamed Elmshurst. The College, run by Samuel Saywell, was often known as Saywell's Academy. The photograph shows the big extension behind, which was built for dormitories and classrooms. BC.

Samuel Saywell took a great part in the life of Bromsgrove, as did so many of those mentioned in this book. There was a strong tradition for anyone of note in the town to take part as a member of the Town Board, the Board of Guardians (the Poor Law Union), or be on the committees of educational establishments, churches and charities. They didn't always agree, which make *The Messenger* columns fun to read, though there were of course many matters - for instance the terrible lives of the nailmakers on whose efforts the wealth of the nailmasters rested, which took many unhappy years to solve.

After the sale of Saywell's properties in April 1915 the Austin Motor Company bought the premises for an Engineering College, but in 1921 sold the College to Bromsgrove School, who brought down their boys from Elmshurst on Stoney Hill and changed the name of the College to Elmshurst. Within a few years,

Samuel Saywell, in 1909, retired Headmaster of The College, New Road.

paraphrasing Bourne,[20] The College became Elmshurst; The Mount on Chapel Walk was bought for the school and became Wendron; Elmshurst on Stoney Hill became Oakley; and Oakley on the corner of New Road and the Crescent became Lupton. One has great sympathy for the postman.

The remainder of the College sale, which included the playing field upon which College Road was built, will be the basis of a later chapter.

One of the personages of the town was Thomas Day, who in the sixties was a land agent and Clerk to the Poor Union, living at Davenal House in Birmingham Road [now housing a doctors' surgery, the Museum and the Tourist Information Office]. His son, Ernest Augustus, was 20 in 1866 and had just completed two years articled to the Birmingham architect Edward Holmes. He was taken on as assistant to his uncle, Henry H. Day of Worcester, but began to practise independently in Bromsgrove at the same time. E.A. Day planned only four buildings in Bromsgrove, two being the Parish Rooms for All Saints Church and, with F.J. Yates, the recently closed Meadows school in Stourbridge Road. The others, built in 1866, were also his first two commissions – a villa for James Lea, Overseer to the Local Board and Surveyor, who previously lived on Station Street at Waterloo Cottage, and a very

The Newlands in 1900, built in 1866, architect E.A. Day, for Thomas White Esq., J.P. and lived in by him until 1908, when it was bought by Victor Drury of the Boot Factory. Sir Michael Drury.

superior villa for Thomas White of the Indigo Factory, called The Newlands.

This is an impressive first house – Day was a lucky young man to be able to plan such a splendid property for his first commission. Set well back from the road it is a classically influenced building with a splendid porte-cochère-style portal – not large enough for a carriage to drive through, but for Bromsgrove a decidedly grand entrance. Most noticeable is the eaves-cornice below the roof, and similar decoration to the porch. From College Road can be seen an attractive triple window, but unfortunately the chimneys have lost their decorative collars.

Thomas White, who previously lived in Worcester Street, was a partner of Captain John Adams who built Perry Hall and owned a woollen and cotton yarn business working from the Cotton Mill, as well as the Indigo and Dye Works near Watt Close – from where the Spadesbourne ran blue with pollution. The 'old blue works' were demolished in November 1901. In 1858, due to his industry, White inherited Adams's works and wealth, and so in 1866 Mr White was able to buy land from William Frances and, wrote Dr. Fletcher,

The garden of The Newlands in 1913 showing the fine conservatory and lily pond. Sir Michael Drury.

> 'built himself a capital house on the north side of the New Station Road. … I knew him well, and had the greatest respect and admiration for him – all the more when I learnt in later days of several noble munificent acts of liberality and justice which he performed from a simple keen sense of honour, which marked his character throughout his whole life.'[21]

After the death of Thomas White in 1908 the house and land alongside was put up for auction. Two busy Bromsgrove businessmen were bidding – slightly embarrassing because they were friends. Victor Drury, boot and shoe manufacturer of Worcester Road, bid up to £998. John B. Wilson, grocer and corn merchant, made the next bid, which bought The Newlands for £1,000. Unfortunately Mrs Wilson was not pleased and refused to live in the big house, so Wilson offered it to Drury for the same price. 'No' said Drury, 'I will pay no more than £998' – and his offer was accepted. Drury moved round the corner from Hillcrest in College Road, and lived at The Newlands until about 1943 when his grandson Dr Drury, later Sir Michael, continued the family presence and had his medical practice in the house. One of Victor Drury's improvements in 1913 was to ask J & A Brazier to build an engine house with a gas engine generating plant to convert gas to electricity, and a motor house (garage workshop) with an inspection pit – he was one of the first motor car owners in Bromsgrove, two others being Messrs Brazier and Goodman; they all had motors in 1905. Dr Paddy Blacker moved into The Newlands during the mid 1970s and the enlarged practice built an ugly separate surgery on the site of Victor Drury's motor house [now Nancy Doyle Clinic] staying until 1994 when the New Road Surgery moved up the road to the empty Waterworks building.

James Lea's villa Fernleigh was smaller, built across the New Road from The Newlands. Lea was a bit of an inventor, and he patented seats and stands for use by 'invalids or weak travellers who experience great inconvenience by reason of the shock to the system, which is received from the vibration of busses [sic], trams, railway carriages, cabs, and other vehicles'. These cushions and stands had springs inside, and were particularly recommended as seats for Bath-chair users or as supports for railway engineers and guards. He lived at Fernleigh until he died in 1904, when he willed his home to the Cottage Hospital; it was sold for £720. [There is now a block of flats on the site which keep the original name.] In part of the building – probably over the stables – there was a school where Miss Ellen Johnson lived between 1879 and 1883, with two teachers and a cook, aiming to educate five girls aged between 7 and 15. The maps show Fernleigh to be a small building in comparison with other houses in the road; one wonders where they all slept! At any one time throughout the period of this book there were about

Fernleigh built in 1866, architect E.A. Day, for James Lea who lived in it until his death in 1904 when he bequeathed it to the Cottage Hospital. Behind the house can be seen the roof and chimneys of Sunnymead. Note the size of the trees, which were planted in New Road in 1878 in honour of Lord Windsor's coming of age.

six small schools, run usually by widows and their unmarried daughters as a means of making some income. They usually lasted only a few years, and to us today it seems very surprising that young girls were sent away from home to be taught by such untrained women.

Shortly after A.E. Day's houses were built came another, Highfield House, up above the road. Here Miss Amelia Taynton and her friend another Miss Johnson also ran a boarding seminary for young ladies, sixteen girls between 9 and 15; in 1881 most of them came from Birmingham. By the end of the 1880s the school was closed and Highfield House became a private home. This has also been demolished to be replaced by smaller dwellings and a block of flats.

Just lower than The Newlands came Holly Lodge, built in 1872 and lived in by Mr Alfred Palmer, printer and engraver, book and music seller, and publisher-editor of the *Bromsgrove, Droitwich and Redditch Weekly Messenger, County Journal and General Advertiser*. This newspaper was first published in 1860 and, as Leadbetter[22] says 'ever since has proved an accurate reflector of the total life of Bromsgrove … Bromsgrove will always be indebted to its editors for their interest in the history of Bromsgrove, and for the publication in its columns of much historical information.' And so say all of us! Leadbetter goes on to list all the editors, including Eric Belk (1940s and '50s) who many will remember – though my own early memories are of the kindly Lionel Wheat (1970s).

Mr Palmer died or left Bromsgrove in 1878, and John Cotton, auctioneer, estate agent and architect, sold Holly Lodge by auction together with a piece of building land opposite, both bought in at £1,850. Holly Lodge itself is now much extended, known as Wayside residential home.

On the land opposite Holly Lodge a pair of houses was built by Braziers in 1898 for the widow Mrs Bolding. She lived there with her daughter and son-in-law Joseph Fitch, J.P., Bailiff of the Court Leet in 1896. He carried on the family tradition of brewing at the large Bolding Brewery behind the Dog & Pheasant in Worcester Street, which they owned. Garlisters, on the corner of the Crescent, and its twin, Oakley, were built with no expense spared, having the latest mahogany fittings in the bathrooms, oak block floors and costly gates hung on stone pillars with

Holly Lodge (now Wayside Residential Home) built in 1872 for Alfred Palmer, printer and publisher of The Bromsgrove Messenger, *which from its beginning in 1860 has taken an interest in local history.*

Lupton House in 1978, a pair of houses previously known as Garlisters and Oakley, built in 1898 on the corner of New Road and The Crescent for Mrs Bolding and her son-in-law Joseph Fitch of Bolding's Brewery. In 1920 they were bought by Hugh Bateman-Champain, famous Gloucestershire cricketer, used as a Bromsgrove School boarding houses and renamed. J.C.Page.

Bath stone caps. In 1920 Oakley was bought by F.H.B. Champain – Hugh Bateman-Champain, the then famous Gloucestershire cricketer – who built new latrines and renamed it Lupton, opening it as an Out-House for Bromsgrove School. Champain was followed by Major Ernest Mashiter as Housemaster, and soon both sides of the house were amalgamated, remaining as part of the school until it was sold in 1979, to be developed for flats.[23]

In 1878 Bromsgrove celebrated the coming of age of Lord Windsor of Hewell Grange by planting an avenue of lime trees up New Road, from the Hop Pole to Marlborough Avenue. The trees did well, too well for the 1954 District Council, who started a programme of felling the 76 year old trees because roots were thrusting through the tarmac.

In the 1870s the only buildings on the west side of the road were Fernleigh and Sunnymead (discussed in Chapter Nine), but soon shops began to creep round the corner from the High Street. Mr William Jefferies had already taken the prime corner site, as grocer, tea dealer and provision merchant, and his warehouse

William Jefferies of Battlefield House and Charford Lodge, grocer and tea dealer on the New Road High Street corner, painted by his son E.C. Jefferies in 1869. Mr Jefferies died in 1896, his son Frederick taking over the business.

Drawing of Sunnymead by architect F.J. Yates, built in 1873 for James Parry, retired nail factor. It was quite a grand house, with seven bedrooms and two dressing rooms, drawing room, dining room, breakfast room and all the latest in kitchen facilities. There was a stable and coach house, kitchen garden and orchard. See Chapter 9 for more information. BC.

behind was built before the New Road. Messrs J.B. Wilson bought the premises in 1950/1951, and in 1953 Spain's radio shop moved from the High Street and opened in the first of the three lock-up shops, and bought the warehouse for storage. By the 1970s the corner shop became the National Westminster Bank and between Spain's and the bank a brick-walled strong room was built. As this is written Spain's is one of the very few privately owned shops left in central Bromsgrove.

The second shop was a jeweller's, opened for a short time by Mr Greene, and taken over between 1898 and 1900 by Mr Rose, describing himself rather

The corner of New Road and High Street in 1975. Mr. Jefferies the grocer owned these premises for many years and built the tall warehouse behind. When the National Westminster Bank took over, a brick-faced strong room was built against New Road and can be seen in the photograph. BC.

No.3 New Road, showing a fine collection of clocks for sale. Run between 1898 and 1900 by Mr J.W. Rose, this was one of the shops later bought by Mr Spain. HC.

unbelievably in the directory as 'jeweller and monumental mason', and living in the cemetery lodge. He was one of the legendary Rose family who for several generations had been vergers of St. John's. This shop was also bought by Mr Spain.

In the 1950s De Greys restaurant of the High Street opened a snack bar in the third shop, followed in 1957 by Hilda White who renamed it the Windsor Café, with permission to play music from a radiogram between 8.30am and 10.00pm, 9.00pm on Sundays. After closure of some years it reopened as the Phoenix Café, known for its bacon butty breakfasts – but sadly that flame died out rather soon.

Beside the shops were entries to two small squares of nailmakers' cottages, and behind

No.5 New Road, a restaurant during the 1950s and 1960s. The Phoenix Café opened after the closure of De Greys Snack Bar and the Windsor Café. BC.

50

these was the abattoir. As this is written the abattoir, once a hive of activity behind Partridge the butcher's shop, is being brought back from dereliction. It was built at the time when every butcher had a small abattoir behind his shop, and often had pigsties as well. Here beef cattle would be led from market, penned in the yard, then killed, hung and prepared for sale, all on the same premises.[24] After the closure of the abattoir a car sales operation used the yard behind, which is now a car park.

Next up the road was a small brick building with a large window and small door, corners and door surround in white glazed bricks, used by solicitors Cresswell and Russon. Much later it was the offices of the Registrar of Births and Deaths, then was the office of the National Farmers Union, and was pulled down in 1994. At this time there was talk within the District Council of making an inner ring road by continuing Windsor Street through the back areas of the High Street buildings, emerging in Worcester Street. Fortunately this did not come to anything, the group of shops was refurbished, and the New Road car park opened where the nailmakers' cottages had been.

The house (No.8), now used as offices for John Sanders estate agents, was built at the beginning of the 20th century as a private house, and was lived in for some years by the Bowen family who ran the glass and china stores at 71 High Street.

Later houses in our period include Nos. 20 (Wayside) and 22 (Ellerslie), and Nos. 21 (Westview) and 23 (Sunnyside), almost opposite each other and all built

The old abattoir behind Partridge's High Street shop, where meat was killed, hung and prepared for sale. Most butchers had their own abattoirs and pigsties until the mid-twentieth century, when this one was closed and used for other purposes.

No.6 New Road, an odd looking building. The white plastered wall hides the house behind, now demolished. Solicitors Cresswell and Russon used the building, as did several other small businesses. BC.

Wayside (No.20) and Ellerslie (No.22), built about 1882 and photographed in the early 1900s. HC.

about 1882. Ellerslie from the beginning incorporated No.20, for it was used as a Methodist ladies' school. It was run by Mrs Gray and her four daughters, all in their thirties, though 'school' seems a grand name for an establishment with only ten pupils. All boarders, the girls ranged from 10 to 18 years, some coming from homes quite a distance from Bromsgrove. The school continued until at least 1908, longer than most of the dame schools of the period. Following its demise the house was used in succession by numerous Wesleyan ministers until at least the 1940s. By some strange quirk of history the drains from Victoria Villas in the Crescent passed through the garden of Ellerslie, causing some problems for future owners.

Over the road Westview (No.21) was also used as a ladies' school between 1897 and 1903, run by Miss Emily Whitehouse, her father Henry, a retired farmer, her mother and brother; there were only three boarders aged 12, 13 and 14, so it is possible that other young ladies attended who lived in Bromsgrove. The house was built by 1883 and lived in between 1889 and 1891 by James Amiss the grocer and tea dealer in the High Street. Later occupants were there for similarly short periods until Frederick S. Jefferies, grocer from the corner of New Road, moved in in 1927 staying until the 1940s; he was Bailiff of the Court Leet in 1935, described as a 'dapper friendly little man with a "pork pie" trilby hat and flower in buttonhole'. During periods of shortage he regularly took to the Unionist Club some very tasty cheese which, cut into squares, he shared around. Very brief occupants during WWI were the Brookes family, whose son, Eric Guy became a pilot of the Royal Flying Corps, was awarded the DFC, and was killed in action in 1918. [Westview is now occupied by a chiropractor.]

Sunnyside (No.23) appears only once in censuses and directories – in 1901 when the popular Dr. Richard Wood lived there briefly with his wife and daughter, who was a governess.

A house in Ednall Lane, though at the time often referred to as being in New Road, was Fairview, in existence by 1883. It was a six bedroomed house with appropriate reception rooms and a good garden. Several well known Bromsgrove names are in the list of tenants – James Lea; Thomas Sanders; Charles S. Boswell, solicitor who was there from 1891-1893; T.E. Ince, High Street grocer, from 1895-1908. The house was sold in 1905 for £640, Mr Ince the sitting tenant

A recent picture of Westview (No.21) and Sunnyside (No.23), built about 1882. After several occupants, including a school, Westview was lived in between 1927 and the 1940s by Mr F.S. Jefferies of the grocer's shop on the corner of New Road and the High Street.

paying £30 p.a. to live there. Philip Brazier of the building family was living there in 1927, having demolished the old house and replaced it with a new white rendered one, but he left in 1929 when the family firm built Thatcholme for him in Conway Road.

Chapter Six

Aston Fields 1840-1880s

Meanwhile Aston Fields was growing fast, though was still without an official name. We left this tiny village, lower Finstall, in the 1840s, at the beginning of its new railway age. As we saw, there was immediate building of cottages for railway workers down by the station, but as the Wagon Works grew and the line became busier so did the need for labour.

The First, Second and Third Aston Fields, farmed by Mr Griffin of the Dragoon [now the Ladybird], bordering the New Road were opened up for building, as were the two fields facing the Stoke Road. All these had been owned by Francis Tongue Rufford, a banker, solicitor and land speculator, as had been the railway land, but it was Mr Samuel Yates the auctioneer who owned the Aston fields when they were sold to the Bromsgrove, Stoke Prior and District Building Society[25].

Henry Griffin's life changed with the village, from being victualler serving the local farmers to becoming a hotelier keeping a cab for the use of railway passengers. The Dragoon was a brick-built two storey public house where Banner's forecourt is today. Stables and outbuildings were on the corner of St Godwald's Road.

The Bromsgrove and Stoke Prior Land Society invested in several parcels of land for building. A field by the railway was purchased in 1870, divided into 30 plots, and the three Aston Fields were bought from Samuel Yates in 1871, their 6½ acres (2.6 hectares) balloted as 39 plots. It took many years before all these plots were built on, which is the reason why the houses in Carlyle, Middlefield, Stoke and South Roads are in the main so individual. Many of the new owners built a pair of houses on their plot, in order to maximise their income by rents. The longer ranges of terraced houses were put up by building firms such as Braziers and Tilt, while tradesmen like Henry Wheelock, who ran a coal business from Pear Tree Cottage [now the Post Office/Co-op], also bought several plots and built cottages to rent out. Regularly there were advertisements in *The Messenger* for the sale of plots for building in what was sometimes described as New Town.

Even by 1848 there was considerable concern amongst the community of churchgoers at St Godwald's chapel that the children of the local workers were getting no education. The nearest national schools were in Bromsgrove at St John's or in Stoke Prior, both too far to expect many children from Aston Fields,

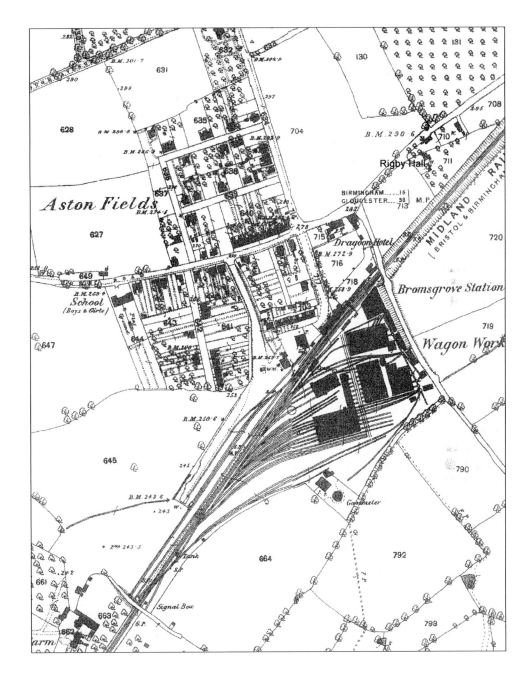

Surveyed in 1883, the map shows how Aston Fields and the Wagon Works had grown since 1840. By 1883 the Finstall Board School had been built, but not St Godwald's Church nor the Primitive Methodist schoolroom on the corner of Carlyle Road and New Road. OS.

A plan showing the Allotments and the names of the Allottees of the Railway Station Estate and the Aston Fields Estate bought by the Bromsgrove and Stoke Prior Land Society in 1870 and 1871. WRO, BA 848.

thus the School House was built on glebe land near to the chapel. Here, with a succession of schoolmistresses – were they not paid enough? – the school stayed until 1881, with the number of pupils ranging between 40 and 80. The school was inspected in 1861, and described as:

'a small rural infant School, with a few elder girls, the discipline is fair, the writing very fair, and the needlework good; [the school] has been mainly supported by the voluntary contributions of those who reside in the vicinity. Its contiguity to the Bromsgrove Station makes it of especial benefit to the families of the workpeople … we regret to hear that certain 'scruples of conscience' do not permit the Directors of that flourishing Company to tender any assistance towards its maintenance.'[26]

However the Directors of that flourishing Company were not totally hard. Each year there was a summer excursion for their workers and families. In 1861 500 workers, wives, families and friends climbed aboard a special train that the Directors had provided – at low fares, not free! – to take them to Bristol.

Stoke Chapel's school house fashionably covered in ivy when it was for sale as part of the Finstall Park estate in 1920. When the building of Finstall Board School made the little school redundant it was converted into a home, known as Finstall Cottage, lived in for many years by Mrs Cotton, stepmother of John and William Alfred. BC.

'The train, consisting of fifteen carriages, was very tastefully decorated. A large crown, about four feet in diameter, was placed on the top of the centre carriage: this had a very imposing effect. A part of the Queen's Own Worcestershire Cavalry band accompanied the excursionists, and enlivened the company by playing some popular airs.

On arriving at Bristol the party proceeded down the Quay, to examine the shipping; here a very pleasing incident occurred. The Captain of an American frigate invited the party on Board; this was readily assented to, the band playing a favourite air, and the party tripping it on the fantastic toe, to the evident delight of the captain and his lady. ... the party [returned] home about half-past ten, evidently delighted with the day's amusements. The band playing the National Anthem, and the company giving three hearty cheers, terminated the proceedings. It is very gratifying to be able to state that the greatest decorum and good feeling prevailed throughout the day.'[27]

By 1868 the community had grown so much – the 1871 census records 618 where in 1861 there were about 150 – that the ecclesiastical parish of Stoke Prior was split in two to become Stoke Prior Parish and St Godwald's Parish, the latter including both Finstall village and Aston Fields. A vicar was appointed to St Godwald's, Rev. J.H. Bainbrigge, who with his wife lived in the house they built, known as the vicarage or, later, St. Godwald's, some way down St Godwald's Road [now the Primrose Hospice]. The colourful polychrome brick house was designed in 1869 by architects Payne & Talbot of Birmingham and built on a plot of land previously part of Finstall Park estate.

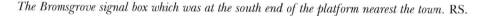

The Bromsgrove signal box which was at the south end of the platform nearest the town. RS.

This growing community now needed tradesmen to provide them with the wherewithal to live. Ale was already provided by the Dragoon, Walter Parry ran his grocery business at Aston House from 1872 (it had recently been built on the corner of New and Stoke Roads by Jonathan Brazier, on land sold to him by Samuel Yates) and Mrs Newman opened her drapery and haberdashery. Money orders and telegraphy were available at the Railway Station, and no doubt coal for home warming was bought from the dealers who stored their coal at the Station.

By 1880 Brazier's ten Aston Villas were built in Stoke Road alongside Aston House, and in New Road, the house on the corner of Middlefield Road. Malvern Place followed, then Rosedale (No.132) and Roseleigh (No.130), built by Mr Tilt whose daughter was named Rose, and the pair of houses on the corner of Carlyle Road. Hestonleigh (No.120), Bryn Melin (No.118), Lyndhurst (No.116) and Warwick House (No.114) were built in 1899, possibly owned by Robert Smallwood of Rigby Hall.

About half of the plots were already built along Carlyle and Middlefield Roads, including Fern Bank House and Cam Cottages. Derby Villas were on the market in 1876, and Fern Bank House, in 1879 lived in by Benjamin Witheford, was later occupied by Arthur Pickering who had premises in Bromsgrove High Street as a 'wholesale clothing manufacturer, hunting suits a speciality' and later was Managing Director of Carlyle Road's clothing factory. Olive Place in Stoke Road was occupied by Charles Bates from 1879 and between 1895 and 1904 was lived in by the Dolphin family – Mrs Emma Dolphin was a

St Godwald's, built as his vicarage in St Godwald's Road by Rev. Bainbrigge in 1869, architects Payne & Talbot of Birmingham. Note the chimneys, and the tall window which was on a sash into the wall above and could be raised high enough to act as a doorway.
J. Deighton.

William Dolphin's 1880s advertisement for 'bassinets, mail carts and mangles'. The Dolphin family lived at Olive Place.

dressmaker, while of the menfolk, William was a carpenter and furniture dealer and George was caretaker at the Workmen's Club.

Many of the members of the Workmen's Club were, naturally, workers at the station or the Wagon Works and when the Midland Railway Co. took over there was major expansion. There were odd moments of drama: one night in 1851 rumours of a fire at the Wagon Works reached Bromsgrove, and people flocked along New Road to view what they thought would be the remains of their working place – but thankfully it was only a small fire in a cask of charcoal noticed by the night watchman who successfully doused the flames with water from a hose.

Another fire, not at the station, was more serious when one day in 1866 Finstall House was in flames. Seeing the smoke the Stationmaster telegraphed for the gentleman tenant, Mr Palmer, a solicitor, to come from his Birmingham office, while the local vet galloped to Bromsgrove to call the volunteer fire brigade's horse-drawn fire wagon. A body of about a hundred men from the Wagon Works rushed to help, and made a human chain with buckets scooping water from the pool near the Finstall road. They were joined by numerous Bromsgrove people, including some boys from the Grammar School [Bromsgrove School], who had seen the flames from the town and run along the New Road to help. The roof was entirely destroyed, together with the floors of the rooms down to the basement, though much costly furniture and many valuables were saved, for the men fighting the fire by the house were throwing carpets, furniture, paintings and other chattels out of the windows. A day or so afterwards Mr Palmer – who had been completely uninsured – went down to the Wagon Works and gave a day's wages to each man who had helped with the fire – for which generosity the men in turn, through *The Messenger*, thanked Mr Palmer.

Finstall House had remained the property of the Brettell family until James Shaw JP bought the estate in the 1850s. After Shaw's death his daughter Edith and son-in-law William Everitt moved in. Their marriage in February 1860 was a splendid affair and after the service at Stoke Prior Parish Church the company 'partook of a sumptuous dejeuner ... A ball in the evening terminated a happy day. The children of the three schools in the parish were regaled with buns and wine ...'

The house is thought to have been built in the 1770s, a fine stone classical building. Everitt made it a splendid house, with six family bedrooms with dressing rooms (the *en suite* is nothing new), a billiard room, and

Finstall House (later known as Finstall Park) was the grandest house in the area, built in the 1770s but much extended by Mr. William Everitt. CC.

Finstall House garden front and croquet lawn. The extensive grounds included 46 acres of parkland, bordered on the north side by a splendid sandstone wall, and still the largest green space in the area. CC.

a spacious Lounge Hall – 34ft by 18ft (10 by 5½ metres) – with panelling and a handsome stained glass window which led into a 42ft (12½ metres) Drawing Room with an ebony mantelpiece. Some of the extensions – done between disastrous fires – were planned by John Cotton in 1884, when it became known as Finstall Park.

Finstall parkland was often opened for the use of Bromsgrove people, a regular occurrence being its use by the local soldiery. In May 1863 the 2nd Worcestershire Battalion's Drill was held in the park, with 500 all ranks participating. The park was open to the public and the shops were closed in Bromsgrove town while its inhabitants streamed along the muddy lanes and across the fields to have a fine day out. Such events continued throughout William Everitt's ownership, and he was a welcoming host,

Worcestershire Volunteer Officers in 1872. Seated from r. Captain Bourne of Grafton Manor, unknown, Adjutant Lewis, Captain Lewis. Seated on the ground far right is Captain Blick of Droitwich, next to him Lieutenant Avery of Redditch. The uniformed officer in the back row is Lieut. J.R. Horton of Bromsgrove. The Bromsgrove Volunteers regularly met at Finstall Park and Hewell Grange. BC.

providing splendid celebratory repasts on special occasions such as the opening of the Cottage Hospital, his wife encouraging the children at the school with small gifts at Christmas.

Everitt was a Birmingham business-man, but his real love was horses and over 40 years he built up a very successful stud farm up the Finstall Road, his bloodstock racehorses becoming known throughout the country. Here at Finstall Cottage Farm [now Penn Manor estate] were 17 loose boxes, stallion yard, mess room, saddle rooms, more loose boxes, etc., the head groom living at Clovelly House.

There is a nice snapshot memory of Mr Everitt and his near neighbour, Mr Smallwood of Rigby Hall, written by one who once worked at the station.[28]

Mr Robert Smallwood, J.P., owner of the Rigby Hall estate between 1864 and 1900. CC.

As I remember these gentlemen, Mr Everitt was of medium height, with a pleasant face and a manner that was always affable. Mr Smallwood was a tall, upright man, who always wore a gold monacle. Both the gentlemen had first class season tickets between Bromsgrove and Birmingham, and used to travel backwards and forwards nearly every day. Their morning newspapers were always left at the station, Mr Smallwood having *The Birmingham Gazette* and Mr Everitt *The Post*.

Rigby Hall front in the 1960s. Built in 1838 it was extended in 1844 by Birmingham architect Charles Edge, and altered again in the early 20th century.

Rigby Hall, its land originally part of the Finstall Park estate – probably sold by Richard Brettell because the railway was about to slice its way through his fields – was built as a gentleman's residence in 1838, though it is possible the land was purchased by Henry Ellins, George's brother, as early as 1805.[29] Nailmaster George Ellins,[30] aged 40 in 1840, was Rigby Hall's first inhabitant and about this time he was the major shareholder in the Birmingham & Gloucester Railway Company, and also was on their books as a Contractor to the company. His stay was short and Rigby Hall and its 24 acres were put up for auction on

Rigby Hall garden front in the 1960s. The gardens were a feature of the property, with numerous glass houses and a tennis court.

20th June 1843, together with several acres at Finstall. The prospectus described George Ellins, Esq. as the 'occupier', giving the impression that he did not then own the property.[31] The family's fortunes had declined sharply during the early 1840s, and by the 1850s gentleman George was living a poor man's life as lodger with a cordwainer (shoemaker) in Droitwich.

However, during his time at Rigby Hall Ellins had created an attractive domain, described in the Sale particulars as a Mansion House, with coach houses and stables, conservatory, vineries, peach houses, five acres of pleasure ground and twenty acres planted with a 'rare and choice collection of Apple and Pear Trees'. It appears not to have been sold to James Holyoake until March 1844 the following year[32] when Birmingham architect Charles Edge was put in charge of alterations[33].

Several short stays followed, including Charles Taylor in the 1840s, and Thomas Kinder, owner of the railway coach building company, in the 1850s.

Tree-lined Rigby Lane, deep and narrow, that led to Rigby Hall from New Road.

John Corbett, Salt King of Droitwich came in 1861 while The Grange at Stoke Heath [now Avoncroft House, part of Bromsgrove School] was being built, but then in 1864 Robert Smallwood arrived from Edgbaston and put down strong roots, remaining at Rigby Hall until his death in May 1900. He lived a stylish life, with eight servants and several cottagers in his employ, adding some 60 acres, a Lodge, servants' wing, farm buildings and a melon house to his property during the 35 years he was in Finstall. He was on the Bromsgrove bench for 35 years, and Chairman for twenty.

After the change in ownership to the Midland Railway Company, the Wagon Works' labour force grew. In 1867 two new wagon shops were built together with a large smithy – 28 smithy hearths and two steam hammers of five tons each. In 1872 working conditions for the men were improved when their weekly hours of work were reduced to 9 hours per day, 54 hours per week, working of course all day Saturday. A year later Mr T.G. Clayton took control and the works were again expanded and reorganised, and by 1875 there were 600 men in the workforce. Can you imagine 600 men tramping down New Road every morning from the courts off Bromsgrove High Street, from Stoney Hill and Sidemoor, trooping past the Dragoon and round into the narrow lane to the Wagon Works gates? But this success was not to continue and two years later there was dismissal of a large number of the workers. There was no question of any compensation from the Company; a large proportion of the men on the railway had come in from other parts of the country bringing their families, so there was no help to be had from their kith and kin. If they had been paying long enough into a 'club' there might be some regular support, but many found they had to swallow pride and apply to the Guardians of the Poor, or move into cheaper dwellings or even, if they had been in Bromsgrove for less than a year, having to return to their parish of birth.[34]

Chapter Seven

The Old Road to the Station and the Building of the Crescent

Local historians, using directories and censuses for much of their information, find great problems over names of roads. Today we have nice signs telling us the names of Station Street, Ednall Lane and the Crescent, but during the period we are discussing there were no such labels in a small town like Bromsgrove. Names here evolved, in the main, as descriptions and the town was small enough for everyone to know them: the street leading to the market became Market Street, the same applied to Church Street, Chapel Street, Little Lane, St John's Street, Stourbridge Road – and, of course, New Road. Before the railway the road leading up to Ednall Lane from Worcester Street was also known as Ednall Lane – in fact a group of little alleys was sometimes described as 'the Ednall Lanes'. However, it was natural when the station opened to begin to call it, since it was the route to the new railway, Station Lane or Street or Road, often including the part we today know as Ednall Lane. The origins of the word Ednall are unclear, but a manuscript of 1601 tells us that 'Ednile Gate' or 'Edenhill Gate' – the gate presumably at the border of the Manor – was purchased by one Thomas Biggs.[35]

Confusion for us also applies at the time the New Road began to have offshoots. Those who first built houses in Wellington, Clive and Carlyle Roads or on the Crescent often described themselves as living in New Road – even though all those roads had been given their official names when first built. The old names also continued a surprisingly long time – there is a Sale map[36] that as late as 1900 shows 'Bromsgrove Old Road' instead of Clive Road. The same map used 'The Avenue' instead of Marlborough Avenue. All very muddling.

Strangely, as has been said previously, before the new road there were few larger houses on Station Street, and as you reached the top of the hill from the town you saw numerous gardens and orchards on the south side of the road. The 1840 tithe maps shows many narrow strip plots along the backs of the High Street buildings, the boundaries of most of them going back to mediaeval times, though by the 1840s these garden plots frequently changed hands.

Leaving Worcester Street the narrow entrance to the lane was fixed on the north side by the Wheatsheaf pub, and on the south side by what we now call the

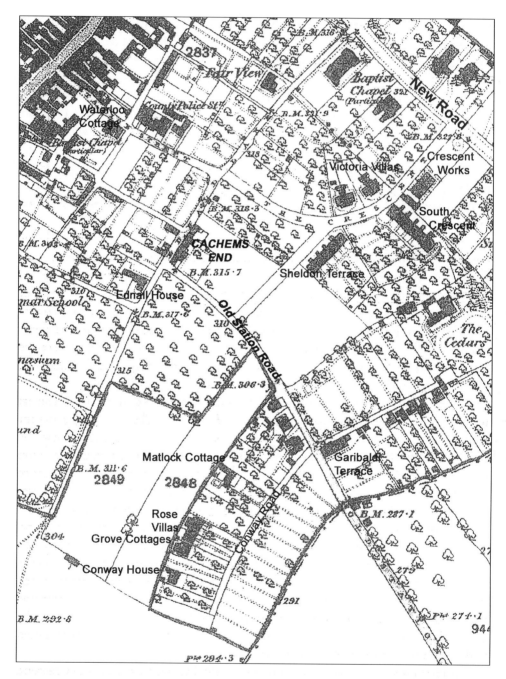

From the 1883 survey showing Station Street, The Crescent, Ednall Lane and Old Station Road. Before roads were built this area was full of orchards. OS.

Merchant's House. This timber framed building is fifteenth century in origin, though had additions at the rear – the early eighteenth century stone house is shown in the photograph. All of these properties were removed in 1962, the Merchant's House fortunately being rebuilt at Avoncroft Museum of Buildings in 1965.

Behind the stone house were three boulders. These were not the only boulders around the town; John and William A. Cotton were enthusiastic boulder hunters, and made a list of where they were to be found near Bromsgrove[37]; their friend John Humphreys, dentist and naturalist, deduced

Three boulders in Station Street, seen facing up hill outside Giles's Carriageworks.

these were glacial deposits, brought down from the Arenig Hills of Snowdonia. They were big enough to be a nuisance when roadways were being built, and it is said that trenches were dug around the largest so that they dropped below the surface, being too big to break up or remove. Two of them may still be seen, one each side of the main entrance to Bromsgrove Cemetery, brought there from beside the weighing machine previously at the junction of the Strand and Rotten Row.

On the north side of Station Street, on the site of an old Workhouse, a smart new police station for the new County Police force was built in 1840. This had four cells for short sentence prisoners, and accommodation for policemen. Previously there had been a four cell lock-up at the old Workhouse in the Strand at the top of the High Street. The police station was to become Melbourne House, but more of that later. Behind the police station was Paradise Row, tiny cottages commemorated today by the name of the lane. Opposite the police station was Waterloo Cottage, for many years lived in by Meacham Lea, accountant, land agent, schoolteacher and father of James Lea. Meacham Lea took in day pupils, charging 8 shillings per quarter (40p) to teach reading, 10 shillings per quarter (50p) to teach reading, writing and English grammar, and £1 per quarter to teach land surveying as well. James, his son, was also based at Waterloo Cottage working as a surveyor, dealing in guano[38], and running a coal depot on their land, until he moved to Fernleigh, New Road in 1871. In the 1880s Charles H. Green sold gold and silver watches from Waterloo Cottage.

Facing you at the top of Station Street in 1880 was a new road, the Crescent, cutting through Mr Frances's Barn Close field, curving round towards the New Road – though it was not Mr Frances's field now – our canny estate agent friend

Samuel Yates had bought the whole of the 7 acre (2.8 hectares) Barn Close, south of the New Road, in 1871.

Ednall Lane went north from the little cross roads, along the mediaeval back lane parallel with the High Street, past gardens and fields and the house known as Fairview, across the New Road, where it became College Walk. This went up to the gardens of The Mount (Wendron) where the path turned down towards the Chapel. In the other direction the narrow lane went past Ednall House (The Lion House) and the cottages opposite, leading through the orchards and past the King Edward VI Grammar School [Bromsgrove School] until it reduced to footpath size and went through the large pasture known as Kiteley's Close and on down to the Charford Mill.

This little area on Ednall Lane was called Catchems End well into the twentieth century, but the name seems now to have been forgotten. There are many other places called Catchems End including at Bewdley, Brewood in Staffordshire, Hatton in Warwickshire and one in Northamptonshire. The theory is that they are on the border of a mediaeval town boundary over which the constable of the manor was not allowed to pursue a miscreant.

If in 1883 we had walked down Old Station Road from Ednall Lane we would have found pasture and orchards until we reached the five new houses on our right, then Conway Road with a few newly built dwellings, and on our left Garibaldi Terrace, both built on long narrow fields that were previously gardens and allotments.

Conway Road was so christened after Conway Villa, which was built, as were the other houses in the road, with gardens to the front of them and none behind, so that the sun was on the gardens all day long. This land was one of the first plots

Rose Villas (Nos.14-18 Conway Road) built in 1879.

Conway Villa (No.28 Conway Road) built in the 1870s.

bought in 1867 by the Bromsgrove, Stoke Prior and District Building Society, though it was a number of years before houses were built. The first was the block of three Rose Villas, then Grove Cottage, Conway Villa and Matlock Cottage – the latter in 1875 the residence of William Garnett Taylor, lint manufacturer of Charford Mill; the path through Kiteley's fields to Charford must have been an element in his choice of site for his house.

Montgomery Terrace (Nos.8-12 Conway Road), not built until 1901.

FRONT ELEVATION.

Left: Matlock Cottage (No.4 Conway Road) built in 1875, probably for William Garnett Taylor, lint manufacturer of Charford Mill. Right: Architect G.H. Gadd's drawing of Mr. Ledbury's Conway Road pair of villas, Heathcote (No.26) and Braeside (No.24), built in 1904. WRO.

The houses on the corner of Conway and Old Station Road, Poplar Villa and Glenthorne Villa, were joined, the latter lived in from the 1870s by Albert Nicholas, teacher of music ('the tonic sol-fa method') and Walter Fawke, Professor and Teacher of Athletic Exercise. Professor Fawke, then in his fifties, had been a Drill Sergeant with the Old Scots Greys, and fought in the Crimea at Alma (when he was slightly wounded) and Inkerman and took part in the charge of the Heavy Brigade at Balaclava[39]. He was a 'fine, tall man' and very popular. He gave awesome 'demonstrations of feats of strength, skill, and dexterity, with the broadsword, sabre and scimitar'. 'He could cut a sheep in half with one blow of his sword, or cut an apple in two on a man's hand, with the same weapon.'[40] He taught sports at The College, and was on the Hospital Management Committee, for which he once organised a display by the Gymnastic Club, raising £3 13s 6d. After 68 years in Bromsgrove, in 1899 Fawke decided to move away, and a group of friends gave him a memorable farewell dinner at the Dog & Pheasant; he was presented with a sedan chair, listened to an ode written by John Cotton, and enjoyed many stirring speeches referring to his gallantry.

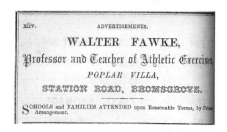

An advertisement placed by Professor Walter Fawke, whose career as a soldier in the Crimea taking part in the charge of the Heavy Brigade made him one of Bromsgrove's notable characters. BR.

Poplar Villa was an appropriate name in those times, for Old Station Road was lined with poplar trees; in 1881 there was a big storm, when 'a score or so of the poplars were uprooted'. However some remained and there are still people who remember them.

The five tiny houses of the original Garibaldi Terrace[41] had already been built by 1866 when Mr Timmins bought them at auction for £400. This little terraced block was demolished in the mid twentieth century and half a dozen houses built on the land. Further up Garibaldi Terrace were five larger cottages, several with nail shops and long narrow gardens at the back, built in the 1870s, which are still there today. The Garibaldi land was one of the early Bromsgrove, Stoke Prior and District Building Society's estates, bought in 1863, twelve small lots, most of them long and narrow, and not all built upon.

Our walk along the tree lined Old Station Road then crosses the parish boundary into Stoke Prior and becomes completely rural, with no more houses until the Broom House Farm.

Garibaldi Cottages (Nos.12 & 14) not much changed since being built in the 1870s.

The earliest reference found for Broom House Farm is in a tax record from 1240. The present Broom farmhouse was built mainly in the 17th century of local stone, the eastern range is timber framed from the 15th century and there is a small Victorian addition of 1869. There are 17th century farm buildings [the barn is now a dwelling]. During the first half of the 19th century it was part of 200 acres (81 hectares) farmed by the Nash family who owned much other acreage in the area, but in 1863 it was sold at auction to a Charles Shaw of Edgbaston as an investment property for £11,000. By

Broom House in 1973 from the Bromsgrove Lower School field known as Broom Field pitch, now covered in housing. A few years later the barn was sold and restored and is now a dwelling. J.C. Page.

1910 the farm had shrunk to 36 acres (14.5 hectares) (Bromsgrove Urban District Council had bought several of its acres for use for new sewage beds for the town) and was sold by the executors of Miss Alice Rogers and her sister Mrs Sophia Carter (Dutton). Although the farmland was split into two lots, both were bought by the wealthy young Old Bromsgrovian Charles Whitley for £3,495.

Fashionably covered in Ivy, Broom House as it was photographed for the 1910 Sale prospectus. BC.

Whitley, aged only 22, had recently inherited a large sum after the death of his father, a Liverpool brewer. Having been very happy at Bromsgrove School, and knowing it needed a more secure financial footing, he had already given a massive £5,000 to the school's Endowment Fund; shortly afterwards his money anonymously paid for the building of the Kyteless teaching block. Having bought Broom House Whitley presented the farm and its lands to the school, an action which gave the school an immediate small income and use of the Broomfield and Long Lands as playing fields for the junior school. After World War II, on the school's return from Llanwyrtyd Wells, Broom House was put into use for junior boys, initially under Mrs Jane Boyer.

In the 1950s the school benefited from the sale for housing of the land along Old Station Road, and in the 1980s from selling the remainder of the fields for Broom Park housing. The house itself was bought and carefully restored by Alfred Wood, whose knowledge and experience in town planning was of the greatest support to the newly formed Bromsgrove Society in 1980.

Whitley himself volunteered for service in World War I, and was killed in action in 1916, aged twenty-eight.

The Crescent from the 1870s

The first houses built in the 1870s were John Sheldon's attractive terrace of dwellings now known as South Crescent. The gardens of the six houses were very small at first – maybe Mr Sheldon hoped to build more on his plot of land – but gradually land was cultivated to make the pretty gardens there today.

The next houses to be built were the two pairs of Victoria Villas (Nos. 4, 6, 8 and 10), built by Brazier & Weaver in 1876 for Alfred Bennett the draper and designed by Bromsgrove's architect John Cotton. You may remember that in 1871 Samuel Yates the auctioneer and estate agent had bought the seven acres (2.8 hectares) of Barn Close. In 1873 Alfred Bennett paid £100 5s 6d for the second of his two plots. Bennett built these houses as an investment, but he was still happy to pay extra for Cotton to decorate the stone drip mouldings with animal heads and foliage bosses, use blue and buff bricks to pattern the walls and

One of the two pairs of Victoria Villas on the curve of The Crescent, designed by Bromsgrove's architect John Cotton, and built in 1876 by Brazier and Weaver for Alfred Bennett, High Street draper and milliner (2000).

add sunflower finials at gable tops. The houses have had numerous extensions in recent years, but still have a lot of their original charm.

Notable among the inhabitants of these villas were Walter Parry the nail manufacturer in No.2, who lived there until 1891 when he crossed over the road to live in South Crescent. Edwin Coxell, Registrar of Births and Deaths, lived in No.4 until 1895, while No.1 was where Alfred Bennett moved on his retirement from his drapery establishment in 1886. He lived in the house until 1901, after which his widow stayed on until at least 1916. Perhaps the most interesting of the inhabitants of these houses was David Raimbach, who was Headmaster of the School of Art until 1898. This was the year when the Art School Committee asked Raimbach and his deputy, G.B. Benton, to resign and apply for their own jobs, on the grounds that there were not the funds to pay for both posts. Even worse than this was that a young outsider named Walter Gilbert also applied for the headship – and got it. Unsurprisingly Raimbach and his wife left Victoria Villas after this, moving to Willesden in Middlesex to try to make a living from his paintings, leaving Gilbert to change the artistic and creative life of Bromsgrove (see Chapter Sixteen).

Not all the plots sold so well as those of Victoria Villas – Yates disposed of his land quite slowly. There was some resistance to his high selling price when he held a Sale of the southern part of the field in 1877. However John Sheldon did buy two plots after the Sale and quickly put up another row of five cottages, known then as Sheldon Terrace, facing towards the sun and with their back entrances along an alley from the Crescent.

Although the Crescent was regarded as a refuge from the smoke and noise of the High Street and Worcester Road, there was one occupant who in 1872 had opened a nail manufactory, the Crescent Works, on the corner of New Road, directly opposite The Newlands, the grand home of Mr White. Henry William Lewis was, and continued to be, a stone and marble mason working from Rock Hill, but diversifying now into wrought iron nailmaking. It

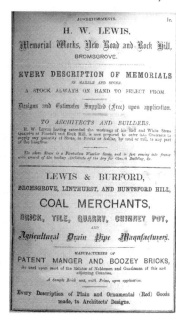

An 1880s advertisement showing the commercial interests of Mr H.W. Lewis of the Crescent Works – memorials from Rock Hill and Finstall Quarries; an offer to supply coal, stone and ashlar to any part of the kingdom by road or rail; and drainpipes, quarry tiles and 'manger and boozey bricks (bricks especially made for agricultural use) as used by most of the estates of Noblemen and Gentlemen of this and adjoining counties'.

seems that Lewis was renting out 'standings' for 48 nailers, and he also had equipment for the making and repair of nailers' tools. The result was hot smoke and clouds of dust coming from the building. When he came to this site he was surrounded by pastureland, but when elegant new homes were built there was friction with his neighbours, bringing some testy correspondence in *The Messenger* about the state of the Crescent road in 1881. However by November that year, after only nine years, Mr Lewis sold his nailing business (though not the building) to nail factors Eliza Tinsley & Co., who already had premises in the town, and in 1884 was offering the manufactory to let. By this time he was back on Rock Hill concentrating on his first business, and in 1889 offered the site for sale as a plot of building land; this was not successful and on his death in 1901 the Works was again put on the market. Possibly to be able to control activities, the plot was bought for £760 by Mr Fitch of Garlisters, across the road. After this the works were taken on by the School of Art, where metalwork was taught, and also by the Bromsgrove Guild, but more of that in Chapter Sixteen.

Chapter Eight

Warwick Hall Estate and Houses for Merchant Princes

Warwick Hall was a farmhouse that slightly belied its name; it was never the grand house of the area. It has a small sixteenth century house at its core, with an 18th century wing and plenty of Victorian and modern additions. Around it were the usual farming necessities of outbuildings, barns and pigsties, and during the nineteenth century the land worked by the tenant was a swathe of fields bounded on the west by the brook running down to the Sugar Brook and on the east by Dragoon Farm fields – some 83 acres (33.5 hectares). In 1865 the New Road cut across the 9 acre (3¾ hectares) Large Meadow to join and widen the old lane down to the Dragoon and the station, which did not please the tenant farmer, Joseph Russon.

All this land was owned by the Manor of Stoke Prior and under the control of the Ecclesiastical Commissioners.[42] From at least 1799 until 1878 the Sanders family, Sarah the mother followed by Sarah the daughter,[43] were the Copyhold tenants.[44] The farm was held in trust for Sarah the daughter from 1872 by two land agents, a Mr Rigden, a solicitor from Salisbury and James John Tomson of Barnt Green House [now the Barnt Green Inn], who was also agent for Lord Windsor of

Hewell (not involved in this property), but it seems from conveyances that these two gentlemen later bought the family's tenancy.

Alongside the Warwick Hall land were the three fields of Fringe Green Farm [Newton Road today] and 15 acres (6 hectares) at Sallow Brook (land along the willow lined brook that joins the Spadesbourne, now under the by-pass). These two tenancies, also Copyhold, were acquired from the Nott brothers by Rigden and Tomson, thus adding to the profitability of the Warwick Hall estate.

Warwick Hall in 1878, a drawing by John Cotton for Joseph Russon, tenant farmer. CC.

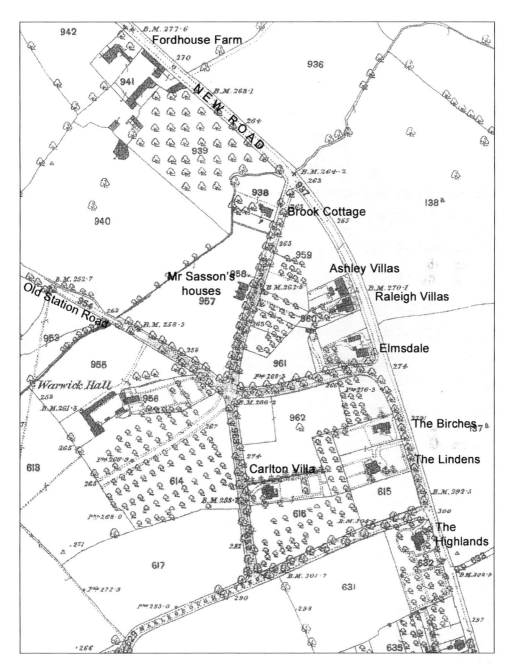

From the map surveyed in 1883 of the Warwick Hall estate, showing a few houses built along New Road, and just three properties on Wellington Road. OS.

On 31 July 1878 the Ecclesiastical Commissioners agreed to enfranchise the land (free the land from copyhold) for £830, which was paid in September, but in the meantime part of the property was put up for auction that August. After the auctioneer, our old friend Mr Yates, had given 'a capital description of the land, and of its value as building sites for the accommodation of some of the "Merchant Princes" of Birmingham', there was fierce bidding. Although the land had been divided into five Lots it was first offered as a whole, at which all 42 acres (17 hectares) were sold for £9,500. There was 'much excitement ... evinced amongst the company as to who [was] the purchaser', for James Lea, land agent, had bought it on behalf of a mystery buyer.

It seems that the tenant farmer, Joseph Russon, came into some funds at this time, for he wanted to improve the farmhouse, going to John Cotton to draw up suggested alterations. The proposal[45] was presumably too costly and over-ambitious, for it was a simpler extension that was built. Joseph Russon continued to live in the farmhouse, its land holding depleting round him, though most of his income would have come from his job as land agent to Lord Edmund Talbot, owner of the Grafton Manor estate.

In December 1878 came the really big Sale of 72 acres (29 hectares), when Henry Corbett, solicitor of Bromsgrove, took the bidding to £11,567. The mystery of ownership was not solved until the following summer when *The Investors' Guardian* announced the registration of The Bromsgrove Warwick Hall Estate Company, with a capital of £7,800 divided into 78 shares of £100 each. The shareholders included several familiar Bromsgrove names: William Llewellin, corn merchant; Frederick J. Yates the architect and son of Samuel Yates the auctioneer; the two solicitors Henry Corbett of Bromsgrove and Frederick Corbett of Worcester; William Davis of Malvern Link; Oliver Giles of Clifton, Bristol (also of Bromsgrove of the wagon building family); and Samuel Saywell M.A., proprietor of The College Academy. Of these gentlemen William Llewellin held the most shares. The Company invested not only in Warwick Hall land but also other land for development particularly in the Lickey area, and was still in operation in 1905, though it had sold Warwick Hall itself by 1884.

The Company came into ownership of all the estate on 7 November 1879. The next day a large proportion was sold on to two men – William Llewellin and Charles Field the Younger, whose purchase apparently covered 72 acres 2 roods 12 perches. Of these 19 acres 35 perches, (A on the first Sale plan) cost William Llewellin £4,784 4s 8d. Other plots were bought directly from the Warwick Hall Company at this time, including Mr Albutt's two plots, and those of John Cotton and William Weaver (see 1891 Sale plan).

In December 1879 Samuel Yates held a Sale of Warwick Hall land at the Golden Cross to dispose of 17 acres (6.75 hectares) divided into 43 'building allotments

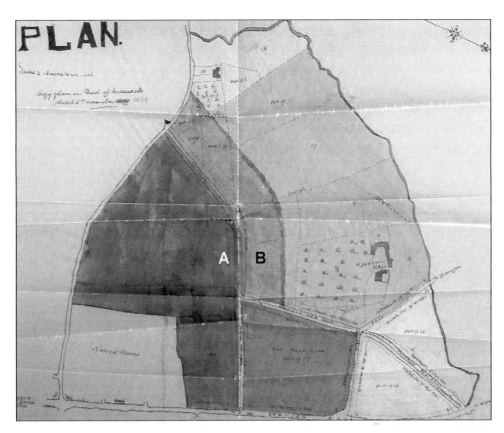

A fragile Sale plan of the Warwick Hall Estate used in 1899 but originally prepared for the Sale of 1879. The plan shows how the first Lots sold followed the traditional field shapes. The rectangular field bottom left contained the three Aston Fields, now Carlyle and Middlefield Roads, never in ownership of Warwick Hall. The road at the bottom of the plan, 'New Station Road', is New Road, and leading from it 'Old Station Road' i.e. Clive Road and Old Station Road. The road on the left boundary is Stoke Road and the right hand boundary is the brook. William Llewellin and Charles Field the younger together bought Plots marked **A** *and* **B***, Llewellin thereafter selling on* **A***, and Field selling* **B***.* Privately owned.

suitable for the erection of villas and other residences'. The bidding this time was more cautious, though after the Sale there was a fair amount of buying at a price under the reserve. As happened with plots allotted by The Bromsgrove, Stoke Prior and District Building Society, investors bought and later built pairs of houses, or just kept the plots, sometimes for many years, until they felt the time was right to build on them.

There were strict restrictions on builders and those who purchased the houses, who were asked to sign a Deed of Covenant relating to facilities. The Warwick Hall

Company agreed to arrange the building of the roads and footpaths but the cost would be borne by the landowners in proportion to their frontage – Mr Law of Kidderminster won the contract to make the roadways. Once the drains, gas and water pipes were laid they were to be inspected by the Company at a charge of two guineas (£2.10p) for each villa, and one guinea for each 'ordinary house'. The building line for villas should be a generous 25ft (7.62 metres) from the roadway, boundary walls were not to exceed 4ft 6ins (1.37 metres), villas should cost £400 or more, and no factory or noisy trade could be carried out – especially not nailshops. The result would be a pleasant area where inhabitants could live in 'quiet enjoyment'.

The names of the new roads were chosen by the Warwick Hall Company to honour those regarded as heroes – the Duke of Marlborough, the Duke of Wellington, Baron Clive of India and for the road that was never built, Lord Beaconsfield (Disraeli was ennobled in 1876), the latter showing the Tory inclination of the Company's partners.

It was now that the big changes began. In 1879 Mr Law began to lay the new roads – Wellington Road being excitedly described by *The Messenger* as:

> 'a main thoroughfare leading out of the New Road at the stone bridge, in an oblique direction, to the corner of the orchard at Warwick Hall,' and Marlborough Avenue and Clive Road, of 'commanding width, provision being made for the houses to be erected thereon to be placed sufficiently back so as to admit of trees being planted on either side'.

> 'We hear also that preparations are making for the erection of one villa residence at the corner of the old road, and in the course of time, and that not long, the frontage to the New Road will in all probability be fringed with a class of houses which the contiguity of the situation to the railway station and its easy distance from Birmingham, will command'.

New Road

That first villa was Elmsdale (No.94), designed and lived in by architect F.J. Yates, on the corner of New and Clive Roads, standing as an advertisement for what could be built on the estate. Elmsdale has been lucky in its owners, and there have been few alterations to its external design, apart from the demolition of its stable block for the sale of part of the garden for other houses to be built. Elmsdale was designed to look good both from New Road and Clive

Elmsdale gable facing New Road with six ceramic medallions.

Left: Elmsdale (No.94 New Road) was built in 1879, the first house on the Warwick Hall estate, architect F.J. Yates. It was probably built as an example of the quality of houses expected by the Warwick Hall Company of which Frederick Yates was a shareholder. Right: The rear of Elmsdale. Although this part of the house holds the kitchen quarters and faces the original stable yard it nevertheless was built to look a fine house when viewed from New Road.

Road, and it is not as large as it appears from its frontages. It is in the Gothic revival style, with several pointed arched first floor windows, their tympana decorated with interesting ceramic medallions (there are two blocks of houses, Nos. 32-40, in Wellington Road that had the same feature [only one medallion remains] – was this also designed by F.J. Yates?).

F.J. Yates, who was only 30 when living in the house, was there for just two years until early 1881 when he left with his tail between his legs, moving to a small house in Perryfields Terrace. Things were going badly downhill for young Frederick. In June 1881 he had to dissolve his business partnership in Perryfields Brick Company with his friend and brother-in-law, architect George H. Gadd, and with William Davis, brickmaker. In September he could no longer put off the filing of a petition for bankruptcy – nor could his father Samuel, who with debts of £4,000 removed to Malvern to live in a

Frederick J. Yates, architect, son of Samuel Yates, whose bankruptcy in 1881 took him to work in Birmingham. Pike.

boarding house (even though still advertising his services in Bromsgrove as an 'Estate and Financial Agent').

How had this happened? It is easy to say the Yates's had overstretched themselves – which they probably had – but they also had misjudged the land and housing market when Bromsgrove was going through troubled times. The nailing industry was in a very bad way[46] – a combination of greedy nailmasters and middlemen, and the emergence of new fangled machinery – and Bromsgrove relied upon it. As Walter Parry, nailmaster said, 'one machine in Birmingham would turn out as much as a hundred men here'.

Samuel's liabilities were high, though he was able to offer one shilling (5p) in the pound to his many creditors. Frederick was in a worse position; his liabilities were some £8,000 with assets of only £717. Frederick was truly in liquidation.

ADVERTISEMENTS.   xliii.

S. YATES,

Auctioneer, House & Estate Agent,

NEW ROAD, BROMSGROVE,

AND

RICHMOND ROAD, MALVERN LINK.

A CONSIDERABLE number of desirable FREEHOLD INVESTMENTS, BUILDING SITES, and BUSINESSES, in Bromsgrove, Malvern, Worcester, and Birmingham, FOR SALE.

A number of HOUSES, comprising FRONT SHOPS, COTTAGES, &c., TO LET.

MONEYS to be ADVANCED on MORTGAGE of REAL PROPERTY, from £50 and upwards.

MONEYS ADVANCED on GOODS for *bona-fide* SALE.

All kinds of INSURANCES EFFECTED.

ESTATES, LANDS, and BUILDINGS SURVEYED and PLANNED, at the shortest notice.

A MONTHLY REGISTER of PROPERTIES FOR SALE and TO LET in Bromsgrove, Malvern, and Districts, may be had upon application, personally or by letter.

OFFICE HOURS FROM TEN TILL SEVEN.

An 1881 advertisement placed in Palmer's Bromsgrove Directory by Samuel Yates, the year his business went into bankruptcy. BR.

However this young man was not flattened by his trouble nor by his debts to Bromsgrove traders, and he bounced confidently into Birmingham where in 1882 he opened an office in Queen's Chambers in Colmore Row. He had previously had the benefit of being articled with respected Birmingham architects Bateman and Corser, and thus had suitable contacts. In Bromsgrove before his bankruptcy he had been responsible for Sunnymead in New Road (1873), Dodford School (1877), the Meadows School (with E.A. Day, 1879) and, astonishingly given his record, in 1883 he was entrusted with the design of the Wesleyan Chapel in New Road. He became moderately successful in Birmingham was responsible in the 1890s for Nuneaton Cottage Hospital, and was owner of properties in Gladstone Road, Sparkbrook, Birmingham, where he lived until his death.

Elmsdale meantime was without a tenant, and it took a full six months during 1881 of advertising in *The Messenger* before the property was lived in again, rented this time by George Burrows, late of the Golden Cross. In 1890 Mr James Sutton, a leather currier of Aston in Birmingham, bought the property for £880 and rented it to William Finney, the Aston Fields flour miller and cornchandler. After Finney's widow left, Mr Sutton lived at Elmsdale himself, until his death in 1918.

As can be seen from the Warwick Hall Estate 1891 Sale plan, building on the plots was sporadic. The first to be built were large villas on New Road.

The Highlands, the most splendid of all [now gone], was built in 1881 for James Laughton, Registrar of Marriages and nail manufacturer in Mill Lane (employing 72 men, 72 women, 12 boys and 5 girls), who moved up New Road from Sunnylawn. The Laughtons were followed in the mid 1890s by John Green, who had a nail, chain and rivet manufactury in Mill Lane and moved up New Road from Ashley Villas. John Henry Green was in the middle of the nailmakers revolt of 1891, when the nailers accused him of undercutting payment and taking no notice of the agreed list price. Knowing that other nailmasters would take on striking nailers from Green's workshops, more than a hundred nailers marched on 1st April from Sidemoor to his manufactury. Green capitulated and things went quiet for a while. By the end of the year, however, with popular support, much of it financial, from working men all round the country, the nailers of Bromsgrove became unionised, and a strike took place. Soup kitchens were provided by wives of several tradesmen but Bromsgrove was a divided town. So divided that when Mr Thomas White of The Newlands, an employer himself and a magistrate, made derogatory remarks in court about the striking nailers he had his face slapped by another magistrate, Mr John Amphlett. Full descriptions of the unrest are in *Glory Gone: the story of nailing in Bromsgrove*.[47]

The Green family stayed at The Highlands until 1905, after which it had several owners. The house came up for sale in 1930. The house was very well appointed, as the estate agent said, with good-sized rooms, plenty of fitted cupboards in the china pantry, four large bedrooms, and three reception rooms. There was electric light installed throughout, but the only power points were in two of the reception rooms and three of the bedrooms. Mains drainage, 'Company's water and gas', and P.O. telephone were connected. Outside there was 'an excellent sectional Motor House (for two cars), with asbestos tiled roof, folding and sliding doors and concrete floor. Electric light.' The ornamental grounds included a tennis court, rock garden, rose beds and well planted kitchen garden. Altogether a fine gentleman's residence, which was bought by Mr J.F. Breininger, and later sold to Mr Edward B. Alabaster, the opthalmic surgeon, who sold off the lovely garden, orchard and tennis court to the south of his home. There Braziers built two houses in 1936, The Orchard (No.112) and Newton (No.110) – Newton named because it was built for Mrs Sherwood who had moved from Newton Farm, which was later to become the site for Garringtons.

The Birches and The Lindens, both built in 1881, both now gone, were built on one large plot by Miss Jane Auster, whose parents had lived till their death at Grimley Hall in nearby Finstall. Living at The Birches, which was built by Brazier & Weaver for £684 10s, Miss Auster was followed in 1886 by the respected Dr Roger Prosser who retired and died there within a year. His wife Mary was one of the Walford sisters, artists all, who were living down the road at Raleigh Villas. From the 1920s to 1943 members of the Russon family were living at The Birches, which at some point came into the hands of the Trevorrow family of Grafton Manor estate. During World War II the Birches was used by a branch of Nonington College of Physical Education from Kent that had been evacuated to Grafton Manor; it is now owned by Worcestershire County Council.

The Lindens, was owned until 1894 by Henry Wheelock, coal merchant at the railway station and director of the brickworks at Linthurst, Blackwell, then by solicitor Charles Boswell. Still later Miss James came, who in 1910 married the 73 year old Samuel Saywell, proprietor of The College school in New Road, a marriage that lasted the four years he had left of life. After the Saywell Sale in 1915 the house name was changed to Drayton, when it was lived in by Mrs Wilkinson and her daughter, who by 1943 was running a small preparatory school on the premises.

More properties were gradually built along the stretch between Clive and Wellington Roads, though not as grand as their predecessors. On John Cotton's land he built Raleigh Villas (Nos.86/88) in 1880, rented out by him until his

The Lindens (1881), later known as Drayton, built with The Birches (1881) in New Road by Miss Jane Auster, architect John Cotton. BC.

death in 1934.[48] Raleigh Villas is notable for the one triangular bay window still intact, carried by the roof of the bay window beneath. Amongst Cotton's tenants was William Hadley, son of the wealthy nailmaster Enoch Hadley of Barnsley Hall, whose own son rejoiced in the name of Hyla. Mary Scroxton – widow of the printer, painter, publisher and poet J.H. Scroxton – less well known as sister-in-law of Samuel Yates – was living next door. For sixteen years the most interesting occupants of Raleigh Villas were four of the eight Walford sisters, Amelia, Elizabeth, Hannah and Amy. Though all were artists, it was Amy who took an important role in Bromsgrove's Arts & Crafts movement and the Bromsgrove Guild, making the beautiful brass lectern in Tardebigge Church, the bronze Boer War memorial in St John's church and the rood cross at Dodford. Amy was also Principal of the Bromsgrove School of Art between 1900 and

Raleigh Villas (1880, Nos.86/88 New Road), architect John Cotton, which he built as an investment property. Both houses originally had the unusual triangular bay window carried by the roof of the bay window beneath.

1905. She later left Raleigh Villas to live with her older sister Mary in The Birches. Amelia was living at Raleigh Villas in 1900, but shockingly died after eating an infected plum pudding. Her sister Elizabeth and their servant also ate the pudding and were ill, but not quite so inconvenienced.

Ashley Villas (Nos.82/84) next door to Raleigh Villas also have 1880 on their date stone, though they were still being built in April 1881, and were an investment property for James Laughton of The Highlands. By October they were still not finished – and Laughton advertised for tenders to complete them. Was the first builder a rogue? Originally their polychrome bricks would have made them lively in looks, but for many years now they have been covered with render. One of the beauties of this row of Victorian houses is that they all have walled gardens – a restriction placed on the builders by the Warwick Hall Estate Company.

Also rendered is Thorndale (No.80), or as it was later known, Crofton Lodge. This plot was first bought by Charles Field the Younger, draper of Nottingham House in the High Street, who sold it on within a month to James Giles, bricklayer of Sidemoor, who let the land lie fallow until December 1887 when it was bought by Philip Levans. Levans was brother-in-law of James Lea of Fernleigh, was an estate agent and Sheriff's Officer on the High Street, and Clerk to the Local Board; he built just one house on the plot in 1888, and remained at Thorndale

Right: Thorndale, later Crofton Lodge (No.80 New Road), built in 1888 for estate agent Mr Philip Levans who lived there until the 1930s. The side extension gave him the opportunity to put in an attractive oriel window. J.C. Page.

Bottom: York House (No.90 New Road), built in 1897. A very strikingly designed house with Arts & Crafts touches, built on a narrow plot that has been well handled by the unknown architect.

himself until the 1930s. An addition to the front of the house was a pleasing oriel window on the first floor.

The plot beside Elmsdale also lay fallow and it wasn't until 1896 that it was split in two and fruiterer, town crier and bill-poster Henry Albutt, who had bought the plot (how did a bill-poster make enough money to buy three large plots in all?), and sold half the land to J.K. Elkington. The Elkingtons built Orrysdale (later changed to March House, No.92), after promising 'as soon as reasonably can be to plant a quick set fence at a distance of nine inches within the western boundary', staying until 1917. A traditional house, probably with no bay windows when first built, and without porch or garage, March House looks small compared with its tall close neighbour, York House (No.90) which as the date stone tells us was built in 1897. It is a striking Arts & Crafts house, unusual for Bromsgrove, with attractive brick detailing, clearly designed by a good architect. Although built for George Bower, retired innkeeper of the Coach and Horses, living on Stoney Hill, who bought the plot from Henry Albutt for £69.7s – it was bought in 1898 and lived in until his death in 1920 by Arthur Pickering, Managing Director of the clothing factory in Carlyle Road, one of the major employers of the neighbourhood. Bower's monogram is on the house, yet he does not appear to have ever lived in it.

Holly Dene (later Foxhollies, No.78) was built about the same time as York House on a plot owned by Mr Taylor. Lived in initially by a railway timekeeper, in 1916 John Henry Hardy, a bit of a martinet, and his wife moved in, bringing up their closeknit and rather eccentric family – Wilfred, Laurie, Doreen and Geoffrey (known as Sam), all buried from the house in which they were born – not quite – Geoffrey left his home a few months before he died. Laurie, a quiet man, had shown his true colours in WWII, when he was the naval officer in charge of landing craft on Anzio beach.

Next door were the last of the early built houses – two pairs, smaller than the others, which probably bears out the theory that there was less money available for building on land which had been bought on a flight of expectation of profit. No.76 was lived in by the Bond family from 1888, husband George dying in 1897, leaving his widow Ellen and daughters Jessie and Mary, schoolmistresses both, and William who became a clerk. No.74 is first mentioned in a directory in 1897 as being lived in by architect George Henry Gadd, married to Sarah (daughter of Samuel Yates), with his five children. Of these the youngest, G. Cyril Gadd also became an architect (designer of L.G. Harris's brushworks at Stoke Prior). Next door are Vailima (No.72) (Vailima was the village on Samoa where Robert Louis Stevenson died in 1894) and Columba (No.70), which as the datestone tells us were built in 1904 by JJ – possibly as an investment by John Jones, the nail factor of Birmingham Road.

Sales in 1881

By 1880 the Warwick Hall Estate Company was paying itself an annual dividend of 10 per cent per annum, and in 1881 the Company was advertising 'eight of the most eligible Lots to be sold by private contract' – 'This Property will very materially increase in value by time, it being one of the most healthy resorts in the neighbourhood'. Lot 16 was bought by Mr W. Ward at 1s 6d per yard (probably the corner plot of Clive and New Road), Lot 27 by Mr J. Weaver at 1s 3d (probably the corner plot of Clive and Wellington Road), and Lot 26 by Mr J. Read at 1s per yard – builders all! 'The reserves were low and the remaining Lots are to be sold by private treaty at a very moderate price.' Three years later Warwick Hall itself was bought by Mr Quintus C. Colmore, solicitor of Birmingham – presumably on behalf of W.E. Everitt, Esq., owner of Finstall House, who never lived there but is shown as owner of Warwick Hall on the 1891 Sale plan. The same year John Cotton auctioned another group of plots, Lots 9, 10 and 11 on Clive Road, though they were not sold.

The 1891 Sale

The next big Warwick Hall Company Sale was in 1891, when the Company hoped to sell the remaining plots in Clive and Wellington Roads, twelve plots on the east of Marlborough Avenue and, as can be seen from the illustrated plan, 32 plots down a Beaconsfield Road which was never built. Note also that already on the plan are mapped 'on the broad Avenues ... the Lime, Plane and other choice Trees', only a few of which are still ornamenting the roadsides today.

The largest Lot, No.92, down by the Stoke Road at Fringe Green included rich meadow land and two farm workers' cottages, Cotswold and Ivydene (Nos.130 and 132 Stoke Road), lived in by Messrs Clinton and Everton. 'Each house has its own Artesian Well, yielding an abundant supply of the purest water, and would be of inestimable advantage for a Brewery, Mineral Water Manufactory, or other trade purposes.' Their style gives a date of the 1840s or '50s, and their cheerful polychrome stripes are still looking good today, though both cottages are extended. They are older than nearly all the dwellings in Aston Fields.

Cotswold and Ivydene (No.130 and 132 Stoke Road), built as labourers' cottages in the 1840s or '50s for the Warwick Hall estate. The photograph doesn't do justice to the bright red and blue bricks that stripe round the building.

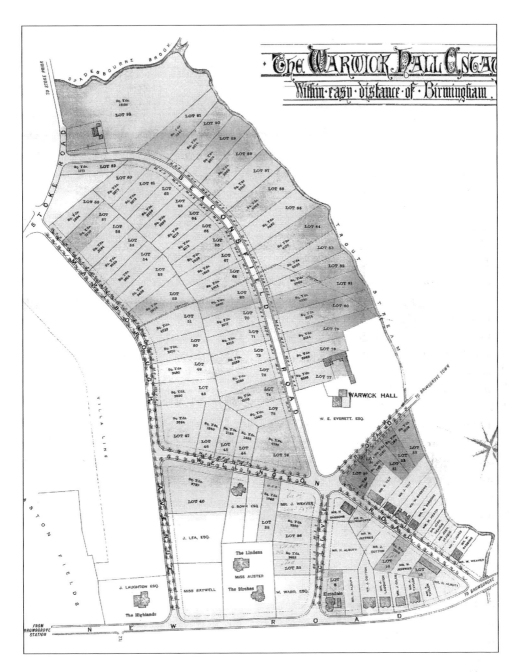

1891 Sale plan of the Warwick Hall Estate. This shows to whom plots had already been sold either by the Company or by William Llewellin and Charles Field. At this point Wellington, Marlborough and Clive Roads had been laid, but Beaconsfield Road was never built. BC.

Lot No.18 on the plan was on sale this time as Lot 1; here the four semi-detached villa residences, Kinver Terrace, Nos.1-7 today, were rented to Messrs Hemming (insurance agent), Tavenor (draper's assistant), Brooks and Garner (blacksmith) who were 'well supplied with water' and paid an annual rent of £44.

The 1891 Sale was clearly not successful – the Company had incorrectly gauged the amount of interest from those 'Merchant Princes' of Birmingham; indeed, most people living in the larger new houses already built on the Warwick Hall estate and in others in the area, were well-off local traders or owners of local businesses. The smaller terraces or semi-detached properties were rented as we have seen, mainly to clerks, railway workers or shop assistants.

Wellington Road

In 1881 Wellington Road was just opening up for building. By 1883 there existed three properties. Brook Cottage (No.8) was the first (now showing no sign of its age) with garden going down to the 'trout stream', divided to be lived in by Mrs Sassons, retired grocer and by Joseph Jones, a carpenter, who also owned the plot of land next door. Further down the road, on land also owned by the Sassons family, was built a solid pair of houses, Nos. 22 & 24; and then nothing else on this new road, until Mr Bown's beautiful home which he christened Carlton Villa, later to became Redthorne. George Bown was a well-to-do ironmonger and retailer of

agricultural implements in the High Street, who was ambitious – both of his sons went to Oxford – but gave his services to the town as most of the wealthy did in those days.

Carlton Villa hit the headlines in March 1895 when a hurricane hit Bromsgrove, to be vividly described in *The Messenger*. All Saints' Church lost a pinnacle, several chimneys fell through roofs, including the Hop Pole in Birmingham Road, and at Carlton Villa 'the top was blown from a chimney and made a great hole in the roof. ... a mass of masonry, consisting of ten courses of bricks from the chimney, and weighing about a ton, fell into the garden and then rolled through the hedge into the field beyond, where it lay in a solid lump.' Mr Colville of Conway Villa suffered a similar problem. 'Trees fell in all directions ... Practically every road in the district was blocked by fallen trees ... the case of the Old Station road is certainly worth a mention.' Gales twenty

George Bown, the prosperous ironmonger and agricultural implement dealer in the High Street, who lived at Carlton Villa (now Redthorne) in Wellington Road.

Left: Carlton Villa, now Redthorne (No.53 Wellington Road), built for Mr G. Bown in 1882, who lived there until his death in the 1920s. Right: A fearsome storm in March 1895 ripped the roof off Carlton Villa and severely damaged other Bromsgrove buildings. This drawing illustrated a detailed report in The Bromsgrove Messenger.

Postcard of Wellington Road in 1911, facing towards New Road. The terrace with bikes leaning against its wall is Nos.37-41; across the road the corner plot is still unbuilt.

years earlier had blown down a dozen of the black poplars and Lombardy poplars lining that road; this time 'further toll was levied upon the latter, and a number of the elms lining the approach to the Broom House also went down before the blast. In Finstall Park alone, twenty-three trees were felled.'

Soon more semi-detached and terraced houses arrived, in the main built for rent to artisans, traders' assistants and railway workers. In 1891 there were a foreman fitter, a railway wagon repairer, a railway coach spring maker, a railway timekeeper, a journalist, an insurance agent, a blacksmith (Henry Hedges, who had

Waterloo Villas (Nos.19-23 Wellington Road), architect John Cotton, which he built in 1883 for investment and owned until his death in 1934.

moved from Stoney Hill, and whose descendants still work in the same line today), a draper's assistant and a commercial traveller – quite a mix.

A larger detached house, Glendene, on the corner of Wellington and Clive roads, was built by Henry Sassons in 1888, who lived there until 1902 when he sold it for £600 to Mrs Rogers. Later it was lived in by J.M.H. Wilson of Barclays Bank

Glendene, now considered to be No.10 Clive Road, on the corner of Wellington Road with the original gate. This early 1900s post card shows Elmsdale in the centre, maturing trees lining the roadway, some of them lopped, and a grass bank behind them on the right.

Left: Glendene, built in 1888 for Mr Henry Sassons, whose family owned at least two other properties in Wellington Road, on the corner of Wellington and Clive Road, seen from the air in 2008. Mrs Cole. Right: The wrought iron gate decorated with a squirrel, probably put in place at Glendene by Mr George H. Whewell, Secretary and Managing Director at the Bromsgrove Guild.

before he moved to College Road in 1936. After this George H. Whewell, Secretary and Managing Director at the Bromsgrove Guild in its last declining years, moved in and added the wrought iron gate decorated with a squirrel and some good glass in the porch.

The most unusual large block is Cedarbrook, built as three homes by William Weaver the builder, on the corner of Wellington and New Roads, one house facing New Road and the others Wellington Road.

The Wellington Road face of the Cedarbrook block (Nos.2-6).

Cedarbrook (Nos.2-6 Wellington Road), built by William Weaver, builder. Unusually designed so that the front of No.2 faces New Road.

Warwick Terrace in Old Station Road, built by Tilt in 1899.

During the remainder of the nineteenth century other groups of houses were built to accommodate the rising number of lower middle classes. Round the corner in what we know as Old Station Road, though then it was an extension of Clive Road, is a group of five pairs of houses known as Warwick Terrace, built by J. Tilt around 1899. By 1891 he had already built the two blocks of four dwellings in Wellington Road, whose gardens abutted on those of Warwick Terrace; both of these blocks boasted a ceramic medallion in the central gable, similar to Elmsdale, though one of these has now gone. Along Wellington Road to where it meets Clive Road can clearly be seen the Victorian houses; during the Edwardian period there was no building here and a number of plots remained empty until the 'twenties.

Living in Wellington Road at this time was Philip Green describing himself as an architectural draughtsman, who in 1904 was the architect of Mornacott, No.12 College Road. He was born in Birmingham, but was in Bromsgrove at Charford House in 1891. Next door to him for a short period was George Bankart, the Bromsgrove Guild plaster craftsman, in rented accommodation with his young family until he moved to Cedar Drive, and Thomas Green, nail manufacturer, one of the several Green families in the nailing business.

Ceramic roundel on the centre gable of Nos.34-40 Wellington Road, built by Tilt prior to 1891.

The next tranche of building in Wellington Road was between Clive Road and Marlborough Avenue, when Cherry Lea (No.58) was built, and in 1905 Braziers built Nos. 47 and 49 which they rented out. These were the last to be built looking back towards traditional Victorian/Edwardian styles. Cherry Lea (now known as Rivendell) was built for Mr Thomas Gilbert, who had bought the plot of land from George Bown in 1903; Bown had bought it in 1892 from the Warwick Hall Company after the 1891 sale, while Mr Gilbert had already bought the land on the east and at the end of the plot.

Left: Postcard of Wellington Road in 1928, taken from Marlborough Avenue, showing White Cottage (No.60), architect probably G.H. Gadd. The field on the left of the picture was used for growing strawberries. Note the avenue of trees, planted almost fifty years previously. Right: Nos. 47/49 Wellington Road, a pair of three storeyed houses built in 1905 by Albert Brazier for renting out, and sold by him in 1920.

Left: Crossways (No.43), architect probably Philip Green who lived here during the 1930s and '40s, built on Mr J. Weaver's land on the corner of Wellington and Clive Road. Right: No.45 Wellington Road, architect probably Philip Green, also on Mr J. Weaver's land. Here lived Miss Fanny Scale, headmistress of the Meadows School in Stourbridge Road.

Then there came something different - some attractive Arts & Crafts influenced houses, most of them rendered in white. White Cottage (No.60), next to Cherry Lea, opposite Carlton Villa (Redthorne), was one of the early ones, built c.1910, its architect G.H. Gadd – surprisingly unlike his own home Redlands round the corner in Marlborough Avenue which he built in 1902. The large plot on the corner of Clive and Wellington Roads owned by Weaver was not built until 1913 when two delightful houses added to the streetscape, thought to be by Philip Green who lived in his latter years at Crossways. The smaller house was lived in for some years by Miss Fanny Scale, headmistress of Meadows School in Stourbridge Road.

Clive Road

Clive Road was also slow to take off. It wasn't until 1889 that Redcliffe (No.3) and Hollydene (No.5) were built for Charles A. Davies, manager of a brass tube works; these two houses, built high above the road, though joined, are not the same in design. Davies lived at Redcliffe until 1894 when widow Mrs M. Amiss moved in. The Firs (No.13) came in 1900, designed by G.H. Gadd, and occupied by Edwin Elks, a railway signal

The Firs (No.11) built in 1900 and Nos.13-17 Clive Road built after 1901.

A postcard of Clive Road showing Redcliffe (No.3) and Hollydene (No.5), a pair of three storeyed houses built in 1899 for Mr Charles Davies, manager of a brass tube works. Opposite is the stone wall of Elmsdale.

inspector; by 1903 Grasmere and Burnside were lived in by a father and son, George Butler, who even in his seventies was working at home making sword scabbards, and young Frank who was next door, a Secretary for the Temperance movement. Gradually the short road filled up – but only on the south side. Mr Henry Albutt, fruiterer, town crier and bill-poster, hung on to his orchard on the north side as he did with his plot on the corner of Wellington and New Roads. Neither was built on until the mid-20th century.

Marlborough Avenue
Marlborough Avenue, joining the New Road at the top of Black Hill, first saw a builder's wagon in 1893 on the south side of the road, on part of the arable Top Aston Field. This was bought from the Company in 1879 by William Llewellin and Charles Field the younger (of the High Street draper family), though not put on the market as building plots until the 1890s.

Beechwood (No.5) was the first to be built in 1893. This solid understated house set an example for the other houses to be built on the large plots in the road, and was bought and lived in by Henry Stone Whitfield, tailor, clothier, hatter and hosier, and owner of the large clothing factory in Carlyle Road. He was at Beechwood until

97

his death in 1905, and held in the family until 1918, when it was bought by Mr W.C. Kerr of The Highlands – though he did not move into the house himself until the late 1920s.

The second house was at the far end of Marlborough Avenue – Blenheim – apt title for a house in a road of this name. Here, on his retirement as Stationmaster at Bromsgrove Station, lived William Gimson until he died in 1898, Mrs Gimson staying on until the 1920s. The Gimsons had previously lived in the Stationmaster's house, known as Station Villa, on Station Approach [currently under threat of demolition]. Sydney

Beechwood (No.5) was built by Henry Stone Whitfield, a proprietor of the Clothing Factory in Carlyle Road, who lived in the house until 1905.

Blenheim in Marlborough Avenue, which was built in 1895 and demolished for Springfield Avenue in the late 1950s. The architect and builder of Blenheim are not known. This watercolour sketch, c.1914 by Philip Green, architect. J. Pearce.

Brazier of the building firm lived at Blenheim in the 1920s and '30s, followed by Mr Stephen Schilizzi, later a Housemaster at Bromsgrove School. Blenheim was demolished in the mid-20th century when eighteen homes were built on the site, now called Springfield Avenue.

The carved stone pediment and frieze above the window of Vitznau (No.20 Marlborough Avenue). The initials in the central cartouche are TG, for Thomas Gibbins.

Tom Gibbins, innkeeper of the old George in Worcester Street, moved into Vitznau (No.20) in 1897, hoping to enjoy retirement with his wife in this leafy road, but unfortunately leaving her a widow the same year. In his memory she gave an eighteenth century marble and stone font to St Godwald's church. Vitznau is the most decorative of the four semi-detached villas built by Tom Gibbins, and has the initials TG carved in the stone lintel above its front room window. Fairholme (No.18), next to Vitznau, was lived in at the beginning by Edmund Grove, who with his wife Rosannah had retired from farming in Fockbury. He too died in 1906, aged 77, his wife staying on until 1914. No.16, Branksome, was lived in first by bank manager Charles E. Davenport and his family, but soon afterwards rented by the dental surgeon Arthur Ward who had moved from Birmingham. He advertised his Tuesday evening surgeries at Branksome, when fillings and all types of operation were carried out, including extractions using gas, ether or cocaine as anaesthetics for a fee of 2s 6p (12½p). The

Left: Fairholme (No.18 Marlborough Avenue) and on the left Vitznau (No.20). These are two of the four houses built for Thomas Gibbins in 1897. Vitznau was more decorative than the others, built to be lived in by Mr and Mrs Gibbins. Right: Llanfair (No.1) and Wyona (No.3 Marlborough Avenue), in 1979. J. Lloyd Taylor.

Normanhurst (No.7) was built in 1902 for Henry Sassons, furniture dealer in Birmingham. The family remained in the house until 1932. The architect of this splendid house is unknown, but he made a feature of the decorative hung tiles on the front gable.

Redlands (No.8 Marlborough Avenue) was built by architect G.H. Gadd in 1901 to be lived in by himself and his family, where they stayed for 26 years. BC.

last of the four houses, No.14, was occupied by Victor Drury until 1901 when he moved to the even smarter new College Road, the house then being taken by the recently widowed Mrs Dipple. Following Mary Gibbins' death in 1921 some land she owned was auctioned, including an unbuilt plot on the corner of Wellington and Marlborough Avenue, and another opposite her own home. This was bought by George Green the estate agent, who then built Withymoor (No.13) and lived in it for many years.

1901 saw the building of Llanfair (No.1) and its pair, Wyona (No.3) by George Gray, tobacconist in Bromsgrove High Street and Deputy Registrar for Marriages, who moved into Wyona and rented out Llanfair. Here lived the Manager of the Midland Railway Carriage & Wagon Department, Robert Swales, who bought his home from Gray in 1922.

Normanhurst (7) was built in 1902, largest in the road, into which Henry and Rosa Sassons moved from Glendene (on the corner of Wellington and Clive Roads); his four daughters aged 3, 6, 8 and 9 were looked after by a resident Nanny, sister of the family's cook. Two of the Sassons girls remained unmarried, and stayed in Normanhurst until 1932.

Redlands (8), over the road, also came in 1902. The architect G.H. Gadd designed this for himself, and moved round the corner from New Road with his family of five – though this family did not aspire to a Nanny. Here the Gadds stayed until 1928. Working mainly in and around Bromsgrove, G.H. Gadd was responsible for houses in Wellington Road, but also for Bromsgrove High School, later Parkside School 1909-12 (with A.V. Rowe), the remodelling of the Queen's Head in 1907, several houses in Stoney Hill, and alterations and additions to the Cottage Hospital and the Institute & School of Art. For some time he was Architect for the Bromsgrove District Council, and his practice office

Napleton (now Athlone, No.15 Marlborough Avenue) was built in 1902 for William Ledbury, whitesmith and blacksmith of Worcester Street. The photograph for this postcard was taken when Marlborough Avenue was still surrounded by fields of strawberries.

was in the Town Hall Chambers where George Cyril joined him in the 1920s. Another notable family living at Redlands was that of John Nicholls of the button factory, there in the 1940s.

Napleton, now Athlone (No.15) was completed in 1902 for William Ledbury, whitesmith and blacksmith of Worcester Street. The quality of his work can be seen from the fleur de lys and the Art Nouveau style weathervane which decorate the house. Originally there were wrought iron gates, which are now no more; they were not taken away during the 'war effort' as so much decorative ironwork was, because they were regarded as a necessity, since Mr Halfpenny's cows were regularly taken up Wellington Road to graze in the field opposite and took any opportunity to wander in. The house was built by William Weaver, who dug a well in the cellar, which had to be regularly pumped out after rain to avoid flooding. Sadly Ledbury too was not able to enjoy his new home for long, for he was dead by 1907. Mrs Ledbury sold Napleton in the 1920s to Thomas McDermott who renamed the house Athlone, as it is known today, after his birthplace in Ireland, and he inserted the sandstone name stone into the chimney. McDermott was a leader in bringing moving pictures to Bromsgrove; in 1928 he ran the Playhouse Cinematograph Hall in Worcester Street, and by the 1950s was running this and the

The fleur de lys that decorates Napleton (Athlone) was made by William Ledbury's smiths, as was the weather vane on the roof.

Left: Architect Philip Green built Wayside (No.54) for himself in 1907. Although in Marlborough Avenue the house faces Stoke Road, as does No.63 across the road. A later resident was Major Bridge who was Headmaster of Watt Close school during the 1940s. Right: No 63 Marlborough Road, thought to be planned by Philip Green.

Regal cinema. In the 1940s he sold Athlone to his brother, and on the profits from the movies went upmarket to buy The Oakalls estate[49].

Philip Green, architectural draughtsman, was mentioned earlier as living in Wellington Road in 1901, aged 35, with his young family; by 1907 he had saved enough money to be able to build himself a new house, Wayside (No.54), in the Arts and Crafts style, on the corner of Marlborough Avenue and Stoke Road. This was one of the first of the attractive white-rendered houses to be built there, and it is conceivable that Philip Green designed more of them. By the mid 1920s there were several in Wellington Road and three in Marlborough Avenue, leading the way for most of the later architect designed dwellings in the immediate area to be in this style. He was also responsible for Mornacott (No.12), in College Road. Philip Green was a great supporter of St Godwald's church, and in 1900 he designed a new pulpit and organ case, followed in 1923 by a new organ chamber and the north vestries with their attractive doors; however his piece of work most familiar to us all is the Aston Fields war memorial, which was built in 1920.

Where Rutland Drive is today was originally Hillfield, planned by architect

Chesterton (No.32 Marlborough Avenue), built in 1927 by Braziers.

Arthur Bartlett who was responsible for the beautiful Arts & Crafts church at Dodford. It was built in 1910 for Walter Hesketh Scott, solicitor, who moved in from St. Godwald's, St. Godwald's Road. Some twenty-five years earlier W.H. Scott had taken on his father Thomas's role as clerk to the magistrates and clerk to the Commissioners of Income Tax and Land Tax. Thomas Scott had brought up his family in The Cedars in the 1880s.

Half way down Marlborough Avenue, on the bend, there is a path leading to Long Acre (No.34), lived in by Archibald J. Davies, Bromsgrove Guild stained glass artist, but up until the mid 20th century this path led to the backlands worked as market gardens, grazing and orchards by Mr Halfpenny and Mr James Evans. But it was not a new path – originally it was one of the network of footpaths that were the main links between hamlets and Bromsgrove town; this one took people from Fringe Green Farm on the Stoke Road right up to the old Station Road.

Aston Fields' War Memorial designed by architect Philip Green to remember those who gave their lives in World War I. The names of those who died in World War II were added later.

The Last Big Sale

During the years after 1891 small parcels of land were offered for sale, often by purchasers of Lots in the early Sales, which in the main had been bought by builders or canny – or not so canny – investors. The last big Sale was in 1918 when Warwick Hall itself and 26 acres (10.5 hectares) came on the market. Most of this land was offered in small Lots as being suitable for smallholdings and market gardens, but in the end came into the hands of building firms, for in the mid twentieth century this land was used for Warwick, Brueton and Hampton Avenues. The attention of 1918 purchasers was drawn to 'the Main Sewer of Bromsgrove District Council along the north-western boundary, following the Brook, thus affording opportunity of obtaining drainage facilities of considerable value'.

Warwick Hall was sold by private treaty before the sale. By now it was clearly a gentleman's residence, with all 'mod cons'. Not only had it large reception rooms but also a conservatory 42ft long

Warwick Hall in 1918 when it was sold as a gentleman's residence with 26 acres (10.5 ha). BC.

Warwick Hall garden front as it was in 1910, with the then fashionable ivy covering the castellated extension to the sixteenth century farmhouse. BC.

(12.8m) and a 'handsome billiard room'. There was a bathroom for its four family bedrooms (with mahogany fittings, hot and cold), a W.C. and hot-air linen cupboard, with two servants' bedrooms on the second floor. The gardens included a croquet lawn, a substantial summerhouse, a pavilion and a tennis lawn. There was also an entrance Lodge with two bedrooms – still to be seen at the entrance to Warwick Hall Gardens, though the 'expensive wrought-iron entrance gates, pillars and lamps' have disappeared. In 1924 the house, lodge and some land were on sale again, when Mrs Matthewson became the occupant for some twenty years until the 1940s. In the 1970s the house was altered to become a residential home for the elderly, with many extensions to the property, and twenty-five houses were built on Warwick Hall's gardens.

Brookfields, a house built around 1906 on part of the orchard very close to Warwick Hall, and let to Mr R.T. Hall, approached by a long carriage drive from the corner of Wellington and Old Station Roads, was sold for £920. Notable amongst its facilities, and also of Warwick Hall's, was a motor house or garage among the outbuildings. Brookfields also disappeared for the building of Warwick Hall Gardens.

The two-bedroomed Lodge to Warwick Hall in 1918, built after 1901, together with its splendid gates which have now gone. BC.

Cherry Lea, in Wellington Road, let to Mr W.E. Burman, was sold out of the estate for £500, bought by Mr William Corbett, chemist and mineral water manufacturer of the High Street. Although a five bedroomed house it did not have a motor house. It was described as having 'Entrance Porch, Square Hall (with fireplace), Dining and Drawing Rooms', and the usual kitchen quarters. *The Messenger* gave no other prices, except that a smallholding of 3 acres 3 roods 8 perches (just over 1 hectare) was sold for £165, and good prices were achieved for plots of land adjoining the other properties in the road. Who bought these fields? Very possibly it was local builders or groups of businessmen with an eye to the future needs of an expanding town, but for many years more Mr J.H. Halfpenny and Mr James Evans were tenants using the land on both sides of Marlborough Avenue for grazing, market gardening and fruit growing.

Chapter Nine

The Cedars Estate and its Owners

When Samuel Yates, the busiest property speculator in Bromsgrove, bought Barn Close where the Crescent is built he also bought the pastureland alongside. In 1870 he put up a fine new house, more than probably designed by his recently trained architect son Frederick. It was set well back from New Road, with a lodge at the gate, the only New Road house with such grandeur. The Cedars was built with its main entrance facing its garden and orchards, the kitchen quarters at the back against the boundary wall. There were stables, built with a back access down 'a cart track' that later became known as Garibaldi Terrace. Here Yates lived for a couple of years with his family, offering the house for rent or sale, until one day John Sheldon, a newcomer to Bromsgrove, arrived wishing to buy the house and land – so Samuel moved his long suffering wife into yet another home – Torbay Cottage in Station Road.

The only available photograph of The Cedars, taken in 1967. To the left of the house, which faces south, is a range of greenhouses. There is a great similarity between this house (1870) and Sunnymead (1873). R. Alton.

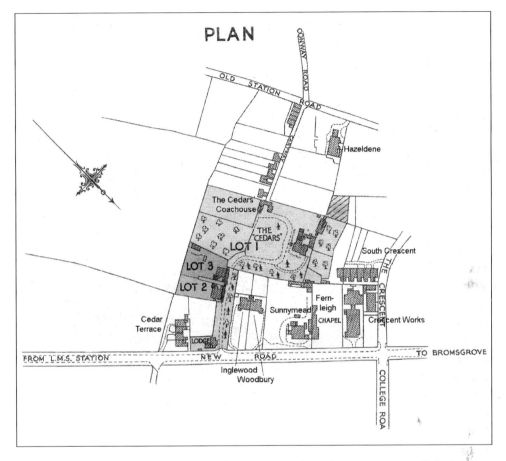

1946 Sale plan of The Cedars. Inglewood, Woodbury and South Crescent were built by John Sheldon, as was Sheldon Terrace in the Crescent (not shown on this plan); Sunnymead was probably bought by John Sheldon in 1883. Note that Garibaldi Terrace is marked as a Cartway, originally for market gardeners to reach their plots, and later to become the back entrance through the stables' archway into The Cedars. BC.

Little is known about John Sheldon before he came to Bromsgrove. He was born in Great Bridge, Tipton in 1826, but appears on no later censuses, giving credence to a theory that he had lived in India and also on the continent, where he made his fortune working as a bridge engineer.[50] Having purchased The Cedars in 1874 he lived there for a year, and then for two years he gave his address as Umritsur Cottage, New Road (another hint of an Indian background) which has not been identified. He then bought a further plot of land against the Crescent where he built the attractive terraced row known as South Crescent and lived there

South Crescent in The Crescent was built in 1877 by John Sheldon who added his crest to the first and the sixth house in the terrace and lived at No.6 until 1882. These charming houses have extended gardens in front, though these were not added to the properties until much later.

Left: John Sheldon's carved wood crest on No.1 South Crescent. Right: Sheldon Terrace was built by John Sheldon in 1877, just off The Crescent. It remained in his possession until his death, when in 1891 it was sold to Mr. G.A. Klosz for £1,260.

himself in No.6 between 1877 and 1882, looked after by a housekeeper. He rapidly became part of the Bromsgrove social scene, and in 1879 was Bailiff of the Court Leet. The Cedars meantime was rented out to Mr F.A. Harrison. Sheldon's next purchase was in 1877 of two plots of land off the Crescent where he put the five cottages, Sheldon Terrace.

By 1879 Cedar Terrace had been built, in a different style from the Crescent buildings – more like The Cedars, with cheerful brick string courses. These four houses are bigger than their looks, having three bedrooms each, and described at the 1917 Sale as having cellars, a shared pump, and being 'roomy, well-built, and always commanding good tenants'. A good extension to No.1 was built in 2008, planned to fit in with the old building. Notable tenants in these early years were Henry Dickinson, a master at the School of Art (No.4), Arthur Bartlett, architect of Dodford Church (No.1), and Alexander McEwan Allan (Mac), the Bromsgrove Guild modeller and designer (No.4).

Sheldon's empire grew in 1882 with two good villas built on the drive to The Cedars, again built with their main entrance doors and reception rooms at the back, facing across their gardens towards the fields of Fordhouse Farm and the sun. The simplicity of the exterior of these two houses belies their interior, for they were planned

NEW ROAD, BROMSGROVE.

A postcard of 1919 showing Cedar Terrace (1879) and the Thomas White Homes (1886). Note the row of trees planted in the broad footpath along New Road, all now gone.

A 1965 aerial photograph of Inglewood (left, No.38 New Road) and Woodbury (right, No.36), built in 1888. The pair of conservatories (only Woodbury's is now extant) add a touch of individuality to the buildings. Privately owned.

to be spacious and comfortable – so comfortable that Walter H. Scott, solicitor of St John Street, lived in No.1 for over fifty years. The previous occupant, who was in the house for just four years, was John Humphreys, the respected Professor of Dentistry at Birmingham University, who had started his working life as a chemist in Bromsgrove High Street. He was a man of great enthusiasm and had many interests which he studied with intensity, from prehistoric man to trees, boulders and ferns – his collection of Worcestershire flora was given to Birmingham Museum. In Bromsgrove he took a full part in local government, was Court Leet Bailiff in 1896, thoroughly enjoyed amateur dramatics and was Chairman of the Cycling Club.[51]

Later, work started on the pair of houses, Inglewood (No.38) and Woodbury (No.36). Datemarked 1888, they were designed simply, their notable feature being a

Left: No.2 Cedar Villas in 1970, a pair with No.1, both built 1882. No.2 was lived in for many years by Mr and Mrs Sheldon, while No.1 was the home of Walter H. Scott, solicitor, until 1943. The garden fronts face south. M. Lawrance. *Right: John Humphreys, M.A., Ph.D., M.D.S., F.S.A., F.L.S., F.G.S. When aged 21 John became a self-taught dentist in Bromsgrove; by the end of his life, aged 86, he had become one of Bromsgrove and Birmingham's most respected and learned citizens, knowledgeable and influential in a great many spheres. Humphreys lived in Cedar Drive between 1888 and 1893.*

matching pair of conservatories at each end of the New Road frontage; sadly only Woodbury still has its conservatory. The 1917 Sale catalogue states firmly that they 'occupy one of the best positions on the road, and [because they are set well back from the road] are free from the inconvenience of motor dust'.

In 1882 John Sheldon married, aged 55. Mary Ann Drury, a 43 year old widow, had lived in the High Street with her father William Brown, a plumber, and it seems that Sheldon joined her there, for in 1883 he gave his address as the High Street. The next year, however, the married couple was installed in Cedar Villas No.2 where they lived, one hopes happily, until June 1889. Then their lives were turned upside down.[52]

The respectable Mrs Sheldon was taken to court for bigamy. The case against her was that her previous husband George Drury, though thought to have died in Dartmoor Prison in 1877 (the death certificate was produced) was after all alive – and that she had been informed of the fact before her recent marriage to John Sheldon. Prosecution called her nephew and his mother, both Bromsgrove people, who swore that they had shown and given to Mary Ann a letter from George Drury, and that he had visited them in Bromsgrove. Defence lawyer, Mr Amphlett, accused the witnesses of jealous conduct because Mary Ann had been the sole inheritor of her father's estate, and stressed the good character of his client who denied receiving such a letter. He then called Walter Parry, nail manufacturer and member of the County Council, who had known Mary Ann for thirty years and confirmed her high character and respectability. The judge reviewed the facts of the case. The jury retired.

> 'The jury were absent about a quarter of an hour and returned into Court with a verdict of 'Not guilty'. A slight attempt at applause was made in the rear of the Court as the verdict was announced. Mrs Drury then left the dock; and a scene of considerable excitement took place outside, one lady fainting, while other friends pressed round Mrs Drury to offer their congratulations.'

So Mrs Sheldon became Mrs Drury again – though Bromsgrove appeared to be happy for her to be known in society by the name of her new 'husband'.

George Drury appeared before Birmingham Quarter Sessions in January the following year, accused of stealing portmanteaux from New Street station railway platform on two occasions. He seems to have been a compulsive suitcase thief, for his previous sentence was twelve months' hard labour for a similar offence and earlier he had served sentences of five years and seven years. The Birmingham Recorder sentenced him to seven years' penal servitude, and we hear no more of him in this book.

John Sheldon, however, getting on in years at 64, was probably sadly shaken by all this scandal, and he died a year after the court case in October 1890. Mrs

Sunnymead (see Chapter 5), architect F.J. Yates, was part of The Cedars estate when John Sheldon died, and was then put up for auction. BC.

Drury/Sheldon, however, did not do too badly – she was now owner of a nice little estate, even though much of it was mortgaged. A year later she put some of it up for sale, in five lots, and included in the Sale as Lot 3 was Sunnymead.

Sunnymead, also designed by F.J. Yates, was very similar in looks to The Cedars, and built in 1873 for James Parry, just retired from his family's nail factoring business in Church Road, Catshill. Parry died in 1879 leaving his widow living at Sunnymead until 1883. It is possible that John Sheldon bought the property at this point. Sunnymead was an attractive, gentleman's house, brick, with stone string courses and 'eyebrows' over the windows, entered up an elegant flight of stone steps and a porch with barge boards, as had the two gables. Attached to the side was a very large conservatory. Again, the main front was positioned to receive the sun most of the day.

After William Hadley, a dental surgeon, had lived there for a few years the house was bought at the 1891 Cedars Sale by Ernest Brewster Cotton, his wife Jessie, and their three children. Ernest B. was step-brother of John and William A. Cotton, and a different type of person from those two earnest men – popular, sporting and full of life. He headed the family auctioneering business, and opened branch offices in the area dealing with stock and crop sales and house auctions. However, during the spring of 1912 he became depressed, not only for financial reasons but also dreading the serious illness, Bright's Disease, that had killed his father and step-brother, and shockingly he committed suicide by shooting himself in a field after taking a train to Rugby. His creditors forced an order in Worcester Bankruptcy Court for £6,000, leaving his business and his dependents in disarray. They of course then had to leave the family home, which was bought by Dr Coaker, who had a surgery in the garden, built by J. & A. Brazier. Later residents were Dr C.G. Auld, and Dr. Wilkinson before he moved to a new surgery in Recreation Road. Sunnymead was demolished in the 1960s to be developed as a cul de sac, which kept the same name.

The sale of part of The Cedars estate in 1891 achieved the following: Sunnymead went to William Hadley and South Crescent was bought by W.H. Avery of Fairview in Finstall. The small field between Sunnymead and South Crescent did not sell and was added to The Cedars land; Sheldon Terrace in the Crescent was sold to a Mr G.A. Klosz of London (who later in wartime changed his name to Close).

Mrs Sheldon continued to live at No.2 Cedar Drive, until in 1902 she married again. This was to William Francis Hobrough, Engineer in charge of the Worcester and Birmingham Canal and the Droitwich canals[53]. He was clearly an ingenious and inventive man, who solved many of the construction problems on these waterways. His home was the Bridge House at Stoke Wharf where he 'lived the life of a gentleman', running a brougham and a wagonette and involved in parish and other local affairs. Until his retirement he was joined at Stoke Wharf by his new wife, who by then was 62; her new husband – still working – was 74. After Mrs Hobrough left for Stoke Wharf her home was lived in by George Bankart of the Bromsgrove Guild, until William Hobrough retired in 1908, when the couple returned, Bankart having moved to work in London the year before. Mr Hobrough died four years later, aged 84. Mary Ann lived until March 1917, aged 77.

The Cedars property was put up for auction in six Lots two months later by Smith & Russon at the Golden Cross. Inglewood and Woodbury were sold for £1,230 (for both), Cedar Terrace for £1,000. The Cedars (£1,400) and its lodge (£300) and the two villas in Cedar Drive were bought by Mr A.C. Cutler, who was already living in The Cedars. Nothing more seems to have caused drama after the sale, and this area of New Road was peaceful again, remaining so until Cutler's death in 1946. The Cedars and its grounds were then purchased by Mr Griffin, builder of Catshill for £4,000, who eventually built numerous new homes on the site. A condition of the Sale was that the purchasers of the two villas should pay 'a contribution of Five Pounds per annum towards the upkeep of the Drive'.

Chapter Ten

Preaching and Teaching – Chapels, Church and School

It was on Mothering Sunday in 1851 that a national census was taken of the country's religious worship. What seems to us to be a surprising result showed that over half the population chose not to attend church or chapel on that day, and that fewer than half of the worshippers were Church of England. Most of the worshippers were middle-class, and most of them were nonconformist; absentees were overwhelmingly working class.

With this knowledge all the denominations determined to raise their numbers – though it seems that in Bromsgrove the several churches and chapels were already thriving, and, especially with the growth of population at Aston Fields, there was a need for new buildings. There was the little Stoke Chapel of Ease, but no nonconformist chapels that might better suit the railway workers' families. The gentry – from Rigby Hall, Finstall Park and the larger houses – worshipped at St John's in Bromsgrove or at Stoke Prior, taken in their carriages. Nonconformists from near the railway had to walk up New Road to Worcester Street Baptist chapel, to the Kidderminster Road Wesleyan chapel, or to Chapel Street to the Congregational chapel [now United Reformed Church]. The Roman Catholic chapel at Grafton Manor was replaced by St Peter's church on Rock Hill in 1858, and it is said that in the late 1880s and early 1890s a Quaker Meeting was held at Finstall Farm, at the top of Finstall.

The Baptist Chapel, New Road

The Bromsgrove Baptist church community has a long history[54], longer than those of most Midland towns and, proudly, was a forerunner of the Birmingham ministry. The earliest Bromsgrove records go back to the mid-seventeenth century but by the 1850s the sometimes thriving, sometimes depressed congregation worshipped at the chapel in Worcester Street [now a night-club]. In 1864 the membership was healthy enough to warrant thoughts of a new building. Among the committee members delegated to plan the chapel were our useful old friend Samuel Yates the estate agent, James Parry the nailmaster, and J.H. Scroxton, the influential High Street newsagent, printer and poet, son of the late and much loved minister, John Scroxton.

The 35-year-old Wolverhampton architect George Bidlake, already known for his nonconformist chapels, was asked to design the building to go on an elevated site on the New Road, bounded on one side by Ednall Lane and surrounded by orchards. It is probable that Samuel Yates was instrumental in suggesting the site, part of Barn Close (soon to be the Crescent) which he had recently purchased from Mr Frances. The young would-be Bromsgrove architect John Cotton had only the previous year become apprenticed to Bidlake, so Bidlake had a link with the town, though the builder, Mr Richard Thompson, was from Kidderminster. The chapel was geometric Gothic in style, red brick with stone dressings, built with a view to adding the turret and side galleries in the future – a future that came quite quickly. There was seating for 600 worshippers, though the congregation numbers at the time of building were 170. Imagine the effect this bright brick had – there were no buildings on this side of the still very new road, so it would have been a dramatic sight as one walked up from the High Street.

Left: The architect's drawing for the Baptist chapel in New Road, built in 1866. The tower was added a few years later. George Bidlake was a specialist in nonconformist churches, his architectural practice in Wolverhampton. John Cotton of Bromsgrove was articled to him from 1865-1867. His son, W.H. Bidlake was for a few months partner with John Cotton, and became one of Birmingham's most important architects. CC. Right: A 1974 photograph showing the splendid tower added to the Baptist chapel. Baptist church archive.

Behind the chapel the schoolrooms for 250 children were opened in October 1888, built by Messrs. J. Read & Sons, to plans by Mr W.T. Layton, a member of the building committee – 'the aim had been to get a useful rather than an ornamental building'. It is still being useful today.

By 1891 the chapel itself was 25 years old and in need of refurbishment; on re-opening it must have looked glorious, having an interior 'rich in design and colour'. The 'warm willow-green, relieved by a frieze of terracotta outlined with Indian red, and a stencil ornament of the

The Baptist Sunday Schools in Ednall Lane, built in 1888, with four memorial stones set in the brickwork.

same colour on the terracotta'. The chancel walls had 'a scroll in terracotta, upon which is written ... "Enter into his courts with thanksgiving"; the chancel arch was decorated by 'geometrical ornamental stencilling and a serrated border in dull blue'. The 'gasoliers, gas brackets and ironwork to gallery and rostrum front are picked out in positive colours and gold ...,' the whole design by Mr C.M. Barber of Hereford.[55] Some 85 years later Bidlake's Gothic building was tired and expensive to run, and the community built another church on the site in 1976. Then fourteen years later, in 1990, another new church with a slim metal spire took its place, and thus it is that there have been three churches on one site.

From Church School to Board School

During the 1840s the church school near the old Stoke Chapel had proved adequate to house the number of children requiring a little reading, writing and arithmetic. But by 1880 there were so many – about 56 in the 3-5 age group, and 160 in the 5+ group – that the government's Education Department requested Stoke Prior School Board to establish a school in Aston Fields near the railway station. A one acre (0.4 hectare) plot on Further Hither Furlong was bought from the John Jones Newton Farm estate and a competition announced, for which there were eight entries. John Cotton's design 'Convenience and Economy' was chosen, with Alfred H. Parker of Worcester's 'Utility' second. Bromsgrove builders Tilt and Fisher built the school, the painting and plumbing was done by Mr Brown, and the wrought iron railings were made by Mr Hedges. The patent pitch-pine school desks on iron standards and other furniture came from the Midland Educational Co. of Birmingham, supplied in three heights to suit children of different ages. The architectural style was Gothic, with roof dormer windows for ventilation,

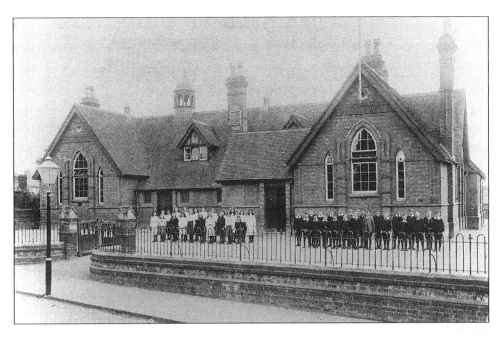

By the time this photograph was taken, after 1901, there was already a porch extension spoiling the lines of John Cotton's design. Note the bell turret and on the central chimney the monogram for Stoke Prior School Board. Mr William Hedges of Worcester Street made the wrought iron railings, Mr William Brown of the High Street did the painting and plumbing, and the builders were Messrs. Tilt and Fisher. BC.

prominent chimneys (one with carved date stone) and a bell cot of open timberwork on the roof with a weather vane on top. By 1886 the school needed separate infants and 'baby rooms', which were built behind the main block.

The Board was fortunate in their choice of headmaster, Mr Charles H. Tunbridge, who settled in Aston Fields for thirty-eight years. There not being a teacher's house attached to the school – although planned it was never built – he and his wife Victoria (who taught the infants) lived in New Road, though not a settled existence. They started off in Roseleigh (No.130) in 1882, had moved up the road into Hestonleigh (No.120) by 1900, and then next door to Penshurst (No.122) in 1903, first renting the property and then in 1908 buying it from William Quinney of Finstall. It was Mr Tunbridge who set the tradition of a high standard of music in the school at Aston Fields, for with the help of Mr Smallwood of Rigby Hall he raised funds to buy a seven guinea (£7.35p) harmonium. With the help of their elder daughter, also Victoria, the Tunbridges worked extremely hard on extra-mural activities, taking responsibility for education of adults as well as children by running evening classes.

Finstall Board School grew as the population multiplied, was extended in 1886, and continued to flourish until new schools were built off Rigby Lane – Aston Fields Middle School on Drummond Road in the 1970s and Finstall First School in Carnforth Road in 1992.[56] Today the much-altered old buildings are used as a training centre. Drummond Road was built on some land used for Allotments, known as Fourth Wheelers Close in the 1840s and part of Fordhouse Farm. The Middle School was built on Rigby Hall orchard land.

St Godwald's Church

The little chapel of ease at Aston Fields, seating only 130, was becoming noticeably too small for the growing number of people coming to live in the village. The main expansion of Aston Fields was yet to come, but even so, the 1871 census lists 618 inhabitants, and the 1881 census showed 997. In 1883 the churchwardens decided that a new church must be built, double the size of the chapel, with 240 sittings, and a small part of the Dragoon fields was given by Mr William Robson, late owner of the Warwick Hall estate, who had moved to Bournemouth. John Cotton, who had just so successfully designed Finstall Board School, was invited to draw plans, with the instruction that cost was of vital importance (when is it not?). Indeed funds were so tight that Brazier & Weaver's stone mason was not allowed to complete carving on

St Godwald's Church (built 1883) and the Vicarage (1897). Although John Cotton designed the church with a steeple the parish could never afford to build it and had to make do with a small bell cot on the porch where the steeple should have been, and a small turret over the crossing.

Interior of St Godwald's church, architect John Cotton (1883). The south organ chamber was added in 1923, architect Philip Green. The walls are yellow brick, with good stonework detailing and arches; some of the corbels were uncarved because of shortage of money.

some corbels; however, it was to be built to be capable of enlargement. Sandstone was brought down from Mr Fetherston's quarry in Finstall, a gift from the wealthy farmer. It was built with nave, south transept and chancel, but no north transept, organ-chamber, vestry or tower. Cotton could not resist showing a turret over the porch on his first drawing, but this has never been built.

Many were sad to leave the little chapel, which had occasional use until 1960. One writer to *The Messenger* mourned:

> Only those who have been associated with the place are able to appreciate the charm that was attached to it ... The peacefulness of the surroundings, only disturbed by the occasional passing of a train down the "bank" – they were not so numerous in those days, and the Sunday traffic was very small – seemed to clothe one as with a garment. I can seem to hear the Vicar, Mr Bainbrigge, conducting the service (he was not possessed of a particularly pleasant voice); I can hear the wheezy harmonium, and the weak voices of the ladies in the choir "leading" the singing; and see the homely, motherly face of the Vicar's wife. There were never many of us, and it all seemed so homely and friendly.'

In 1923, Philip Green of Wellington Road was able to add the organ chamber and vestries to the new church, having already designed the organ case and the pulpit in 1900. Mr Avery of Fairview, Finstall gave a brass eagle lectern. William Robson paid for the east window designed by Temple Moore, in memory of his wife Sarah, whose family had owned the Warwick Hall estate since 1799, while A.E. Lemmon of the Bromsgrove Guild in 1937 designed a two-light window in memory of Barbara Ethel Palmer for the south transept, one of its lights showing St Cecilia the patron saint of music. His son Peter later designed a window celebrating church music, full of musical allusions.[57] Another member of the congregation was Celestino Pancheri of the Bromsgrove Guild of Applied Arts, who was then working in the old Dragoon stables; he embellished

The memorial to the Normandy Landings on 6 June 1944 in St Godwald's church was carved in Clipsham stone by Robert Pancheri.

A.E. Lemmon painted the patronal banner of St Godwald's church in 1927, the saint as a bishop with the village church in his hand. On the left he painted the old chapel with a train descending the incline; on the right is a detailed picture of the Wagon Works in a rural background. The fragile treasure was restored in 2007.

the 1897 reredos in 1924 and his son Robert in 1946 carved the memorial to the Normandy landings in Clipsham stone.

Until 2006, quietly crumbling away in the church chest, was a fragile silk patronal banner. It was painted by A.E. Lemmon, also of the Bromsgrove Guild, in 1927. This shows St Godwald cradling the new church in his hands, while scenes from parish life, including the Wagon Works, are depicted behind him. Funds were raised to restore the banner, which is about to be safely displayed behind glass on the wall of the church.

In 1883 the Ecclesiastical Commissioners also agreed to grant £1,500 for the building of a parsonage – the Revd. Bainbrigge was still living in the house he had built in St Godwald's Road [now the Primrose Hospice], but he died in 1896, followed in 1907 by his widow. The house, St Godwalds, was put on the market and was bought by Joseph Tilt, the builder, presumably to rent out since he never lived there. The new Gothic style vicarage was not built until 1897, when Lewis Sheppard of Worcester was asked to plan both this and the parish room. The vicarage was built alongside the church with big hipped roof and tall chimneys, and surrounded by gardens. It is now superseded by a newly built vicarage placed in front of the old one, which is to be refurbished as flats.

Another addition was the Parish Hall in 1897, costing £430 and also built by Joseph Tilt. This made a tremendous difference to both congregation and the community, not only being used for the Sunday School but for adult classes, concerts and other activities. It was so successful that it was extended, built on land offered by Mr Edward Ansell of Rigby Hall (at a nominal rent) with the intention of starting an Institute 'for innocent recreation and a thoroughly healthy tone'. Rather duplicating the Working Men's Club, the new Institute had classes for all, as well as cards, dominoes and billiards – but no alcohol.

The church congregation greatly benefited from the house building on the Warwick Hall Estate and from the numerous terraced houses built along Stoke Road and Carlyle and Middlefield Roads. The gentry from Finstall Park and Rigby Hall, though benevolent towards the children of the parish, on Sundays still went up New Road in their pony traps to worship at St. John's in Bromsgrove. Several Warwick Hall Estate residents have already been mentioned, and it was these well-off middle-class people, together with wealthy local farmers, who were the backbone of the new church.

The Wesleyan Methodist Chapel, New Road

The Aston Fields nonconformist community was drawn primarily from the railwaymen and the agricultural workers of the area, while the Bromsgrove Methodists appear to have relied upon numerous shopkeeping families for their flock.

Aerial photograph c.1960s of the Methodist Church with tower still in place, and its Schoolroom behind. The chapel was of red brick with stone detailing, its roof with alternate bands of green and grey slate. Next to it on the right are the Crescent Works, and far right across the Crescent is Lupton House. Across the lawn on the left is Fernleigh. Privately owned.

The mainstream Methodist congregation in Bromsgrove, known as Wesleyan, had been in existence since at least 1823 when they were meeting in the Congregational Chapel [now United Reformed Church, Windsor Street].[58] By 1832 a new chapel was built in Kidderminster Road, opposite St John's, with seating for 240 people. Fifty years later when the roof fell in the congregation decided to build a new chapel on a site owned by Thomas White, opposite The Newlands, for which they paid £400.

This was to be a Bromsgrove build. F.J. Yates was the architect, Joseph Tilt of the Hop Pole in Birmingham Road was the builder, and stonework was by Mr Griffin of Rock Hill. The new chapel with room for 350 seats, and its schoolroom for 300 children, was completed and opened in 1884 with, as always, massive debts. The group had done its best to raise funds, and though two years previously John Cotton held a Sale of the chattels from the Kidderminster Road chapel, selling its pulpit, the gas standards and the seating, there was still £2,500 to be raised. However, the debts did not stop the building of a twenty-seater gallery and installation of an organ (£80) nine years

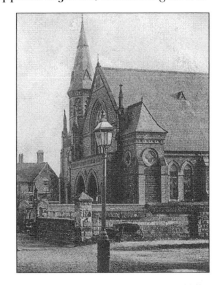

The Wesleyan Methodist Church built 1884, showing detail of its brick and stone Gothic design by F.J. Yates.

To celebrate the 50th anniversary of the building of the church in 1934 a new larger organ was bought, the rostrum was moved to accommodate it, and choir seats built on either side. An electric blower was installed for the organ, and electric light for the congregation. Brian Henderson shown here at the organ in 1983. B & J Henderson.

later. The chapel itself was, again, Gothic, red brick with Mr Griffin's stone dressings, and a colourful roof with alternate bands of green and Bangor slates. The stubby octagonal turret was decorated with moulded stone pinnacles and set on a tall stone lantern. Gas light fittings, including three handsome coronas suspended from the roof, were made by the excellent Messrs. Stock, Son and Taylor of Birmingham[59]. In the 1930s the organ was enlarged, and the choir, previously in the organ chamber, was brought forward into tiered seating.

In the 1970s the turret became unsafe and was removed. Then the widely told story is that one day the Baptist elders of the chapel down the hill asked a surveyor to inspect their building. Not knowing the area, he went to the Methodist chapel in error and gave it a thorough survey. He found severe problems in the drainage system and pronounced that the sandstone foundations were dangerously wearing away, and the Methodists felt fortunate – or not – that the surveyor had come to them. The costs of looking after the chapel, as well as the other two Victorian chapels in Bromsgrove (Birmingham Road and Carlyle Road) became too high for their modest congregations to support, and so the decision was made to sell the three buildings and build one new Methodist Centre on the site of the old almshouses on Stratford Road. On closure of the New Road building the organ became redundant and was sold to Ham Parish Church, in Surrey. One treasure was moved into the spanking new building in 1983 – a small stained glass window by Bromsgrove Guild artist A.E. Lemmon, depicting St. Cecilia, patron saint of music. The dedicatee of the window was Harry Irish, organist, who died in 1956.[60] The New Road site was then redeveloped to build the Raglan Court block of flats.

By the 1970s the tower was in bad repair and the congregation were unable to pay the cost of restoration, and so had it removed, but continued to worship in the church until 1983 when the building was demolished. Chris Roberts.

Benjamin Tilt, builder, lived at the Hop Pole in Birmingham Road. He and his son Joseph built the Wesleyan Methodist Chapel, Finstall Board School, Aston Fields clothing factory, the Police Station and Court House. BC.

Primitive Methodist Sunday School, Carlyle Road

During the early nineteenth century some Methodists believed that their church had moved too far away from the beliefs of Charles Wesley, and that their worship and the places of worship should be simpler, with leadership from lay people, and even from women evangelists, rather than ministers. They believed themselves to be true guardians of the original, or primitive, form of Methodism and were popular with the Bromsgrove nailers and rural working class, though known to outsiders as 'Ranters' because of their evangelical enthusiasm. Growing in numbers, the Aston Fields Primitive Methodists, who began by meeting in a cottage, and later in a tent, acquired the corner plot on New Road in order to build their own place of worship.

The Primitive Methodist Sunday School, now the Salvation Army. The four memorial stones laid in 1891 can just be seen behind the fence. F.J. Yates was architect, and the builder J. Read & Sons of Bromsgrove.

It was however felt that a Sunday School rather than a chapel was of greater immediate importance, and with the support of F.J. Yates, the architect, who offered his work at half fee, the small Sunday School was built by J. Read & Sons, builders of Birmingham Road. No fewer than four memorial stones were laid on 11 April 1891 at the site on the corner of Carlyle Road and New Road, and on 7 June the opening ceremony was held. The building had one large room and two classrooms, plus a little kitchen and storeroom, and cost £450. It was tucked away at the back of the site in order to allow for the later building of a chapel to front New Road, while in the meantime the new schoolroom was used for services.

During the early part of the twentieth century the two groups' views moved nearer together and in 1932 the Primitives formed a union with the Wesleyans, which may have been the reason why the chapel intended for the corner site of Carlyle Road in Aston Fields was never built. Since 1983 the little building has been the home of the Salvation Army.

Labelled Finstall Mission, 1905, *this postcard shows a large group outside Nos.6-10 Carlyle Road. On the far left is a cross, then clergy – probably the Rev. G.T. Fieldwick – and choir members, followed by women and girls wearing splendid hats, the men smartly dressed in bowlers and caps.*

Chapter Eleven

'The meeting broke up in confusion' – Bromsgrove's Struggle for Progress

As early as 1825 an Act of Parliament was passed to enable a gas company to light the town, the inhabitants paying the company if they wanted to take advantage of its benefits, though this did not come about for ten years. 'The service-pipe will be laid at the Company's expence [sic] to the inside of the Houses adjoining the public Street; the interior fittings to be fixed by the Company's Workmen at the expence of the Consumers'.[61] The Company put restrictions upon the length of time that lamps could be lit – except for Saturday evening when they could be burnt until midnight. Arrangements made by the Town Commissioners to light Bromsgrove, for a District Rate of 6d (2½p) in the pound, caused regular grumbles: Dr Collis in 1861 complained about 'ineffectual lighting of the town and the Church Steps', the answer being that 'it is left to the discretion of the Company on which nights to light the gas at the full of the moon', but there was also 'some delay in lighting the lamps in some parts of the town, only one man being employed'. There were no lamps at all other than in the High Street, Hanover Street and St John's Street; certainly none were in New Road or Stoney Hill, and Aston Fields too was dark.

By 1870 the Gas Company at its offices in Gas Square off Worcester Street, had in its showroom 'a grate full of incandescent material, which can be extinguished at will', especially useful 'where apartments are seldom used, e.g. dressing rooms, offices, the drawing room for an hour's music in the evening'. Not everyone agreed about the value of gas even ten years later, when a letter to *The Messenger* pronounced 'I do not myself believe that gas ever will be extensively used for heating purposes, because habit in these matters is everything, and it will be long before the habit of open coal fires disappears'; this however was from a proponent of the even more new-fangled electricity.

Before the great gas ownership row started in the early 1880s the Gas Company proposed to supply Aston Fields with the service at the same cost as Bromsgrove, providing the ratepayers of the district agreed – and a unanimous vote gave permission for the Company to 'break up the roads and footpaths for the purpose of laying down the mains ... the Gas Company to be held legally liable for the perfect state of repair for six months afterwards'.

However, Bromsgrove Gas Light & Coke Company, privately owned, had also offered itself for purchase by Bromsgrove Local Board, saying – or threatening – to expand their area out to Aston Fields and rural communities rather than improve gas facility and reduce prices in a town where the inhabitants could not afford to pay, and also to invest in production of electricity. The Board refused to buy, causing bitter recriminations amongst the townsfolk. 'Electric lighting must be for householders

'Be Modern – Use more Gas' exhorts Bromsgrove Gas & Coke Company via its Sentinel steam wagon c.1920. Note the smoke stack from the boiler through the roof on the passenger side, and the solid tyres.

and by householders' ranted a letter writer; the Company has 'regarded their customers much as a feudal lord in the middle ages regarded the wretched serfs attached to the glebe'. Another objected strongly to the Company's powers 'for the benefit of a few capitalists at the expense of every ratepayer and gas consumer ... Instead of every working man in Bromsgrove being able to burn gas ... the increased capital of the Company will be absorbed in carrying gas to adjoining parishes, to light a few gentlemen's residences, and to give value to building estates'. He quoted the success of other municipally owned gas companies, particularly that in Birmingham where so much profit was being made – 'twenty-five thousand pounds per annum' from which 'a magnificent Art Gallery is being provided for the town'.

Some 120 Bromsgrove ratepayers, headed by Herbert Millington, Headmaster of Bromsgrove School, petitioned the Local Board via *The Bromsgrove Messenger* on 23 January 1882 to:

> 'take into consideration the propriety, advantage, and necessity of PURCHASING, at a reasonable valuation, or by arbitration or otherwise, the BROMSGROVE GAS CONSUMERS' COMPANY LIMITED, for the conjoint benefit of the Ratepayers and Consumers.'

On 13 February 1882 the renamed Gas Consumers' Company held their shareholders' Annual Meeting, during which solicitor Corbett, Chairman of the Local Board *and* a shareholder of the Gas Company, said 'during the whole of his experience as a member of the Local Board ... he had never seen so much spleen and bad spirit shown as had been exhibited in this gas question'.

On 23 February 1882 there was a special meeting of the Local Board, where unofficial arbitrators Mr Benjamin Sanders, Clerk to the Board, and Dr Prosser, surgeon, managed to defuse the situation and, if the Company withdrew the electricity proposition, and agreed to reduce the price of gas, in return giving the Board the option of purchasing the Company within three years, then both sides would find things acceptable. Mr Jefferies, grocer, Board member and chairman of the Gas Company, hoped 'that from this time forth they would all live as friends and neighbours (hear, hear)'.

So Aston Fields did not immediately get all that it required. In 1891 Bromsgrove Local Board offered to put gas lighting along New Road from Stoney Hill to Elmsdale (on the corner of Clive Road), if the ratepayers of Finstall and Aston Fields agreed to put in lamps from Elmsdale to the station, partially paid for by the railway company. This would mean forming themselves into a Lighting Area, and to this end a packed meeting of ratepayers was held at Finstall Board School in Stoke Road. It was agreed that there should be fifteen lights on this stretch, 'lighted from 1st September to 30th April, from sunset until six o'clock in the morning for the convenience of the men who went to the railway works at the latter hour (applause).' There were grumbles from those living in Wellington Road who would have no lamps, but as Mr Bown (of Wellington Road) pragmatically said, 'the only way to get Wellington Road or any other road lighted would be by voting for the scheme, and if it was not lighted today it would be tomorrow.' There was a decisive result of 72 votes to 4 to accept the offer, which came about in 1892.

Meanwhile there had been two other important matters that brought forth strong opinions – sewage and water.

'Fever feeds on filth', wrote Dr Fletcher, surgeon, in a letter to *The Messenger* in 1869. Filth in plenty there was in Bromsgrove, and Fletcher insisted that 'by appropriate structural work all the excremental produce of the population should be ... promptly and thoroughly removed'. Another wrote of Worcester Street: 'several of the necessaries, with the bog-holes thereto, are set up by the side of the public thoroughfare, and are indecent in the extreme, being in some cases all but doorless, and open to the full view of all passers, which with the combination of stinks is enough to poison the whole neighbourhood. The next filthy place is the large open ditch at the bottom of Worcester Street, wherein the town drainage is emptied.' One of the worst described was in Foundry Yard, with one closet for twelve houses and 56 persons.

Sanitation in the town left a lot to be desired, but even in the newly built areas covered in this book there was trouble. Lavatories, which were usually in a 'bog-house' in the garden, drained into ash pits or buckets; these were cleaned out by the night soil man, who would empty the pit and remove the refuse on a horse and cart. It was not unknown for the night soil men to take the ashes in barrows into the street and tip it all in the road, leaving an oil lamp on top until the horse and cart came to pick it up the next day. It was not until the 1870s that the invention of the water closet became viable as an alternative, and that was dependent on financial considerations and a piped water supply. The closet had a built-in 'stink trap', or S bend, recognisable to us today, designed to eliminate the smell from the drain.

Open drains bordered the roads, so what with sewage, other domestic rubbish and mud, roadways were often very unpleasant for walking, in hot weather were very smelly and in very wet weather those living at the lower end of an incline must have suffered from an accumulation of disgusting sludge.

January 23rd 1869 brought a rowdy town meeting of ratepayers to consider the sewage question. On the table were plans to build a main sewer from the workhouse in Birmingham Road [now Bartleet House] to an existing sewer in Worcester Street, with additional pipes for St John Street and Hanover Street. Those against the project were vocal. Mr F.J. Halfpenny blamed the damming of the Spadesbourne by the Town Mill for causing stagnant unsanitary water; others from Stoney Hill, Mill Fields, Catshill and Sidemoor objected to their rates being spent on sewage in the town. An opposite view came from John Russon of Warwick Hall, who spoke as a Poor-Law Guardian; he said that the previous July

'there were twenty cases of fever and diarrhoea on the books of the Union. ... The poor', he said, 'suffered very much from sickness through fever and other preventable diseases, and it was very hard when perhaps three or four persons in one family were laid down at one time. The sewerage was objected to on account of the expense, but they ought to consider their health before their pockets'.

At this Mr Halfpenny created a diversion by blaming the poor state of the nail trade and the oppression of the nailers by foggers for ill-nourished families – but also he blamed idlers who drove their wives and children to work for them. Dr Prosser, hovering between being for or against, agreed that drainage into the brook was not advisable

THE
SEWERAGE OF BROMSGROVE
HEALTH & HAPPINESS
VERSUS
DIRT AND DISEASE.

THE OPPONENTS of the former, for some time past, have FALSELY Circulated a Report that the Estimate for the above would amount to £3500, whereas a Contract has been accepted to-day for its completion for £1204 4s. 6d. Figures are Facts, and Facts are stubborn things; therefore, VOTE FOR MEN OF BUSINESS, who rely on FACTS, and not Fiction.

Bromsgrove, August 3rd, 1870.   **A COMMISSIONER.**

A poster dated 3 August 1870, when finally the Local Board took the decision to build sewers. The arguments were between the ratepayers – those who owned property in the town – and those whose interest was in general welfare and prevention of disease. CC.

but felt there should be Government advice. The meeting was brought to a close, and 'broke up in some confusion, after lasting upwards of two hours'.

Meetings of this kind, both of ratepayers and of Local Board members, continued for six years. During this time the Local Board was threatened with proceedings in Chancery because of the pollution of the Salwarpe, and after advice

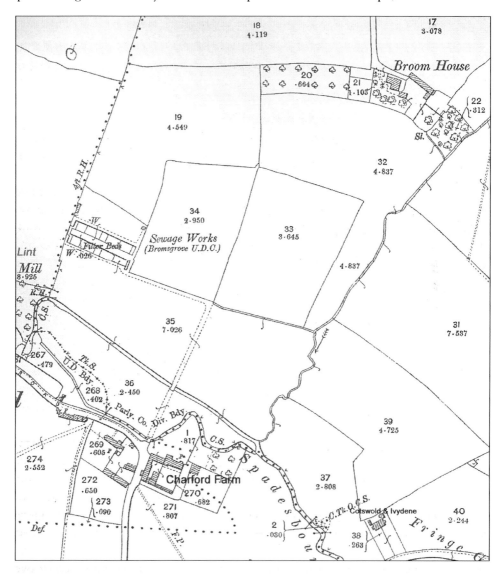

From the 1901 survey showing Bromsgrove Urban District Council's Sewage Works, opened in December 1876. OS.

from consultants their plans at last became more ambitious and a sewage system was built. The main sewage pipe ran to the boundary of the parish, then followed the stream (outside the Bromsgrove boundary) to a field behind the Lint Mill at Charford (also outside the parish boundary). The builders of the new works were Brazier & Weaver, at a cost, including the four acres of land, of £3,500. The opening of the Sewage Works was on 2 December 1876, when the members of the Local Board, having walked to Charford from the Town Hall, spent an enjoyable afternoon of self-congratulation, though their eyes probably glazed when Mr W.R. Taylor, the engineer, described at length the operation of the plant [see Appendix 2]. The day was completed by a dinner at the Golden Cross, where toasts were made to nearly everyone present, even to the Press.

So the Aston Fields community had to suffer the indignity of seeing a splendid new sewage works in their own parish, yet not accessible to them. It was no wonder that there was outrage – yet, as so often is the case, nothing was done for another twenty years and then the great Aston Fields sewage row began.

There was pollution of the Spadesbourne at Charford; there were huge drainage problems outside Finstall Board School on Stoke Road. The rural sanitary authority was not likely to spend money on repairing drains – after all, when there was a complained-of build-up of detritus outside Stoke Prior School, they had simply waited for a rainstorm to wash the nuisance away. Bromsgrove Town Board was asked to accept sewage from Aston Fields, and gave a very noncommittal answer. The meetings to discuss Aston Fields drainage in 1888 were divided between those from the Lower End (Stoke Heath, Stoke Prior) who wanted to leave well alone, and those from the Upper End (Aston Fields and Finstall) who were suffering from bad drainage and neglected roads; but within each group were others who were much more interested in how new drains would affect their pockets. It was finally agreed to ask for a Government Inspector to visit, and Mr Gadd, the surveyor and architect, was asked to prepare a plan of the levels (for which he would be paid no more than £5).

By 1892 and '93 the situation had not progressed very far; large meetings were held of Aston Fields ratepayers and householders who were against the 'enormous and unnecessary expense' of creating a separate drainage district, meetings fully described in *The Messenger*. One meeting was chaired by Mr R. Smallwood, JP of Rigby Hall. He was dismissive of the need to spend £9,000 on draining the village, saying that there were more cases of 'scarlet fever, typhoid fever and all those horrible things' at the lower end (meaning Stoke Prior) – 'it was a few buzzing busybodies at the other end of the parish who had instigated the [Bromsgrove Union Sanitary] Authority, in order that they might hide their own insanitary condition (Applause).' All this was an appalling case of 'nimbyism'; the objecting

133

householders included very vocal businessmen owning highly rated properties, and included Messrs Samuel Saywell, Henry Wheelock, J. Laughton, W.H. Lewis, P. Levans, H.S. Whitfield, George Bown and William Llewellin, all of whom we have met earlier in this book and nearly all of whom owned terraced housing in Aston Fields.

Their protests were to no avail and finally in 1894 the Rural Sanitary Authority proposed to construct main sewers from Finstall at one end, to Stoke Works at the other end of the parish, all run by gravity. The expense would be £10,000, the rate something like one shilling (5p) in the pound. And then another complication came with the refusal of Mr John Corbett, owner of the Salt Works at Stoke Works, to allow anyone on his land to inspect it, and certainly not to purchase any of it for sewage works. At this point the County Medical Officer, Dr Fosbroke, reported his findings.

'At Finstall there were midden closets. There were 35 houses, and there was no system of sewage disposal, and the slop water found its way into ditches, etc. ... At Aston Fields there were some pipe drains, but no system of sewers. The pipe drains conveyed the slop water down the road to the brook or into ditches, and there were a few dumb-wells.'[62]

He continued to report similarly on the whole Stoke Prior parish.

Come June in 1894 the plan changed again, but the Rural Sanitary Authority did at last agree to drain only Aston Fields, taking the sewage to a field between Bant Mill [demolished about 1902; the original name was Baddington Mill, corrupted to Bant] on the Sugar Brook and the railway, just north of Sugar Brook Mill (and stating that if they were called upon to drain the lower part of the parish Mr Corbett had undertaken to sell them the land required for a pumping station). Despite this decision it was not until 1896 that Mr J. Tilt's tender of £3,999 11s was accepted and the work took place.[63]

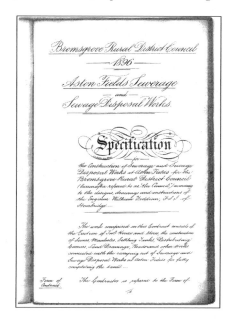

The Specification issued by Bromsgrove Rural District Council for those quoting for 'the erection of Tool House and Stores, the construction of Sewers, Manholes, Settling Tanks, Land Drainage, Roads and other Works connected with the carrying out of Sewerage and Sewage Disposal Works at Aston Fields ...' Mr J. Tilt won the contract. WRO.

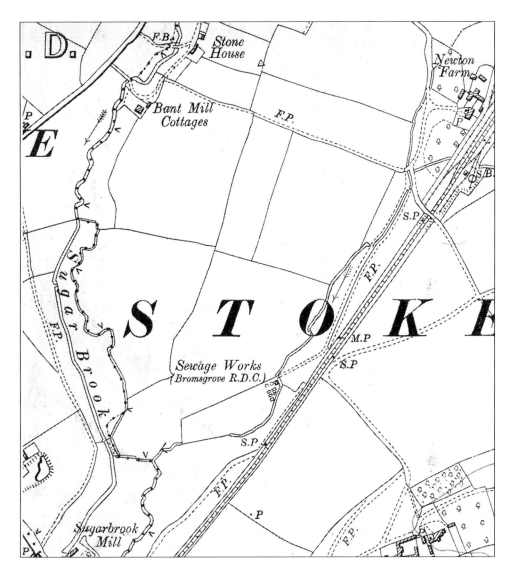

From the 1901 survey showing Bromsgrove Rural District Council's Sewage Works for the waste of Aston Fields. OS.

All the drama of the great gas row and the great Aston Fields drainage row should not detract from another achievement, which caused comparatively few arguments. During the mid 1860s a group of local gentlemen investors, headed by Lord Windsor of Hewell Grange, applied to Parliament under the name of Bromsgrove and Droitwich Waterworks, for permission to bring running water to the area. The first proposal was to take water from Pikes Pool at Finstall (to be piped to Droitwich) and the Spadesbourne Brook near the junction of Brook House Lane and Shepley Lane at Long Eye [Lickey End], piped to Mount Pleasant [just above the College Road junction with Stratford Road], where there would be a reservoir. However the Bromsgrove Local Board was unhappy – if the reservoir were placed at the top of Mount Pleasant the descent of the water into the town would be only 71 feet (21.5m). If it were placed at the rise of the Spadesbourne Brook at the Lickey, the descent would be 241 feet (73.5m). Firemen would then be able to throw water to the top of the church steeple.

It was not till 1877 that the Parliamentary Bill went through delineating the area of supply,[64] though there was opposition from mill owners and other vested interests, but by 1880 sufficient private investment had been made to allow Messrs Howard & Baker of 8, Old Jewry, London to sink a deep well into the red sandstone at Burcot, quickly finding 'a copious supply of remarkable purity'. There were a few hiccups; as we today laugh about 'leaves on the line', so locals then must have enjoyed hearing references to delays caused by 'the immense quantity of water in the well'. It seems that the 100ft (30.5m) deep and 10ft (3m)

The East Worcestershire Waterworks engine house and stack at Burcot, together with the manager's office and cottage, architect C.A. Edge of Birmingham, opened in 1882. The stack was demolished in the late 1960s. G. James.

broad well had to be emptied in order to set up the steam driven pumps – work achieved with some difficulty because of an 'immense influx' of water.

At last, Wednesday 13th December 1882 saw a procession of carriages arriving in Burcot, delivering for the opening ceremony a number of notables, members of the Bromsgrove, Redditch and Droitwich Local Boards, and representatives of the Board of Directors of the renamed East Worcestershire Water Works. *The Messenger* reporter lyrically described the scene. 'Much interest was taken in a large vaulted reservoir, intended for the town of Bromsgrove, which was illuminated for the occasion, and the long vistas of massive piers and arches with the water beneath was very striking.'[65] The only lady present, wife of the Director of the London engineering firm, turned the key to start the engines.

> 'It was a grand sight to see the stately engines put in motion so easily, moving slowly and quietly, but with irresistible power; reversing the order of nature and lifting the pure water from the deep fountains of the far-famed Lickey Hills, to apply it for the use and convenience of man at distant centres of industry.'

Mr Batten, Chairman of Bromsgrove Local Board, told the company that there were now 'hydrants in various parts of the town, and only the other day he saw the energetic volunteer fire brigade attach a stand pipe to a hydrant and throw a stream of water over one of the highest houses in Bromsgrove (applause).'

The London engineer, Mr Yockney, said 'As to the engines, they would in a good day's

Bore hole excavators in 1911 preparing to go down the shaft in a bucket. G. James.

Working down a borehole with hammer and wedge in 1911. G. James.

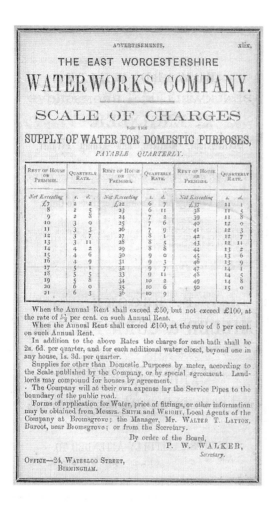

THE EAST WORCESTERSHIRE

WATERWORKS COMPANY.

SCALE OF CHARGES

FOR THE

SUPPLY OF WATER FOR DOMESTIC PURPOSES,

PAYABLE QUARTERLY.

Rent of House or Premises.	Quarterly Rate.		Rent of House or Premises.	Quarterly Rate.		Rent of House or Premises.	Quarterly Rate.	
Not Exceeding	*s.*	*d.*	*Not Exceeding*	*s.*	*d.*	*Not Exceeding*	*s.*	*d.*
£7	2	2	£22	6	7	£37	11	1
8	2	5	23	6	11	38	11	5
9	2	8	24	7	2	39	11	8
10	3	0	25	7	6	40	12	0
11	3	3	26	7	9	41	12	3
12	3	7	27	8	1	42	12	7
13	3	11	28	8	5	43	12	11
14	4	2	29	8	8	44	13	2
15	4	6	30	9	0	45	13	6
16	4	9	31	9	3	46	13	9
17	5	1	32	9	7	47	14	1
18	5	5	33	9	11	48	14	5
19	5	8	34	10	2	49	14	8
20	6	0	35	10	6	50	15	0
21	6	3	36	10	9			

When the Annual Rent shall exceed £50, but not exceed £100, at the rate of 5½ per cent. on such Annual Rent.

When the Annual Rent shall exceed £100, at the rate of 5 per cent. on such Annual Rent.

In addition to the above Rates the charge for each bath shall be 2s. 6d. per quarter, and for each additional water closet, beyond one in any house, 1s. 3d. per quarter.

Supplies for other than Domestic Purposes by meter, according to the Scale published by the Company, or by special agreement. Landlords may compound for houses by agreement.

The Company will at their own expense lay the Service Pipes to the boundary of the public road.

Forms of application for Water, price of fittings, or other information may be obtained from Messrs. SMITH and WRIGHT, Local Agents of the Company at Bromsgrove; the Manager, Mr. WALTER T. LAYTON, Burcot, near Bromsgrove; or from the Secretary.

By order of the Board,

P. W. WALKER,

Secretary.

OFFICE—24, WATERLOO STREET, BIRMINGHAM.

Left: 1880s Scale of Charges *for water in Bromsgrove district, related to the rent paid by the house occupant. With house rent of £21 per quarter the payment was 6s 3d, with further 2s 6d for bath and 1s 3d each for more than one water closet. This was not cheap, and it is no wonder many people continued to use their pumps and wells. BR.*

The offices of East Worcestershire Waterworks in what is now Strand House. Note the horse trough in front of the building, re-erected in 2007.

work send 2,500 tons of water to the different destinations supplied by the company. This weight represented no less than five fully laden good trains on the Midland Railway (cheers), and he remarked that the water was just sufficiently impure to be beautiful. It ... would save a lot of money in the matter of soap alone.[66]

The new system was an undoubted success, though it was many years before every home took its water from the Company – cost of connection and expectation of regular bills allowed only the comfortably off to use water from the Burcot wells. By the end of 1882 the Company had received only 111 applications for a supply of water. Two shillings and six pence (12½p) was charged per quarter if the home had a bath, and a second water closet in the house was charged at 1s 3d (6¼p). This was not cheap and many preferred to rely on private or public wells, most of which were contaminated, or which dried up in the summer months. In 1884 the Medical

Officer of Health declared many of the wells unfit for drinking, but even this had no effect; however in 1886 the Local Board took matters into its own hands and closed all contaminated wells where the Company could provide a supply. Two years later there was an exceptional drought which dried up most of the remaining wells, bringing even more households onto the Company's books.

Matters did not always go well, and water wastage from leaking pipes became a great problem, despite the latest invention to detect water waste – a stethoscope consisting of a rod of wood (fir or ash) with a bellshaped top, one end of which was held at the workman's ear and the other to the ground. Despairingly in 1884 the manager wailed 'It is by no means a rare occurrence for the water wasted in a town to far exceed the quantity that is used'. Household pipes burst because of freezing weather (80% of consumers were regularly frozen up in winter), but also the mains, not laid deep enough underground, could freeze. In 1895 eleven miles of pipes were frozen solid and the Company had to take water round by horse and cart to waterless areas. A few years later an important use of quantities of water was on the streets. Macadamised roads required a ton of water on every 400 square yards of road surface during warm weather to keep the surface solid, a job carried out on average 120 days each year.

Also in 1895 the Company undertook re-washering of leaking taps free of charge to encourage people to report such defects, a splendid system which I remember taking advantage of in the 1970s – a time when the Company re-washered over 25,000 taps and ball valves free of charge every year.

From 1883 water for Redditch was piped five miles to another underground reservoir at Headless Cross, some of which was pumped up into the red brick octagonal water tower with its large cylindrical iron tank,[67] for the supply of Headless Cross and neighbouring villages. Barnt Green, Finstall and Bromsgrove Workhouse were supplied from 1884, while Aston Fields, for those prepared to pay, had to wait until 1886.[68]

Probably under half of the dwellings in the newly built Aston Fields shown on the 1903 OS map have a *P* denoting a pump in their back yards. All the terraced houses lining Stoke Road between the Aston Fields cross roads and Carlyle Road were lucky enough to have their own pump. I think we can assume that for most of these inhabitants in the smaller houses the cost of being put on the mains, and the additional water rate would be out of the question. Even as late as the 1940s water was not supplied to all houses in the town; between 1938 and 1948 166 wells were filled in, and water supplied to 302 houses.

Initially the East Worcestershire Waterworks had its offices in the aptly named Waterloo Street in Birmingham, opening the Bromsgrove branch office in 1889 in the premises now occupied by Thomas Horton, Solicitors. In 1960 part of a field was bought on the New Road alongside the site of Fordhouse Farm, where new flat roofed office buildings were ready for occupation by the Company by 1964.[69] When the Company was taken over by Severn Trent in 1994 the offices were bought by the New Road Surgery.

The last of the services we value so lightly – unless we have to do without them – to reach Bromsgrove and Aston Fields was of course electricity. Despite the subject being raised many times in the 1890s, Bromsgrove was, as usual, slow to take up a new invention. It was in 1894, the last year before the creation of Urban Districts and Rural Districts, and the year that sewers came to Aston Fields, that Messrs Hemming & Co. of Birmingham sought permission to supply electric light to the inhabitants of Bromsgrove. There were more ratepayers' meetings, more squabbling, more headlines in *The Messenger* on 'The Electric Lighting Question'.

The first meeting convened 'to consider the subject of lighting the town by electricity' was held in the Town Hall on Monday morning, 18th August. There were three letters of apology, from Mr. A. Dipple, Mr George Bown, and from Mr Charles Field Junior, all important men and all regretting inability to attend because of the short notice and inconvenient hour. Mr Lewis, representing the Local Board, immediately asked for an adjournment, which, after some discussion, was agreed for the following Thursday evening. Of this second meeting, having named fifty attenders, including all the usual names, *The Messenger* reporter gave up counting and added 'etc.' to the list. For once everyone present seemed to agree. The Vicar said 'There were too many empty houses in the town and what they wanted to do was to attract people who would bring grist to the mill, and he could not help thinking that if they introduced electric light it would at least add to the attractions of the place (hear, hear)'. Mr Oliver Giles of the Crescent said 'he was anxious to see Bromsgrove move forward, and he thought they all ought to try to help the poor old town out of the difficulties it was troubled with. He expressed regret at the lack of enterprise shewn by the nailmasters when machinery was introduced into the nail trade, and went on to argue that they should move with the times, and lift the town out of the slough of despond it was now in'. On this note the meeting closed and it was only a few weeks later that the Local Board agreed to Messrs. Hemming's application, but reserving all legal rights and powers. Mr Oliver Giles emphasised his support, saying that since the railway was so far from the town he thought the next best thing would be an electric tramcar starting at the bottom of the New Road to meet every train.

The Gas Company at this time was renegotiating its arrangements with the Local Board, including the provision of lamp columns, lamps, regulators and fittings, and payment for all requisite repairs. The Company would provide for cleaning and repairs to the glass of the lamps. The two special lamps – Town Hall and Post Office – would be repaired by the Board. Lighting would be provided for half the lamps in the summer months, all the lamps in the winter, lit at sunset and extinguished at 3am. There would be no lamps two nights before, the night of, and two nights after, full moon. The Board was clearly uneasy that the Gas Company had raised, rather than lowered its prices.

Mr Giles' electric tramcar was not an idea plucked out of the air. There had been similar suggestions for many years; in 1864 there was proposed a Halesowen and Bromsgrove branch railway line passing from Bromsgrove Station, through the Warwick Hall farmland and through the field later to be the site of The Cedars. In 1889 there had been plans for a railway through Bromsgrove from Stoke to Birmingham, though this would not provide carriage from Aston Fields station up to the town. This branch line also never was built, and ten years later, 1899, there was another major proposal – for a light railway, or electric tram line, to be built from the station up New Road, joining another line running from Rock Hill to Lickey End, built to carry both passengers and, importantly, goods.[70]

This time it was not only the inhabitants of Warwick Hall Estate and those living on New Road who were interested parties; now there were vocal market gardeners from Catshill who attended the Public Enquiry held in December 1899, as well as businessmen who used carriers to move their goods around the town. The Earl of Jersey and Colonel Boughey, Light Railway Commissioners, came up from London to open the Enquiry, while those living along New Road combined forces to employ Mr R.H. Amphlett Q.C. to speak on their behalf. The proposal included 'passenger cars propelled by Electric power, conveyed by over-head wires, supported by posts of ornamental design which, by arrangement with the Local Authorities, the Post Office, and others can be used to carry electric lamps for the purpose of lighting the thoroughfares, and to support telegraph and telephone wires'; it would be 3ft 6 in gauge (1.97m). This was ground-breaking stuff for Bromsgrove, which had previously kept well away from electricity.

Nimbyism was greatly to the fore once more, with New Road inhabitants clutching at straws – Mr Ernest B. Cotton of Sunnymead said 'a number of people in the neighbourhood were agriculturists, and they took the whole of their produce to market for the simple reason they must bring back certain manures, and they certainly would not use a light railway because they could not bring the manure back'. Mr P. Levans of Thorndale said there 'would be considerable danger from the tramway coming round a corner'. Lord Jersey: 'Is not that the case with a horse and cart going by?' Witness: 'Yes I should think so. ...' Mr Whitfield of the clothing factory said he did not think his female employees 'would receive any benefit if the railway was made; the reason was that after sitting down,

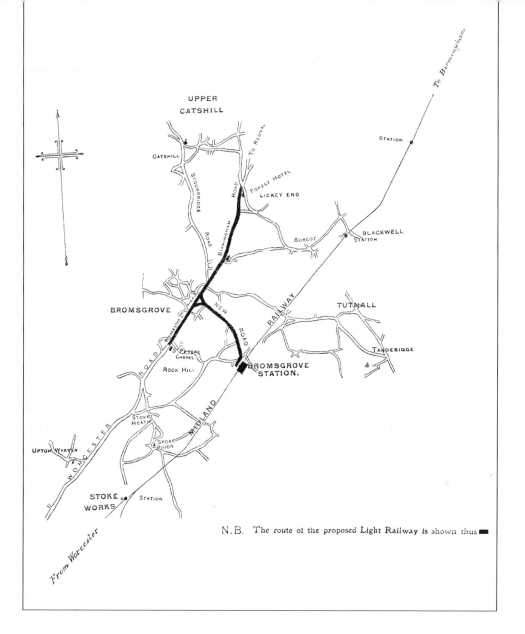

UPPER
CATSHILL

CATSHILL

STOURBRIDGE ROAD

TO REDNAL

FOREST HOTEL

LICKEY END

STATION

To Birmingham

BURCOT

BLACKWELL
STATION

BIRMINGHAM ROAD

NEW ROAD

BROMSGROVE

TUTNALL

RAILWAY

WORCESTER STREET

ST PETER'S
CHAPEL

ROCK HILL

BROMSGROVE
STATION.

TARDEBIGGE

WORCESTER ROAD

STOKE
HEATH

MIDLAND

STOKE
PRIOR

UPTON WARREN

STOKE
WORKS

STATION

From Worcester

N.B.   The route of the proposed Light Railway is shown thus ■■

The 1899 proposed Light Railway would run from the station to the High Street, then down Worcester Street to Rock Hill and up the High Street and Birmingham Road to Lickey End. Although the Urban and Rural District Councils approved the proposition, the idea was gradually forgotten. CC.

as these females did the whole of the day, a little walk was beneficial to their health'. For the other side, Mr Joseph Tilt, builder of Birmingham Road and Mr John Brazier, builder of Worcester Street thought it would be useful for carrying timber and bricks, and also for carrying their men to and from work. Mr Thomas Bott, nailmaster and market gardener of Catshill, said it would save time and money to take produce to the station to be sent off to Sheffield, Manchester, Leeds and Birmingham. The meeting ended with the views of Bromsgrove Rural and Urban District Councils, both in accord that it would be a good thing, especially for the working classes. Four hours after the meeting began Lord Jersey and Colonel Boughey went off back to London.

Of course it all came to nothing in the end. The line through Worcester Street had already been discounted because of the narrowness of the road. The town generally was enthusiastic, as were Aston Fields people, but probably the Directors could not raise the capital needed and though *The Messenger* assiduously and regularly informed the readers of the plan's progress the idea gradually got forgotten, probably to the relief of the big wagon owners who would have lost trade had the tram railway been built. One benefit might have been an earlier bringing of electricity for the use of the townspeople, for it was not until 1924 that the Shropshire, Worcestershire, & Staffordshire Electric Power Co. announced its plans to bring underground cables from a site outside the town. The smart Art Deco company offices were erected in Stourbridge Road [opposite Parkside School], remaining as electricity showrooms for many years.

Telephones had already appeared – very gradually – in Aston Fields and Bromsgrove. In the 1916 Kelly's Directory the only Aston Fields number given was that of J. & N. Nadin & Co, Ltd, the Stoke Road coal merchant – No.67. In Bromsgrove the use of the new gadget was catching on very well with over a hundred lines, and businesses were beginning to realise they should inform the world of their numbers, including the ever forward thinking Mr Victor Drury, Boot and Shoe manufacturer, whose telephone number was 9. Braziers the builders had beaten him to it, however, with No.2.

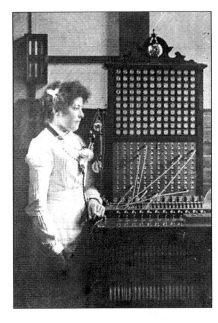

Miss Clymer, telephonist for the Post Office Telephone Service in the High Street. Note the decorative top to the manually operated exchange, which appears to have up to 120 lines. To make a call customers spoke to the operator, Miss Clymer, who replied through the speaking tube hanging round her neck, and then connected them by plugging into the national telephone system. The block of bulbs above related to the points below, and showed the operator when a line was engaged. HC.

Chapter Twelve

Pastimes, Persians and
Pursuit of Knowledge

The inhabitants of Aston Fields, most of whom worked on the railway or Wagon Works, made their own amusements, as was usual at the time. To join in activities in Bromsgrove meant walking up New Road and back again, so very quickly groups of people, often connected with the church and chapel, came together for bazaars, musical entertainment and dances. At home, in better-off families, friends congregated very naturally round the piano to sing popular sentimental parlour songs and familiar hymns and carols. Those without pianos could attend concerts in the church halls, to listen to performances of favourites such as Arthur Sullivan's *The Lost Chord* (1877, printed in *The Ladies Journal*, Christmas 1897):

> Seated one day at the organ,
> I was weary and ill at ease,
> And my fingers wander'd idly
> Over the noisy keys.

or *Love's Old Sweet Song* (James L. Molloy, 1884):

> Just a song at twilight, when the lights are low;
> And the flick'ring shadows softly come and go

reaching an apogee of sentimentality in Amy Woodforde-Finden's 1902 song:

> Pale hands I loved beside the Shalimar,
> Where are you now? Who lies beneath your spell?

Outdoor events took place in the grounds and on the fields of Finstall Park, and even nearer to home there was a Fête and Sports Day on 29 August 1891 at the Dragoon Hotel (presumably on Dragoon fields), with Stoke Works Brass Band, Gittus's steam galloping horses and other amusements – not to mention 'a great quantity of WINE at 2s 6d per gallon to be sold at the Dragoon'.

The previous year the Aston Fields Workmen's Club had been opened. The working men's club movement began in the 1840s, Birmingham being one of the first, and Bromsgrove's Mechanics Institute was opened in the High Street as early as 1849. In the beginning these clubs were not places where working men primarily got together to drink and socialise – in fact there was a clear connection with the ethos of the temperance movement and the clubs were usually a middle-class initiative aimed at the education of working class men. They were built:

> 'to provide wholesome and constructive amusement ... containing rooms to be used for conversation, refreshments, recreation, etc., and others for classes, reading, lectures, and music. A library of entertaining and instructive books, scientific apparatus, diagrams, etc., a supply of newspapers, and some works of art, should be aimed at.'[71]

The Aston Fields Workmen's Club was inaugurated in 1890, and for a year the committee looked for suitable premises in the village. Part of Pear Tree Villa [now the Co-op/Post Office], on the corner of Station Approach and Stoke Road, the previous home of Henry Wheelock (who had moved to The Lindens in New Road the year before), was unused and struck them as being admirable for the purpose – and it was just across the way from the Dragoon. However, Aston Fields men refused to have a totally dry house, and draught beer was on tap from the beginning.

The opening ceremony of an extension to Aston Fields Working Men's Club in Stoke Road in 1929. Built by Braziers (Sydney Brazier is in the light raincoat), this building was extended again in 1971. Roger Brazier.

The building, which included a reading room, a smoke room, and space for card playing and billiards, had 70 members when it was opened by Mr Robert Smallwood of Rigby Hall on 11 April 1891. Very soon afterwards gardening enthusiasts amongst the members started an annual horticultural show, while other activities included fishing, pigeon racing[72] and boxing lessons. After some years the membership grew too large for Pear Tree Villa and a wooden building was added to the rear. In 1920 when membership was several hundreds it moved along Stoke Road to a new building on the Recreation Ground, where it is today, and which in its turn was extended in 1971. The Rec. originally was 4½ acres (1.8 hectares), and though over the years parts of it have been used for building and car parking, it is still a very valuable green space.

Nearly every dwelling in Aston Fields had a good garden; those deprived of this amenity were of course those in Station Cottages, which were built right up against a cliff of sandstone. Some gardens were filled with sheds housing racing pigeons, many had chickens, and some kept a pig – thus giving plenty of work for Dan Manning, the pig killer of Aston Terrace. Other gardens had well looked-after vegetable patches, with the fruit bushes and apple trees that grow so well in the area. For those enthusiasts with not enough garden there were by the 1920s allotments in the undeveloped field next to Finstall Board School, on a field south of the Wagon Works (reached by footpath from St Godwald's Road), and another field, once part of the Rigby estate, to the north of Rigby Lane – where there are still allotments today.[73] During World War I demand for allotments increased due to food shortages, when some shops, including Banner's, had to close, but after that war many allotment lands were used for housing; World War II again brought demand after the Dig for Victory campaign, when in some cities public parks were dug to grow food.

The Aston Fields Workmen's Club Horticultural Show quickly became an institution, by 1894 needing to be held on a large field on Finstall Road. That year Mr Pickering of the clothing factory was chairman of the committee, organising a large tent for the exhibits. As Honorary Exhibitors Mr Ernest B. Cotton, the Bromsgrove auctioneer, graciously sent down a nice collection of ferns from Sunnymead, while Mr G.H. Gadd sent a display of dahlias and carnations, and Mr Smallwood sent baskets of plants. Judging was done by three knowledgeable Head Gardeners from local estates, who were able to award prizes to the 'cottage gardeners' who were entering their vegetables. The top prize vegetable was a head of celery weighing 15½ lbs (7 kilos), 13 inches in circumference (33 cms), while Mr Pickering donated the 1st prize for a collection of vegetables – a pair of trousers worth 10/- (50p).[74] During the whole day the All Saints Fife & Drum Band were playing, carrying on into the evening when everyone danced.

Bromsgrove town also held the third of its own Horticultural Shows at the beginning of August in 1894, on a New Road field belonging to Fordhouse Farm. This was a bigger, grander affair altogether. The first day, Bank Holiday, saw the horse show. On Tuesday athletic sports and the horticultural fête were held attended by all the local gentry who arrived in their carriages (charge half a guinea – 52½p). There were many classes, and notable among the winners was Mr Ernest B. Cotton – out of thirty entries in the Ornamental Plant section he won fifteen. Mr. Gadd's name was also mentioned as winner of numerous classes. Neither of the gentlemen entered the classes for 'cottage gardeners' – the class system amongst gardeners being alive and well. Bromsgrove Loyal

A late autumn array of preserves, honeycombs and garden flowers at a horticultural show in the Town Hall on 14 November 1912.

Town String Band[75] played, conducted by J.W. Rose, sexton and stone mason from St John's church, and people could enter the ground for 1/- (5p). There was an unfortunate epilogue to this particular Show. A NOTICE was put in *The Messenger*, very carefully composed, saying:

> 'Unfortunately a pair of epergnes was removed from the tent by two Ladies for safety on Tuesday evening last. The owner is requiring them continually and would esteem it a favour to have them at once returned, or will reluctantly be compelled to seek the assistance of the Police.
>
> Signed G.H. Gadd, Hon Secretary.'

An epergne being a silver, branched ornamental centrepiece for the dining table, we hope they were safely returned.

Precursors of today's Three Counties Show were Two Counties Shows (Worcestershire and Herefordshire) which were held around the two counties and were in Bromsgrove in 1906 and 1909. These were such big three day occasions that all the Fordhouse Farm fields on New Road were utilised, and preparations took a week. To avoid problems with mud, over 4,000 railway sleepers were used to firm up a special route from a

Ernest Brewster Cotton, cigar in hand, step-brother of John and William Alfred Cotton. A larger-than-life character, he was estate agent, auctioneer and, when off duty, an enthusiastic gardener. BC.

A ploughing match at the Two Counties Show in New Road in 1906. BC.

Bromsgrove Cycling Club had a very enthusiastic membership, though it appears from this 1903 photograph that women were not invited. The cups displayed are the Rigby Challenge Cup awarded by Mr. E. Ansell of Rigby Hall, held by W. Green (18 guineas – 1 mile flat handicap), the Finstall Challenge Cup presented by Mr J. Boultbee Brooks of Finstall Park, held by J.S. Weaver, grocer and chairman of the Club (40 guineas – 1 mile bicycle handicap) and the Nixon Challenge cup presented by Mr J. Nixon of Tardebigge, held by William Hedges, blacksmith (15 guineas – 120 yds flat handicap). BC.

dedicated Wagon Works siding to take the weight of so many animals coming by train. Exhibited were all farmyard animals and birds, with a special Bromsgrove & District Poultry Show, and there were competitions in riding, driving, tradesmen's turnouts, and wagons with their teams. Very popular was the Band of the Royal Marines, which attracted flocks of people from the town; most of the shops in the High Street were closed all day on the Thursday.

A small selection of other social events held in 1894 shows the variety of people's lives, and includes a dinner for the second anniversary of the Bromsgrove Society of Carpenters and Joiners, and another dinner for the Bromsgrove Rovers Football Club. There was an outing for the New Road Baptist Choir; an operetta, entitled *Little Folks at Play* was performed at the Baptist Schoolroom, while in February an entertainment was given in Finstall by children of the school. On 29 March a presentation of a silver-mounted pipe and a walking stick was made to Mr Timson, Hon.Sec. of the Bromsgrove Quadrille Class; an amateur dramatic performance took place in the Drill Hall to raise money for the Institute and School of Art; the Vicar of Bromsgrove gave a lecture at the Institute on *The Life of Mendelssohn*, and a Photographic Society was formed.

Bromsgrove Philharmonic Society's performance of Elgar's King Olaf took place in spring 1912 in the New Court Theatre (the first Drill Hall), conductor Mr Isaac Burnell, music teacher at Bromsgrove School. Mr Burnell was a composer who had several of his works published by Novello. Note the soprano soloist in the foreground, wearing a hat. BC.

Bromsgrove Cricket Club 1st Eleven in 1960 lined up before the pavilion which was brought with the Club to the New Road ground in 1908. Two of the finest Bromsgrove cricketers were Norman Hedges (front row left) and Alan Pidgeon (front row centre). J Weston.

The three great English games were all represented in Bromsgrove, and two of them have ended up on the eastern side of the town. The Cricket Club[76] was the earliest, playing probably on the School ground (was this later the College field?) in 1842, though interest appears to have subsided until 1861 when the Club re-formed with enthusiastic young players. Mr Gillespy the Market Place barber was the first Honorary Secretary, and the committee included Joseph Creswell, George Fletcher and Joseph Steedman among others. For a while they played on part of the old Recreation Ground in Stourbridge Road, but because it was under threat from a new road, in 1908 they moved to a field off New Road which was part of the Rigby Hall estate, bringing their splendid new pavilion with them. The club paid Mr Edward Ansell £700 for the privilege, a large sum to raise, though Lord Windsor donated £100. Here the club stayed, welcoming the presence of ladies for the first time in 1922. In 1970 they sold the land for the building of Harwood Park for £80,000 and paid £18,000 to buy a field in St Godwald's Road. The new ground was opened in 1974, incorporating the Tennis and Hockey Clubs, which had also played at New Road.

Bromsgrove Rovers earn their paragraph in this book because they began playing in 1885 on a field on Old Station Road. They then moved to the Market Street Recreation Ground in 1887, then to Churchfields, before going in 1897 to a field between the Spadesbourne Brook and Well Lane, off the Alcester [now Stratford] Road. The Victoria Ground has been the home of the Rovers since 1910, land which in 1948 was covenanted to Bromsgrove Council by Mr Charles Crane for the club's use or as open space for Bromsgrove people. There were several other football teams at different times, including one from the Clothing Factory, a Police team, the Wagon Works and another known as the Early Closers – shop assistants who could only play on early-closing day – Thursday afternoons, for shop hours were long, including all day on Saturdays, and sport on a Sunday was frowned upon. Come summer the Early Closers Cricket team took the place of football.

The Ladies Hockey team played on part of the ground in New Road owned by the Cricket Club, and this photograph was taken outside the cricket pavilion. The women's clothing and hairstyles look highly unsuitable for an energetic game of hockey. BC.

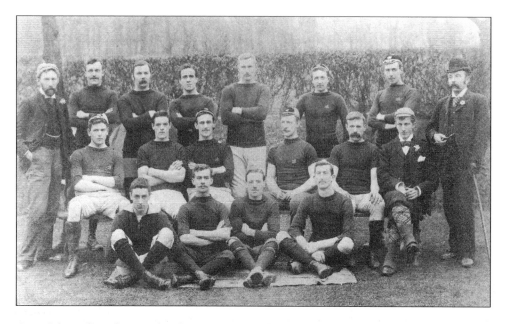

One of the earliest photographs of Bromsgrove Rugby Football Club, taken in 1901, some of the team wearing their caps with pride. Kit for some of the team seems to include knee length trews, while jerseys had both long and short sleeves, while one non-playing member wears a dashing pair of tartan socks.

Rugby – or, as *The Messenger* listed its fixtures, 'Football played to Rugby Rules' – began in Bromsgrove in 1872, and it became one of the first clubs in the country to affiliate to the national Rugby Football Union. Many of the players had learned the game at Bromsgrove School and were keen to continue this energetic sport. In 1924, having been banished from the Cricket field in New Road because of the damage they did to the ground, the Rugby Football Club played on another New Road field belonging to Jack Barnes of Fordhouse Farm, just over the fence from the Cricket Club. They were delighted when Ralph Edwards, owner of the Dragoon, offered to build a small changing room just behind the pub, into which he fitted a bath. Here they stayed, using the Dragoon as a clubhouse, considerably swelling its sales of beer, until 1958. After Miss Albright of Grimley Hall sold them a pitch on her tree lined field in Finstall Park the club gradually acquired more land, which she had covenanted for all time as parkland for the benefit of all. There are now four full sized pitches, two floodlit, plus four smaller ones for mini and junior players.

Another early Rugby Club was that of men from the Wagon Works, named the Crusaders, who were allowed to play on a field adjoining Finstall Park.

There were two exceptional spectacular events that must be mentioned – the Jubilee of Queen Victoria in 1887 and the visit of the Shah of Persia in 1889.

Bromsgrove born A.E. Housman came home on 20 June 1887 for Queen Victoria's Jubilee, joining the crowd on the Clent hills, and the first poem in his *A Shropshire Lad* describes from experience how at least one other beacon fire could be seen from the beacon sites on Clent, Lickey, Malvern and Clee.

1887

From Clee to heaven the beacon burns
   The shires have seen it plain,
From north and south the sign returns
   And beacons burn again.

Bromsgrove's 1887 celebrations for the Diamond Jubilee were masterminded by John Humphreys, and took place on one of Lord Windsor's fields adjoining the monument ground on Lickey. The framework of the magnificent 30 foot (9m) bonfire was made, shockingly to us, from timbers from the old Manor House in the High Street. A torchlight procession

A similar bonfire to that built for Queen Victoria's jubilee on Lickey in 1887. This one was at Breakback to mark the coronation of King George V in 1911. BC.

An 1887 Jubilee crown with the Bromsgrove boar – 'In Celebration of Rejoicing in Bromsgrove'.

153

wended its way from the Golden Cross, the gentry in their carriages, the populace not able to cram themselves on wagons having to walk. There were finally 6,000 people on the hill gazing in awe at the huge flames, which soon devoured the Royal Standard flying from the top of the mound. Twelve dozen rockets were set off, which could have been seen by those watching Finstall's own bonfire in Finstall Park. The dignitaries of the town revisited Lickey the next day to plant an oak tree as permanent recognition of Queen Victoria's fifty years on the throne; unfortunately it died the next year, but another oak was planted in 1889 with iron railings to protect it.

Fireworks were again on the programme on the royal visit to Hewell Grange of Nasser al-Din Shah Qajar of Persia.[77] The Shah's state visit to Great Britain began with great pomp and ceremony in London on 1st July 1889. During the next few days he was graciously received by Queen Victoria at Windsor Castle, was given both a banquet and a ball at Buckingham Palace, and then set out on a royal progress around the country. He stayed first with Mr Alfred de Rothschild at Waddesdon

Left: The Illustrated London News *of 13 July 1889 depicting the Shah of Persia kissing the hand of Queen Victoria during his State Visit to Great Britain.* Right: *Nasser al-Din Shah Qajar of Persia from 1848 until his assassination in 1896. The jewels on his chest would be similar to the ones he protectively covered by his coat on arrival at Bromsgrove Station.*

A damaged photograph of one of the four celebratory arches built to welcome the Shah on his drive through Bromsgrove, surrounded by grubby urchins and a few well dressed children in hats, plus the horse droppings regularly found on roads. The Persian text reads 'O, king, live for ever' painted in blue. The arch is fixed to The Green Dragon on the right, and Mr Harford's boot and shoe shop is on the left – you can just see his shop sign of a boot hanging above the shop. BR.

Manor, accompanied by the Prince of Wales. He then progressed north by train to arrive at Bromsgrove Station on 10th July.

Lord Windsor had warned Bromsgrove Local Board about the impending visit, and asked them to decorate the town with flags and bunting. A public meeting was held to discuss the project, a committee was formed, Bromsgrove people were asked to decorate their houses and shops, and plans were made to erect four celebratory arches – one on New Road near the Crescent, one by the old Hop Pole, one across High Street by Church Street, and one at the top of the High Street by the Alcester Road [Stratford Road]. Architect G.H. Gadd was asked to design three, and the fourth was copied from a previous arch made for the Worcestershire Agricultural Show. 'God save our Queen', 'Happiness to the Shah', 'Good Old Bromsgrove' and 'Long Life to Lord Windsor' were mottoes on the arches. Decoration was done under the surveillance of several town worthies and their ladies, Mr Townsend of the furniture shop going to the extreme of writing 'O, king, live for ever' in blue Persian characters, being lucky enough to have a nephew conversant with that language. The arches, festoons and flags were up by Tuesday evening, and on Wednesday morning the rain fell in torrents. However, as it often does, the English weather turned up trumps and the afternoon and evening 'assumed a holiday appearance'. Shops closed early, large numbers of people arrived from neighbouring towns and villages, and Supt. Jeffrey had a force of over fifty men ready for action.

Worries that the station would not be suitably decorated – for being in Stoke Prior parish the Local Board was not responsible for it – were soon allayed, for despite 'the unsuitability of the object upon which they bestowed their care' the decorations were splendid. The railway Head Office in Derby sent down decorators, and blue and white hangings on a yellow ground were displayed, while festoons of green, blue and white decorated the booking office through which from platform to roadway ran a red carpet.

After alighting with some ceremony at Bromsgrove Station, Lord Windsor accompanied the Shah (who nervously buttoned up his coat over his jewelled chest) in his open barouche with four horses and outriders, escorted by the Queen's Own Worcestershire Hussars. The Queen's Equerry and the Shah's Grand Vizier, accompanied by other important personages, followed in coaches proceeding at a smart rate up New Road. The boys of the College school gave an orchestrated cheer, the populace lining the streets and leaning from windows gave hearty welcome, the Bromsgrove Volunteer Band played the *Persian March* by Johann Strauss II, and the bells of the parish church rang out.

The party rode up the High Street and turned into Alcester Road [Stratford Road], past decorated houses in Finstall, to Hewell Grange where His Majesty admired the illuminated rockeries and fernery and enjoyed a banquet for 40 guests. The next day the Stationmaster, Mr Gimson, in his frock coat and silk top hat, other railway officials and Police Supt. Jeffrey, ensured that the Shah and his entourage caught his special train to visit Birmingham, while Lord Windsor

Lord Robert Windsor-Clive, Earl of Plymouth and Baron Windsor of Hewell (1857-1923). CC.

rushed over to Oakly Park, near Ludlow, where his mother was gravely ill. The Shah visited Elkington's works, Osler's Glass Works and the Birmingham Small Arms Company, returning to Hewell for a quiet dinner on his own, being too tired to join the house party. But that evening 'thousands of people from Bromsgrove and Redditch' were still able to enjoy 'a magnificent pyrotechnic display ... the gardens were a perfect fairyland, ... the fireworks finale was very grand'.

The Shah stayed, according to *The Daily Telegraph* of 12th July 1889, in 'a large bedchamber above the portico of the Grange ... overlooking the garden and lake... His bed is a big four-poster, with canopy, and is of

Hewell Grange as it was when the Shah of Persia visited in 1889, and where he stayed in a room overlooking the lake. This illustration is a watercolour from Humphrey Repton's Red Book 1812.

the venerable massive and Royal order such as monarchs were wont to climb into in bygone days'. The newspaper then tells of the new Hewell Grange, nearly completed, being built alongside the earlier house. The Shah, the Windsors and the rest of the

The 'new' Hewell Grange in 1903. Building began in 1884 but was not completed until 1891.

party were in 'the family home'. This contradicts the story often told that the old house was blown up for entertainment during the Shah's visit, an 'absurd story', said *The Messenger*, which had been first mooted in *The World*. Later, roof beams from the old house were reused as floor boards in the reception rooms of the magnificent new mansion,[78] and the old house was then allowed to become a picturesque ruin to be viewed from the grass terraces.

The following day Lady Mary Windsor-Clive died, and the Shah set off to stay with the Duke of Norfolk, and to visit Liverpool and Manchester before enjoying a day or so of rest with the Duke of Montrose at Buchanan Castle near Loch Lomond. Bromsgrove counted the cost of the visit. All was well, for with subscriptions of £45.8.0 (probably heavily subsidised by Lord Windsor) and expenditure of £45.8.0, Bromsgrove's efforts could be counted a success.

SHAH RECEPTION EXPENSES.

STATEMENT OF ACCOUNTS.

	£	s.	d.
To Subscriptions	45	8	0
EXPENSES—			
Bellringers	1	10	0
"Messenger" Co.	2	12	0
Police Refreshments	1	5	0
School of Art (Muslin)	1	13	4
R. and J. Cordell (Waggonette)	0	13	0
W. Weaver's account	0	8	0
H. S. Harriss's "	2	1	0
T. Hall's "	3	11	0
Jos. Tilt's "	8	8	0
J. Humphries's " (builder)	1	13	0
J. Leadbetter's " "	0	9	0
J. Bryant's "	0	10	0
E. J. Townsend's "	0	17	3
J. N. Creswell (Railway Expenses, &c.)	0	9	6
A. Dipple (Wages paid)	0	15	0
W. Corbett	0	9	0
J. N. Creswell " and Material	1	4	0
Captain Dixon (Band)	6	0	0
Munt and Co. (Hire of Flags)	10	0	0
Music	0	7	6
Stamps	0	2	0
Advertising Statement of Accounts	0	3	6
C. Evans and E. Watton (towards Exps. of Arch)	0	6	11
	£45	8	0

Aug. 2nd, 1889.—Audited and found correct.
J. NASH CRESWELL,
JOHN GREEN Hon. Sec. and Treasurer.

The published account of expenses for Bromsgrove's reception of the Shah. £45 8s 0d income, £45 8s 0d expenses. Lord Robert very likely paid most of the income. Bromsgrove Messenger.

158

Chapter Thirteen

The Railway and Industry
in Aston Fields

By the 1880s the little group of houses at Stoke Chapel, Little or Lower Finstall, or even, as the Census had it, Finch End, had become more than just a railway community, and on the Ordnance Survey map of 1884 it was given the name of Aston Fields. Stoke Road seems also to have been commonly known as Charford Road. Before it settled down as Carlyle Road, that street was known as New Town, Factory Road or Carlisle Road, while Middlefield Road was often quite sensibly called Middle Road.

Gradually more shops opened in the village, and by the 1890s there was Mr Palmer the butcher, conveniently placed in part of Pear Tree Villa on the corner of Station Approach, followed ten years later by Mr John Alcott based in Aston Terrace opposite. Mr Buckley had a grocery shop two doors down from Pear Tree Villa. George Harford the shoemaker and cobbler did a good trade from Carlyle Road, and after he closed his doors Charlotte Hands continued the business in New Road, while Albert Perry was a bootmaker who started in South Road in the early 1900s, ending up in New Road in the 1940s. There was a beer retailer for those not wishing to visit the Dragoon [now the Ladybird] or the Workmen's Club, and Mrs Sarah Wylde had a sack hiring trade in Stoke Road – presumably for coal from the depots by the station.[79]

The Co-op – Co-operative Stores – came to Stoke Road, next to Pear Tree Villa, in 1897. The first ever Co-op was opened in Toad Lane, Rochdale, Lancashire in 1844 by workers who felt that if wholesalers, retailers and customers worked together and shared profits then everyone would benefit. The idea caught on, particularly in industrial working class areas. Customers became members of their local Co-op and were given a number. When they paid for goods – always in cash, no credit – they were asked their number and their membership card was marked. Many people saved up their tokens throughout the year until Christmas time, cashing in their 'divvies' [dividends] in time to buy seasonal extras. The Aston Fields Co-op stayed about fifteen years on this site, then moved along the road into Mr Buckley's building until it closed in 1951. Unfortunately by going against its principles and giving credit its financial position had deteriorated beyond redemption. However, in 2006 the Co-

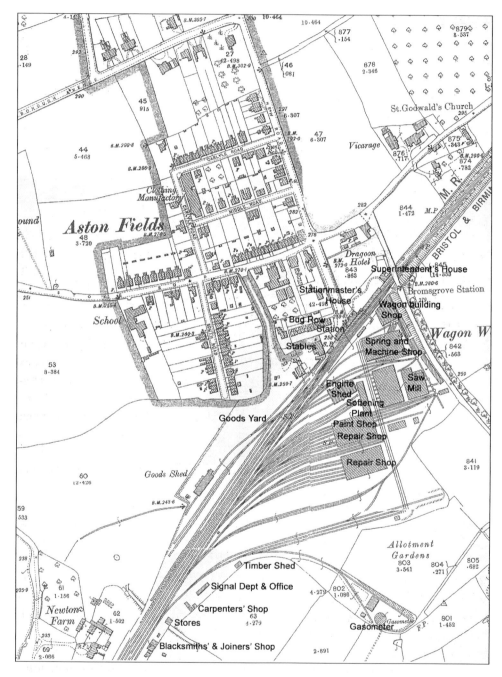

*Comparing the 1883 surveyed map (Chapter Six, page 55) with this, surveyed in 1901, shows
how much Aston Fields and the Wagon Works grew in eighteen years. OS.*

op came back to Aston Fields' corner shop in a different form, but still with divvies.

The Co-op's first building was taken over by Mrs Veale and her pork butchery business, who had been opposite Finstall School. Just at this time World War I was beginning, and Mrs Veale seized the opportunity to take the empty premises and began to provide hot dinners each day for the Workmen's Club next door. The family business thrived and did not close until the 1980s; after this the land behind the shop, originally providing space for pigsties and an abattoir, was developed for a block of flats.

The other butcher that celebrates longevity is Banner's, still a family business, though the shop now offers cooked food as well as joints of beef. Sam Banner opened his shop in the old Dragoon shortly after the new Dragoon [now the Ladybird] was built in 1905. Here, also with pigsties and abattoir on the land at the rear, the shop flourished, and another three generations of Banners have since worked in the firm. Sam's son Eric took over the business after the shock of Sam's suicide, building it up as each generation has done. In 1938 the shop space was enlarged and modernised, and then in 1968 a new building replaced some old cottages, and the first Dragoon was demolished – providing much needed car-parking space today.[80] The last remnant of the old inn is its stable block on the corner of St Godwald's Road, probably the earliest building left in Aston Fields.

The new Dragoon Hotel was, and is, a splendid building, described in the 2007 Pevsner[81] as 'vaguely Jacobethan' but with

A happy Samuel Banner and his mates outside the Dragoon, with his butcher's shop behind, pre 1930 – note the bull painted on the end wall. The friend on the left has old-style workman's trousers that fasten with a fall front buttoned at the sides. D. Banner.

Eric Banner with his son Maurice in the early 1950s. Meat was rationed until July 1954, hence a need to register with a butcher. D. Banner.

The Dragoon Hotel and the War Memorial at Aston Fields, in the 1930s. The station can be seen at the bottom of Station Approach to the right, with the sheds of the Wagon Works behind. Attached to the side of the hotel is a splendid sign – a model of a mounted dragoon soldier. Banner's shop in the old Dragoon is off the picture far left.

strong Art Nouveau influence. It was built by William Weaver in 1905 and no expense was spared in its detail – it was built to impress, particularly for travellers arriving up Station Approach, where there was a hotel sign of a rather splendid model dragoon on a horse. Notable are the stained glass windows, date stone, rainwater head and the grand corner 'Hotel Entrance', alas no longer in use. The old name was lost when the down-at-heel pub was bought and nicely restored by Christopher Bird in the 1990s, renaming it the Ladybird. Where once there was stabling and outhousing and, once upon a time, meadow, is now a car park and the recently built hotel and excellent Rosado's Restaurant.

Since 1855 there had been a Post Office only at upper Finstall, so it was a convenience for Aston Fields people when the Railway Station acquired a letter-box. Another important facility was a clock which was kept to time via the 'telegraphy'. Until the railways came there had been no real need for precision timing in everyday life, and clocks were set by sun-time – so that in the north of England there was a noticeable difference from the time in London. However the railway companies rapidly realised the value of telegraphy, and in 1840 had adopted 'London time' or Greenwich Mean Time all over the country. The clock on the wall of the Golden Cross would have been set to GMT using a reliable watch set correctly at the station, and the other watches and clocks in Bromsgrove would be checked against this.

The busy-ness of Aston Fields in 1880 encouraged the Post Office to open a branch in part of Mr W.T. Clarke's grocery shop at Aston House on the corner of Stoke and New Road. Here, if a letter was posted before 3.00pm, it would be delivered to any address in Bromsgrove that same afternoon. The post box was emptied three times a day, and letters addressed further afield would – with the help of the railway – be delivered the next morning. Licences for dogs, guns and brewing could be purchased; postal orders (just invented) and savings bank business transacted. The office was open 9.00am until 6.00pm, on Saturdays until 8.00pm. Telegrams could be sent from the railway booking office.

In 1899 Enoch Goode – though more likely Enoch Goode's wife – took the Post Office to their house on the corner of New and Middlefield Roads. Enoch Goode not only sold coal from behind the shop, but also in later years moved into footwear. The post office business went into Wilson's shop in 1930 where it stayed until 1961, after which it crossed the road to Pear Tree Villa, where it has been ever since.

Mrs Goode and her daughter outside the Post Office run by her husband Enoch at No.142 New Road on the corner of Middlefield Road. The family arrived in New Road in 1898, Enoch acting as colliery agent and manager for J. Nadin & Co. The coal side of their business was given up by 1908 when he began selling boots. The Post Office moved to Wilson's corner shop in 1930.

J.B. Wilson & Sons' grocery, corn merchants, agents for Gilbey's wines and spirits, in 1908.
The Manager and three assistants stand outside with the delivery man and his pony and trap.
Note the warehouse with a hoist for unloading sacks of corn from wagons; the warehouse corner
is curved to allow the wagons to pass close to the wall.

It was in 1886 that Mr John Broad Wilson took over Aston House, one of the branch premises of a rapidly growing empire that began in 1854. J.B. Wilson clearly had a talent for salesmanship – at the end of his first day's trading in Bromsgrove

From a photograph taken in 1908, left to right: W.C.E. Weston, W.H. Wilson and J.B. Wilson, all of the firm J.B. Wilson & Sons.

High Street his full stock of £20 worth of groceries and other items had sold out. After this success he went from strength to strength, buying three shops in the High Street and bringing his two sons into the business. Originally they sold a wide range of goods, including drapery, hardware and stationery, but gradually reduced these to groceries, wines and spirits, animal feed, farm and garden seeds and fertilizers. Branches were opened in Alvechurch, Belbroughton, Catshill and, in 1886 in

164

Aston Fields. Later came a branch in Stoke Works to serve the salt workers, and in 1942 the Rubery shop was opened. In 1888 William Weston joined the staff, to become a partner in 1909. There is no Wilson involved in the firm today, but there is still a member of the Weston family working from the company's old Market Street warehouse (built by Brazier in 1899), selling animal feed and fertilizers.

Wilson's stayed at Aston House until 1963/4, when the Banner family took over the grocery business. After seven years David Banner began to sell deep freezes for another seven years, together with frozen meat from the family's butcher's shop over the road. The next long-term tenant was James Designs, which sold soft furnishings, and it is currently occupied by a business teaching self-defence. Next door to Aston House in 1958, on a piece of Wilson's land, came a petrol station and motor repair workshop run by a member of the family. This was closed at the end of the twentieth century, and small lock-up shops built on the site, the last plot of this land given permission to build in 2008.

Greengroceries were needed by those whose heavy working life prevented them growing their own. Jimmy Evans, Parish Clerk, began to supplement his small earnings by selling fruit and vegetables from his cottage door, gradually expanding to open a shop in Factory Road (Carlyle Road): extremely useful for those working

Postcard of Stoke Road from the cross roads. Wilson's on the right; the front garden of Pear Tree Cottage – Aston Fields Workmen's Club – on the left with trees, and top left a Union Jack on a flag pole.

Come rain or snow, Roberson's van went out delivering vegetables to its customers. Reg Roberson (right) and Dick Ingram were probably not enjoying this morning in 1990. Note the weighing scales on the van. RS.

locally. Here he expanded into newspapers, and in the 1920s was joined by his son-in-law Caleb Roberson. The Roberson family continued the business, becoming legends for their generosity to customers – Harold Roberson always went to the back of the shop to bring out fresh fruit for his regular customers, and we wondered who bought the slightly old looking fruit displayed on the forecourt. Like Banner's and Veale's, Robey's also delivered their produce to customers' doors, originally by horse and cart, later by van. It was a sad day for the locality when the Robersons retired. [K & K Newsagents is now one of the few shops that still offers newspaper deliveries, and they have a less perishable stock than Roberson's.]

The small group of shops at Aston Fields was joined in 1886 by a steam flourmill, built next to Mr Buckley's shop [probably where today there is a car mechanic and a Chinese take-away]. The mill was a tall building of four storeys,

> 'with a frontage of three yards (2.7 m.) and at the back was built a boiler house and stores for grain. There was a set of stones on each of the three upper floors, and the process of manufacture consisted of taking in the grain at the top and sending it down through each set of stones till it was delivered to the ground floor in the finished state.'

There was gas and piped water, though the East Worcestershire Waterworks Company had not provided the requested fire hydrant outside the building. The mill employed several men, did not make too much noise, and provided an easy source of flour for breadmaking, so was welcomed into the village. The owner was a young man, William Finney, who at the age of only 28 had already opened another milling operation at Moat Mills, a bakery at 180 Worcester Street, and another at 17 Broad Street, Birmingham where he had a large machine bread manufactury. He was living at Elmsdale with his wife and young family. All this investment involved a huge amount of money, even if he was heavily mortgaged, but as we know from the census that his unmarried sister was able to live without working, it seems probable that he had inherited money.

All was going well – indeed on 26 January 1888 'the flour mill was full of grain, the store was filled and every available place in the mill was occupied, and a number of sacks of peas, etc., was stacked outside.' Then in the middle of that night the official in Newton signal box became aware that the mill was on fire. He telephoned Bromsgrove Station, and a porter was sent to the town to raise the alarm; the fire

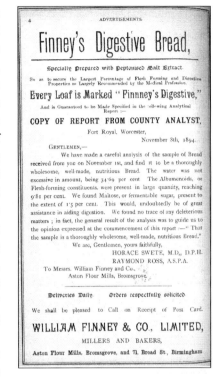

Despite the mis-spelling in the fifth line, this 1894 advertisement gives the County Analyst's report on William Finney & Company's 'thoroughly wholesome, well-made, nutritious Bread'. BR.

bell rang in Bromsgrove at 1.00am, and in what seemed a long twenty minutes later the Volunteer Fire Brigade arrived with a plentiful supply of hose. By this time the fire was 'burning fiercely, the flames being furiously fanned by high wind.' Water was provided from the station hydrant – the water coming from the company's reservoir at Blackwell – but it could be seen that the building could not be saved – flames were streaming out of every window, and creeping through the roof. A hose was played on Mr Buckley's shop next door – thankfully the wind was in a different direction – and another on the store room and boiler house at the back of the mill, which also were saved. The fire engine had to be pulled away because its paint was beginning to blister, the windows of the houses on the opposite side of the road were cracked by the heat, and their front door paint blistered as well.

Bromsgrove Volunteer Firemen in 1895, outside their headquarters in St John Street, Captain Job Leadbetter in the centre, the shiny fire engine behind, and a young lad on the right inching his way into the picture. BC.

'The roof and floors were giving way, and at each fall of débris myriads of sparks sprang into the air and floated away on the wind, simulating a snowstorm with the fiery atoms for flakes, and producing a weired [sic], grand, and awful spectacle.'[82]

After more drama, including two damaged firemen – Mr Hall was struck by a falling brick and Mr Rea bruised himself and 'somewhat seriously injured' his right eye – the flames quietened down. This was helped by cutting off the gas supply that had been flaring persistently all this time. Leaving the heap of brickwork and machinery to cool down, the fire brigade returned to Bromsgrove in time for a late breakfast at 8.00am, and the large number of spectators trudged back home declaring that this was the largest fire there had been in the district since Finstall House in 1866.

It was thought that the fire was caused by overheating machinery, and the damage was estimated at £5,000. Mr Finney's building and machinery were insured for £3,000, but not his stock. Sadly all was not over. Two years and eight months later the shocking news came that William Finney had been found dead, lying against a hayrick in a field near Linthurst church. Near the body was found a little blue bottle, a gold watch and chain, some keys and some letters, one of which, addressed to his father-in-law, listed amounts he owed and where the bills could be found in his office.

The East Worcestershire Coroner held an inquest at the Dragoon with a jury of local men. After hearing from the chemist who supplied young Finney with laudanum, and hearing from business colleagues that he had suffered severe stomach pains for some weeks, the case was deferred for analysis of the liquid in the bottle and of the contents of his stomach. It was only at the second inquest that it was reported that five days' before Finney's death an officer of the Sheriff of Worcester had taken possession of the rebuilt mill. In the end three inquests were held, the jury trying hard not to conclude a suicide. Finally the jury ended up before a judge in Worcester, who told them they could not leave until they had reached a verdict – after which ominous warning they finally agreed – 'Found dead'.

William Finney left Ada, his 27 year old wife, five year old Ada Maria and Kathleen who was one year old. His young brother-in-law George Blakeley joined the family, presumably to help run the business. Mrs Finney senior, William's mother, lived on in Bromsgrove for a number of years, but Ada Finney, after a couple of years living at Raleigh Villas in New Road, disappears from the directories and census – hopefully she remarried. The firm of Finney & Co, millers and corn dealers, continued in business in Aston Fields and Bromsgrove – they were in Roundabout House in 1896 – until 1898. In the first years of the next century J.B. Wilson's were milling at the Aston Fields site, but this did not last, and there seems no trace of the buildings today.

There was very little work available for the women and older girls of the village. The button factory up the Kidderminster Road from Bromsgrove and later Victor Drury's Boot Factory on Worcester Road (which also made shoes and gloves) were the largest employers of women in the neighbourhood, but they were about 1½ miles away, and it was difficult to get a job there. Other work for women could be as a household servant, or the educated could teach – though there were very few positions. It was therefore a matter of some rejoicing when a clothing factory was opened in Carlyle Road in 1886, in a building built, it is said, for Mr T.D. Thomas of Stourbridge, a draper, by Joseph Tilt, builder.

The factory soon became Harries, Whitfield & Co. Henry Stone Whitfield had a draper's shop in Worcester Road, but Harries is more of a mystery. A man named Andrew William Harries lived for a while with his young family in Wellington Road, and was living in Bromsgrove High Street in 1901, shown on two censuses as a commercial traveller. It is possible that he was the sales face of the company,

The clothing factory in Carlyle Road which gave employment to many in the area, particularly women. It finally closed in 1982 and was converted into flats. RS.

while Mr Whitfield looked after both the factory and his draper's shop – which soon began selling tailoring and women's dresses.

It was a good position for the factory. Materials could be easily and quickly delivered from the railway, and equally, goods could be shipped out by rail. An employee of the firm, Mrs Elizabeth Perks, who started working in the factory when she was 13 in 1909, walking up from Broad Street, Sidemoor every day, spoke about her life to *The Messenger* on closure of the business. She worked for a year in the booking department at the factory, before moving on to become one of four specialist buttonhole machinists. Her wages were 3s 8d (18p) per week (more than she would have got from button or boot making), and hours were 8.00am to 5.00pm Mondays to Fridays, plus Saturday mornings. While she worked for the firm it was making men's suits and coats, and it had one dress room and two machinists' rooms.

The business did well. Mr Whitfield moved in 1893 into Marlborough Avenue from the Crescent, staying there until his death in 1905. Another partner in the firm, Henry Wheelock, better known as head of the Linthurst brickworks and for his coal business by the station, died aged 55 in 1901, having added farming to his many interests.

The factory was a convenient source of employment for both men and women, while the Wagon Works appears to have employed only men. The 1901 census

Postcard of Carlyle Road looking towards New Road, with the clothing factory on the right. The children are all wearing hats and pinnies, and a frilly-aproned housewife talks to a delivery man.

shows the importance of these employers to the immediate area of Aston Fields. From a population of just under 900 there were 150 men from the village working either on the railway or at the Wagon Works, and sixty people of both sexes working at the clothing factory. Another 50 had assorted jobs such as gardening, agricultural labour, charring or laundering, or were wagoners or postmen; live-in domestic servants are not included in these figures. This was of course only a small proportion of those working at the two big employers. At the height of its production the clothing factory employed 300 people, though 170 may have been the norm, and though the railway itself had a stable workforce the Wagon Works varied greatly. At its height it employed 600 men, but in 1908 there were 394.

Bromsgrove men were held in high regard in the wagon building industry for the quality of their work. However very gradually there was less demand, and short-time working began to be introduced. Short-time resulted in two branches of the Railway Workers Union being formed in Bromsgrove in 1891 – the Wagon Builders and the Railway Workers. Even so, in the first year of the new century 1,186 wagons were repaired, at an average cost of £2 14s (£2.70p) each. Saturday working was stopped in 1905, reducing the men's earnings and causing unrest. However, the business clung on, and WWI brought a period of frenetic activity, many departments working day and night for nearly five years. In the smithy and

An aerial photograph of the station (left) and Wagon Works (right) in 1925. BC.

fitting shops were built ammunition wagons and gun carriages, as well as smaller items; a total of 39,685 articles. The old sawmill, which had lain idle for 15 years, was brought back to service sawing up timber of all descriptions. During this time over 21,000 trees were cut up, not only to keep the Wagon Works going but also to provide the Derby yard and other sheds as well.

After the war things again got tight for the men, a national problem due to the industry's endeavour to boost profits by reducing wages; this resulted in a strike being called in 1919 by the two unions, ASLEF and the NUR, which lasted for eight days.

Life soon went back to routine, the 7.45am hooter summoning men to work, followed by another call at 7.55 to warn that there was only five minutes left to clock-in. Then the men poured in, many having tramped down New Road, all carrying their

Every repair done at the Wagon Works was fitted with a repair plate. RS.

lunch in red handkerchiefs. Those who remember the handkerchiefs insist they were always red.

Meanwhile during these years the railway station and that other important aspect of railway life, the provision of engines to assist trains to climb the incline, continued their work. At least five bank engines were kept in use, housed in the locomotive shed alongside the southbound platform, to service the number of freight and passenger trains that passed along the line. Many of these needed two or even three engines to bank them up the incline. By the end of WWI the pride of the railway workers was Big Bertha, a specially designed and built engine which became known to railway buffs worldwide. She worked the line between 1919 and 1956, clocking up 838,856 miles on the two mile incline between the station and Blackwell. Big Bertha's last journey up the incline was a splendid one; all the railway men on the site piled aboard the

George Pidgeon, Senior Station Foreman, c.1910. Mr Pidgeon was one of a number in his family who worked on the railway; he retired in 1932. RS.

The great 'engine factory', built in 1840, is on the far right of this postcard of the station c.1910. The bridge carries St Godwald's Road. Note the milk churns.

Thirty-four year old Big Bertha firing up before doing her job banking a passenger train up the line from Bromsgrove Station in October 1953. www.railphotoprints.co.uk.

wagons for her farewell performance, no doubt celebrating their mourning in the usual way. For those men she was certainly more than a collection of bits of metal, and it is touching to see in Finstall graveyard close to the railway two headstones, one for Mr C.J. Bishop (who died in 1990), the other for Mr T.C. Evans (1995), that have an image of Big Bertha on them, fifty years after she had gone.

The railway station itself came under verbal attack during the 1880s. Passengers were aggrieved that the platforms were too low – especially unpleasant for ladies who had to jump 3ft. (0.9m) from the trains, risking showing more than their ankles as they did so. There was much fuss and many

Memorials to two railwaymen in Finstall graveyard, with pictures of Big Bertha etched into the headstones. Clarence Jack Bishop, died in 1990 and Trevor Charles Evans, died in 1995, some fifty years after the great engine was taken out of service.

letters written to *The Messenger,* and eventually in 1889 the station was refurbished, raising the platform, enlarging the booking hall considerably and widening the exit, putting in additional waiting rooms and more up-to-date lavatory arrangements. Another facility was a weighing machine for trade use, which in time took over from the machine at the top of Bromsgrove High Street.

An important part of the railway site was the stable block, which was on the Aston Fields side of the lines. Here were kept the dray horses that carted heavy materials up to town, and here horses could be stabled for a few hours as required. Tuesdays and Fridays – market days in Bromsgrove – were chaotic, as cattle, sheep and pigs were unloaded from trucks to be driven up New Road to the cattle market by shouting men accompanied by barking dogs – only for the same thing in reverse at the end of the day, the animals being loaded back onto trucks to be sent to another destination. The cattle market ceased selling animals in 1972. Each June 24th there was even more excitement, for this was Bromsgrove's traditional Midsummer's Day Horse Fair, one of the most famous in the land. Horses of every breed arrived at the station, many of them from Ireland, Exmoor and Wales, to be ridden and driven up to town:

> 'Bromsgrove Fair specialises in Welsh ponies, not the tame, thoroughly domesticated little Welshman, "warranted quiet to ride or drive," but the Welsh pony, not more than two years old, unshod, wild from his native hills, and entirely without respect for persons or things.'[83]

How the owners of the gentlemen's residences must have hated those days, with the inevitable deposits of manure on footpath and roadway:

Bromsgrove Station from Station Approach in the 1960s.

From 1853 the focus of Bromsgrove's Midsummer's day Horse Fair was in the new cattle market in Church Street behind the High Street. Horses of all types filled the streets of the town, particularly wild little Welsh ponies.

Even in 1950 the tradition of the horse fair continued; this photograph shows a skittish pony refusing to enter his new master's horse box. WRO.

'In the High Street horses were trotted up and down for sale, and the accompanying noise was deafening, the sellers rattling the handles of their whips around inside their hats.' [84]

'Every inn yard and every open space [was] filled with vehicles of divers kinds. The horses, relieved from duty, overflow out of regular stables into improvised stalls, whilst trusses of hay are everywhere much in evidence, and buckets of water, and … business is colossal.' [85]

Fortunately these noisy groups did not pass near the two big houses of the neighbourhood, Rigby Hall and Finstall Park, though it could well be that some horses from the Finstall Stud were taken along on 24th June. Mr Everitt's time living at Finstall Park came to an end in 1892, and after a few years with the Jebb Scotts as tenants, Mr John Boultbee Brooks took their place with much enthusiasm for the stud farm. Boultbee Brooks, a Birmingham manufacturer of bicycle saddles, expanded the breeding to pedigree cattle, hunters and shire horses. Finstall Trojan, Finstall Lady Jane, Finstall Conqueror and Finstall Forest Prince were Shire horse names that brought fame to the village.[86] The best horses were offered for stud. In 1915 the fee was 5 guineas (£5.25p), though tenant farmers were only charged 3 guineas (£3.15p), plus a groom's fee of 2/6d (12½p). A few of the stud farm buildings are still in existence as dwellings, but the surrounding land was used for the Penmanor estate in the 1950s.

Mr Boultbee Brooks was a tenant for 24 years, after which the Everitt family split up the estate for sale in 1920; the house itself was unsold, but was bought at a second Sale in 1924 by Braziers the builders. It was used as a boys' preparatory school for a number of years under Gerald L. Waller, and then went into a state of sad decline. In 1955 permission to build a housing estate in the Park thankfully was refused, though permission was later given to convert the big house into seven dwellings. However in the 1970s there was another disastrous fire, leaving only a small part of the house. Now there are several houses close by, the lower part of the park has been enthusiastically used by the rugby club since the 1890s, and the pastureland is an important green oasis between Aston Fields and Finstall. The most notable remnant of the estate is the ⅛ mile (1Km) dressed sandstone wall that runs from opposite the burial ground to the Finstall House driveway up Walnut Lane. Though damaged by winter salt, it is a splendid reminder of the past life of the 'big house' of the village.

To reach the Finstall wall from Aston Fields one needs to cross over the railway, using the skew bridge.[87] The present bridge is the fourth one. As described in Chapter Two, originally there was a first badly built skew bridge, then Spencer's railway bridge also over the road. It was not a successful passage, particularly in winter, for the navvies had had to lower the roadway to allow enough room for loaded wagons to pass through. This meant that water collected, and there was also a very sharp turn for the road to skirt round Rigby Hall land and pass between the

The original skew bridge built in 1840 took the road under the railway near the back gate to Rigby Hall. The deep cutting needed to allow wagons to pass meant that water and mud collected there in wet weather. This being a main highway and the only road between upper Finstall and Aston Fields there were continual flooding problems, resulting in a new bridge over the railway in 1894. Sayer, 1898.

Rigby Hall gardener's cottage and the old chapel. There were constant grumbles to Stoke Prior parish council who were responsible for roadways, and particular horror when in 1877 Dr. Richard Wood was badly injured when his trap overturned and his horse ran off down to the Dragoon. Building a new bridge was put off as long as possible, but eventually in 1894 quantities of hardcore were brought to build up the road to allow a new beautifully built sandstone bridge to be put over the railway – this is the reason why the first few Finstall Road houses are well below the roadway. The discarded bridge was filled in, but the old footpath to reach it can still be seen between the cottage and graveyard, as can the remains of the grand sandstone gateway to Rigby Hall, which was Listed by English Heritage in 1975.[88]

The new beautiful bridge lasted for a hundred years until it was deemed unfit to carry buses, coaches and lorries. Rather than rebuild it in sandstone it was completely demolished and a concrete bridge put in its place. It was also raised as a preliminary to possible future electrification of the line. The present very high-sided bridge was given a thin sandstone cladding – an unsatisfactory answer. It is sad that, because the walls are so high, we no longer see railway enthusiasts leaning against the parapet, binoculars and cameras poised, waiting for trains to run up and down the Lickey Incline.

The roadway to Finstall from the skew bridge was lined on one side by the sandstone wall, and after WWI opportunity was taken to build the bungalows and a few houses on the narrow land between the railway and the road. This was ribbon development, though one could hardly object when the strip of land was so narrow and not much use for anything else except grazing.

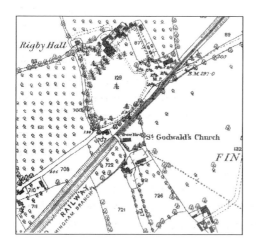 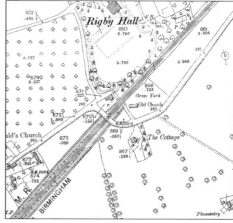

The 1883 and 1901 mapping of the Finstall skew bridges, the first running under the railway, and the second showing the new bridge over the lines. OS.

The Rigby Hall estate had stayed in the ownership of Robert Smallwood, Esq. until his death in 1898, and in 1900 when it was put on the market the sitting tenant Mr Edward Ansell bought all the land for £18,350. There were twelve Lots totalling 174 acres – rather more than the 25 acres Smallwood purchased in the 1860s. Mr Smallwood had also considerably enlarged the house, and George Ellins would not have recognised it, for a grand new wing had been added to the old front, with splendid Doric columns and a mansard roof. The handsome portico entrance led to a spacious staircase hall with Jacobean-style ceilings, which in turn led to drawing room, dining room, breakfast room and billiard room, all generous in size. The domestic wing included a servants' hall, cooking kitchen with hot and cold water supply and soft water pump, scullery, dairy, vegetable and meat larders, cook's pantry, housekeeper's room and butler's pantry. In the servants' yard were a knife house, coal house, ashplace and W.C. There were eight bedrooms, including two suites with bedchamber, dressing-room and bathroom, as well as a nursery suite with nursemaid's and housemaid's closets. Beer and wine cellars made the house complete.

Edward Ansell J.P., a director of Ansell's Brewery in Aston, Birmingham, decided to refurbish the house in 1901, yet only lived there until 1906 when he moved to his splendid new home, Moor Hall at Sutton Coldfield, nearer to the brewery. Rigby Hall with just 24 acres was withdrawn at the Sale for £7,000 and later sold to Mr Wright of Mount Pleasant, Redditch, who sold it on to Mr Albert Eadie, a Redditch bicycle manufacturer. He lived there until 1923 when it went to Mr Ernest R. Jones for £4,000 and he in turn sold it to Worcestershire County Council in 1940. After use as a maternity home and student residence the old house was sold for offices, while Rigby Hall School was built in 1968 on land where the lawns of the big house had been.

Edward Ansell had hung on to some of his land, breaking up the estate which had been so painstakingly brought together by Mr Smallwood, gradually selling off parcels for building. In 1907, in eight lots, he sold the land between St Godwald's Road and the railway line, where later 'Piano Row' was to be built, and later still the houses of St Godwald's Crescent. The second Sale was four years later when in sixteen Lots he sold 'capital building sites' with frontages to New Road on the Dragoon fields, five of them fronting onto Rigby Lane. It was here that in 1927 Braziers on behalf of the Rural District Council constructed sixteen of the most attractive council houses in Bromsgrove. Three years' later Dragoon Fields was built, again by Braziers for the RDC, ten houses which were erected for £3,342 6s 6d.

Chapter Fourteen

The Almshouses and Cottage Hospital

With a growing population in Bromsgrove there was need to look after the impoverished elderly – 'the deserving poor' as the Elizabethan phrase has it. There were 17th century almshouses in Alcester Road [Stratford Road], and in 1885 the Consolidated Charities Trust built two blocks of three houses (planned by John Cotton) when those earlier ones were demolished. The purpose of almshouses is to provide independent living for the elderly who would otherwise end up in the Workhouse. Seeing the need for more such dwellings, Thomas White of the indigo factory and The Newlands planned to give the town three blocks of two houses on his own pastureland land in New Road for 'twelve decayed gentlewomen of 60 or over'. This was one of the 'noble munificent act(s) of liberality and justice which he

A postcard of the Thomas White Cottage Homes built in 1885 for the benefit of 'twelve decayed gentlewomen of 60 or over'.

The Bath stone legend reads 'Cottage Homes erected by Thomas White AD 1885'.

performed from a simple keen sense of honour', as described by Dr Fletcher.[89] Despite his generosity, Mr White made restrictions regarding those who might live at the almshouses – 'no Catholic, Unitarian nor atheist'. He was firmly low church in his belief, a champion of simplicity in worship, and there is a story that when one Sunday the Vicar of St John's wore a white surplice rather than his usual black gown Mr White stalked out, outraged.[90] He was a churchwarden at St John's for several years, gave £1,000 for the repair of its roof, but also supported the cost of All Saints' tower with £400, and gave £700 for the tower of the new church at Dodford.

The very pleasing almshouses were planned by John Brazier and built by his father's firm in 1886, costing Mr White £3,366 12s 5d. There was indeed no expense spared on these homes, which were built in red Kingswinford bricks with 'jambs, mullions, tympaniums, sills, leads, strings, and labels executed in Bath stone'. The walls were built with cavities bonded together with patent terracotta tie bricks – still an unusual method of building at the time. Each house (which was to be shared by two occupants) had seven gaslights and an up-to-the minute drainage system, with water laid on by the East Worcestershire Waterworks Company. There were seven Trustees plus the Vicar: Dr Richard Wood, Messrs Benjamin Sanders, John Green, George

Bown, A.E. Wenham, T. Perkins and Mr Roger Prosser. Miss M.A. Fowler endowed £2,628 while Mr White made a settlement of £200 per annum until his death, when a further £8,000 would become available 'to be invested in Consols … to produce £200 per annum in continuity'.

The almshouses were becoming very decrepit in the 1980s, with a threat of demolition. The Trustees of the time, led by the Trust's Clerk Matthew Horton, were determined to save them and with the help of grants from charitable trusts and local businesses the buildings were modernised in 1985, re-roofed and altered to make two separate flats in each house instead of the

The central pair of Thomas White Cottage Homes in 2001. The tall conifer was removed in 2007.

original shared accommodation. Several of the buildings featured in this book were similarly threatened with demolition at about this time, to the horror of towns-people, prompting a fierce determination to save them. It is a pity that the Thomas White Cottage Homes are the only success stories.

Although Bromsgrove was well set up with medical men throughout our period, it had no hospital. The Workhouse in Birmingham Road had wards to which poorer working class people had to resort when ill, but not only was a stigma attached to this but also the facilities could not suit those with higher expectations.

The most prominent doctors in the 1860s were Dr Fletcher and Dr Charles Horton. Dr Horton lived in The Gables [Nos. 126-130 High Street, currently a pub], which he built for himself and his family in 1851. In the 1870s the prime doctors were Mr Roger Prosser and Dr William Batten. All these men gave themselves the title 'surgeon' – to which they were entitled having passed through the Royal College of Surgeons. The doctors of the 1880s and 1890s were led by Dr Richard Wood and Dr. F.W.J. Coaker. All these men must have spent a large amount of their time riding by horse to outlying parts, visiting the sick in their homes, carrying out operations on kitchen tables, delivering babies, always accompanied by their portmanteaux which held medicines, bandages, splints and surgical tools. Poorer patients inevitably waited until the last possible minute before sending for a doctor, because of the need to pay him – though doctors were used to receiving payment in kind: a chicken, a joint of pork, a dozen eggs.

Since 1884 poor and indigent people could be catered for in the new Infirmary of the Workhouse in Birmingham Road, where there was room for 68 beds. This was built by Tilt & Fisher to the plans of Charles Allerton Edge, the Birmingham architect. The nearest hospitals proper were in Worcester and Birmingham, a long uncomfortable distance for an ill patient travelling in a wagon.

Dr Roger Prosser, at the forefront of the plans for the Cottage Hospital, who lived in a gracious Georgian house in the High Street, demolished for Boots the Chemist. CC.

Dr F.W.J. Coaker, FRCS, who completed 50 years' service as Hon. Surgeon at the Cottage Hospital in 1947. The Story of Bromsgrove Cottage Hospital.

The desire to build a hospital in Bromsgrove was initially driven by the Friendly Societies, particularly the Foresters and the Oddfellows.[91] At a meeting held in June 1876 the group discussed opening a fund for establishing a Cottage Hospital.[92] Having decided to work with this aim, the group managed to enthuse enough people and very shortly a committee was set up, headed by Mr Arthur Ryland J.P., which included not only members of the clergy, the High Bailiff and doctors, but also representatives of the nailmakers, railwaymen and other trades. The campaign was off to a good start, and offers of help began to arrive: Mr John Humphreys, the chemist and dentist, offered free of charge to supply and dispense any medicines required during the hospital's first six months; Mr George Burrows of the Golden Cross gave a donation of 3 guineas and free wine and brandy for the first six months; while within a week employees at the Midland Railway Works paid over to the fund the sum of £23 11s 2d.

The next problem was where the hospital should be, and several offers were made, including Perry Hall [now Housman Hall] which was offered by Edward Housman at a figure of £1,700. The place chosen – though the site was offered only for 14 years – was on Mount Pleasant [Stratford Road, opposite the entrance to College Road].[93] This temporary hospital, converted from a row of cottages, was built for £300, to the designs of John Cotton, in 1877 and was a success, until the lease ran out in 1890 and it was clear that a much bigger establishment needed to be built.

For months Bromsgrove people enthusiastically supported public meetings and made donations: Lord Windsor gave £100, John Corbett £500, while surgeon Sir Thomas Chavasse of Barnt Green quickly donated a male ward with six beds, in memory of Lady Chavasse's father. The site chosen was 'about half an acre on the opposite side of New Road to Mr Saywell's House, on the north side of the Baptist Chapel … bought at 5/- (25p) per sq.yd. from Mr Alfred Dipple and others.' Once John Cotton had agreed to alter his plans by making the buildings face New Road rather than the Baptist Church, he was the clear winner of the competition between four Bromsgrove architects. There were five local doctors on the building

John Cotton (1844-1934) in 1913, architect of the Cottage Hospital, the Institute and the School of Science & Art. These three were the last of his many Bromsgrove buildings, most of which are demolished. John Cotton was an enthusiast for old buildings and local history, and his collection in Birmingham Central Library forms the basis of most of the published Bromsgrove histories. CC.

committee, who attended nearly all the meetings, thus making sure that their needs were provided.

Things progressed at a great speed. By 6 June 1889 revised drawings were ready and builders were invited to tender. J. Brazier & Son's quote of £2,637 was accepted; the final cost, including £820 for the site, was £4,234. On 4 August 1891, after just ten months, the Bromsgrove Cottage Hospital held its opening ceremony.[94]

The Hospital had a central block with corridors to two side 'pavilions' – very fashionable at the time – which were the male and female wards. These held only six beds each, though there was another room on the central first floor of the Hospital if needed. On either side of the main entrance were the day-room and matron's room, and behind were the operating room, stores, nurses' water-closet and kitchen. The yard to the back led to the mortuary, disinfecting chamber and outdoor stores. Matron's room and the day-room had bay windows and a small balcony, with a beautiful wrought iron railing.

Jonathan Brazier (1827-1895), founder of the building firm and father of John Brazier who designed the Cottage Homes.
R. Brazier.

The Management Committee at various times included several of the people we have already come across in this book: Messrs Roger Prosser, J.J. Tomson, J.B. Wilson, James Green, William Holyoake, and James Laughton who was treasurer

A drawing of the 'New Cottage Hospital at Bromsgrove', architect John Cotton, published in The Messenger *and in* The Architect *on the opening of the building on 4 August 1891.* CC.

for 16 years. It was a responsible and worrying role they had, for the hospital was totally funded by voluntary donations. But it was not only such people who supported the hospital. There was always one member of the Management Committee representing the railway and Wagon Works. The Rovers Football Club gave the proceeds of their Easter Tuesday match and did so for many years; a Charity Ball was regularly held; when James Lea died in 1904 he left his house Fernleigh to the hospital, which sold it for £720; John Cotton left Sunnylawn to be used as a nurses' home (though it never was used as such, and was also sold); and annual Hospital Saturdays were held when the working people of Bromsgrove made special and very generous collections.[95] A similar event once organised by Tom McDermott, owner of the town's two cinemas, was a 'Regal Hospital Sunday', which brought in £25.

Mr Thomas White was generous, though by 1902 he apologised for not attending the annual meeting because 'he could not move a step without agony; and, suffering pain himself, he wished to seize the opportunity of doing good to those around him.' He gave the hospital £1,000 that year

The main entrance photographed just before demolition of the hospital. J. Adams.

plus £53 for X-ray apparatus, and left a legacy of £1,000 when he died in 1908. His generosity was matched in 1910 when another legacy of £1,000 was left to the hospital by Mr John Osborne, a plasterer, of Burcot.

Demand for proper hospital facilities grew. In 1898 Dr Underhill reported '172 admissions during the year, of which 134 were cured, 26 relieved, 7 remained as patients, and only 5 died …. When they considered that 93 surgical and 9 dental operations were performed, in a large proportion of which an anaesthetic was administered, he thought they would see the figures were wonderfully good.' The report for 1908 was 282 cases, 31 cases of accident, with 115 surgical and 90 dental operations. There was no mention of deaths in that report.

The allusion to anaesthetic was relevant, for the use of chloroform or gas was still not fully understood. Dr Fletcher, in order to test out the use of chloroform had 'obtained permission to try an anaesthetic on a colt at the Bowling Green Farm. The Doctor succeeded in putting the animal to sleep, but failed in his efforts to wake him.'

The very spartan children's ward as it was when built in 1934, with eight cots and one bed. The architect for extensions was G.H. Gadd. The Story of Bromsgrove Cottage Hospital.

A gate for the Cottage Hospital, made by Bromsgrove Guild. WRO.

The original buildings were of course not large enough to cope with both rising demand and advances in technology. A room was built for the X-ray apparatus (£200 in 1917), Dr Coaker needed an enlarged Operating Theatre (£1,200 in 1926), and the same year a children's ward was deemed necessary though not erected until the early 1930s, when a casualty ward, 6 private wards, a new kitchen and outhouses were built, together with a smart new entrance and waiting hall. The builder again was J & A Brazier, and the cost £7,000. The architect was G.H. Gadd, who in July 1934 presented a gold key to Lord Cobham, who ceremoniously opened the new door. In that entrance hall and around the hospital were placed portraits of benefactors, a bronze memorial plaque to Sir John and Lady Sumner in recognition of their generosity, and by the main door the impressively large mahogany donors' board.

Probably because so many people had donated money, effort and time to the Cottage Hospital it was regarded with great affection. When the threat of closure was announced townspeople were outraged, but to no avail, for the doors finally closed in 1988. Small parts of the stonework were incorporated into the block of flats which now covers the sites of the Hospital, the Institute and School of Science & Art, but the huge mahogany donations board and the paintings of hospital worthies have disappeared.

At the time of the demolition two elderly Bromsgrove people gave their memories to *The Weekly Mail*.[96] Mr Bill Perks (aged 94) remembered when as an employee of the Wagon Works 'one of my mates hit my finger with a sledgehammer and me going up to the hospital to have it stitched up.' And 'whenever

A postcard of the Cottage Hospital showing the necessary retaining wall along New Road, which is in a cutting as it climbs the hill out of the town. One pavilion housed the men's ward, and the other was for women, with extra ward space if required above the central hall.

anyone injured their foot and they could not walk, we used to wheel them on one of the Wagon Works' trolleys to the Cottage to be treated'. His wife, Elizabeth (aged 92) was slightly less enthusiastic – 'We knew it was always there in case of an emergency. For most accidents we used to go to Mrs Harper the chemist next to the Town Hall. She was much better than any doctor'.

Chapter Fifteen

The Institute and School
of Science & Art

The Literary and Scientific Institute in New Road, opened in 1893, was one of Bromsgrove's greatest recent achievements. For many years the organisation had little space in its High Street home and had been struggling to raise money to move. William A. Cotton, who had been Secretary of the Institute for a number of years, had left in his Will after his early death a generous £800 towards a new building which it was decided should go on New Road next to the Cottage Hospital. Lord Windsor, a cultured man with a passionate interest in art, whose great house Hewell Grange by Bodley & Garner was being built, took an interest in the project, heading the list of donors and laying the foundation stone in October 1893. The architect, of course, was to be John Cotton, William's older brother.

The plan was for Cotton's Institute to be built with the projected School of Art alongside, for that was also desperate for premises; they were to be separate, yet together. The builders were Tilt and Weaver, with stonework by Messrs Griffin of Rock Hill, carvings by H.H. Martyn of Cheltenham. It was built high above the road, up steps that divided to lead to the doors of each establishment, and inside were the usual reading room, lending library, recreation and committee rooms, and a 42ft x 24ft (12.8m x 7.3m) lecture hall-cum-gymnasium. In the reading room was a cast iron mantelpiece inscribed *Knowledge is Power*. The unusual and memorable decorations to the otherwise simple rooms were appropriately chosen carvings on the corbels of the reading room and lecture room. These portrayed, as *The Messenger* reported, 'the leading writers of the day in Science, Philosophy, Literature, and Poetry, as illustrated by

William Weaver Junior, builder of Bromsgrove, who with his father for many years partnered members of the Brazier family of builders. The firm was founded in 1865, and is the only 19th century Bromsgrove building firm still in existence, now Weaver PLC.

A postcard showing the Institute, the Cottage Hospital and the Baptist Church in New Road. All that is left of these buildings are a few pieces of carved stone that are incorporated into the Elgar Mews flats that have taken the place of the Hospital and Institute.

Left: The bay window of the Institute which had curved glazing, and a carved stone parapet. Right: The door and porch entrance to the Institute, with the little griffin which has been incorporated into the flats now on the site. Ironwork was done by students of smithing who at that time were learning their skills in the old Crescent Works next to the Methodist Church in New Road.

Darwin, Herbert Spencer (the philosopher who 53 years before had been in charge of building the Finstall skew bridge), Dickens and Tennyson'. The lecture room corbels featured Courage, Honour, Industry, Prudence, Truth and Chastity.

The new Institute was opened with great ceremony on 30 March 1894 by Mr Austen Chamberlain, MP, son of the great Joseph. A year later John Cotton presented a stone tablet (now in Bromsgrove Museum stores) inscribed 'This tablet is erected to the memory of the late Mr. William Alfred Cotton, of Bromsgrove, to whose friendly interest and liberality the building of the Institute was largely due. He died in July 1889.' Of all Cotton's commissions, this was the one most dear to his heart; the Institute was built with enormous care as a tribute to his brother, whose early death caused the architect such grief.

It was not all earnest learning at the Institute; among the clubs based there were Quoits and Bowling, a Chess and Draughts Club, Bridge Club and the Cycling Club, plus Penny Readings, lectures, amateur dramatics and choral and other concerts. Gwyneth Foster used to tell of dancing classes when she was a child in the early 1930s, when in his patent leather shoes the young Robert Pancheri (later to become artist wood-carver) was her dancing partner. Twenty years later, 1952, also in this building, Robert Pancheri was elected President at the inaugural meeting of the Worcestershire Guild of Artist Craftsmen.

The new School of Science and Art was built alongside the Institute during the following year and opened in September 1895. A conscious decision was taken to make the building an example of quality for artisans who would train there to become skilled art workers with iron, lead, wood and stone. There was great depression in the nail trade, resulting in much unemployment, and it was thought that a decorative ironwork industry could be achieved through teaching at the School. Many of the influential people in the town had been deeply concerned about the lack of alternative to the dying nailing industry, indeed there had been meetings to discuss the problem since the 1880s. Ideas ranged from the already popular market gardening to carpet making to sinking boreholes in order to explore the vicinity for coal. In the end it was agreed that decorative ironwork sat comfortably with nail making, and Lord Windsor offered encouragement by saying he would gladly commission students to make some gates for his estate at Hewell.

The carvings on both the Institute and School of Science & Art were done at H.H. Martyn & Co. of Cheltenham, whose name was synonymous with Arts & Craft work in the ensuing decades.

The Institute (1893) and School of Science & Art (1894) in New Road, architect John Cotton. Atop the right gable is the roof tile known as the Bromsgrove Devil. S.Webster.

The quality of the stone embellishments on the School was even higher than that on its neighbour the Institute. Responsible for this was R.L. Clark, the leading sculptor of H.H. Martyn & Co of Cheltenham. Again, corbel heads reflected the purpose of each room. The science laboratory featured Isaac Newton, Friar Roger Bacon (13th century Franciscan philosopher), Thomas Huxley (biologist) and the Birmingham scientist who discovered oxygen, Joseph Priestley. The art room had a massive keystone over the doorway, with John Ruskin looking out, and Sir Frederick Leighton looking in. Others were Christopher Wren, Landseer and Turner, Hogarth, Joshua Reynolds,

Left: Carved stone corbel depicting Hogarth in the Art Room in the School of Science & Art. Right: Lord Leighton the artist, looking into the Art Room from above the doorway, was one side of a giant keystone; facing into the hallway was John Ruskin.

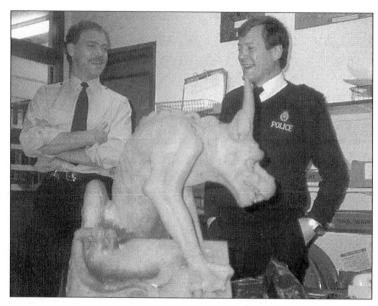

Left: The terracotta roof tile on the gable of the School of Science & Art, known affectionately as the Bromsgrove Devil or the Rousler. Bromsgrove Messenger. *Right: In 1987 the Bromsgrove Devil was rescued by the police, found in a black sack behind a Bromsgrove Chinese restaurant, after he was stolen from the gable of the School of Science & Art.*

Flaxman and Josiah Wedgwood. The builders were Messrs. J. Brazier and Son, and many of the fittings were made by students in carpentry classes. Prominently on top of the building was the roof tile now known as the Bromsgrove Devil, or by some as the Rousler. The terracotta animal is a copy of one of Violett-le-Duc's grotesques on Notre Dame in Paris.

Soon after the building was opened a letter from 'Puzzled' to *The Messenger* enquired what 'animal' it was atop the new School of Art. He suggested that if it was a

The Bromsgrove Devil or the Rousler showing the quality of the modelling and also his chipped left ear, damaged when stolen from the gable of the School of Science & Art. He is now in Bromsgrove Library.

192

cat on the prowl another should be fixed on the roof of the nearby Institute to keep it company. This shows how small the animal seemed to those looking up at it – it is nothing like a cat, as those who visit the Library can vouch! One night in 1987 the Bromsgrove Devil was stolen from its place on the roof, an amazing feat, for the ground sloped steeply below. After the offer of a reward in *The Messenger* (never claimed), one dark night a phone call took the police to a spot behind a Bromsgrove Chinese restaurant. The model was kept in this writer's home for a year, and then it was given a stand and placed in Bromsgrove Library, where it now watches over the reference section and the computers.

Invitation to the architect of the School of Science and Art, John Cotton, on the opening of the building.

Many Bromsgrovians remember these buildings, for they were used in the 1940s as an annexe to the County High School, and in the fifties, sixties and seventies were used by Bromsgrove Technical College. The Art School in the 1950s continued to run classes for practical skills in ornamental ironwork, carpentry, joinery, electricity, engineering and woodcarving – as well as the usual art training. Sheds were built at the rear of the building for carpentry and pottery. The Institute was taken over for Bromsgrove Library by the County Council in 1930, used until 1976 when the new Library in Stratford Road was built. Although in 1986 the Bromsgrove Arts Association endeavoured to save the now very decrepit uncared-for buildings, the County Council sold them for development in 1988. A few of the exterior stone carvings have been incorporated into the design of the block of flats that took their place. Although saved from demolition, all the beautiful corbel carvings of the virtues and famous men, thought to be in a place of safety, were 'lost' a few years later. It is hoped that somewhere they still exist. There are two in Bromsgrove Museum, both damaged – Ruskin/Leighton and Priestley.

Chapter Sixteen

The Police Station and Bromsgrove Guild

We left the Crescent, Ednall Lane and Station Street in the 1880s, after which there was much building in this corner of Bromsgrove.

The Police Station in Station Street, with its lock-up and small house attached, was becoming too small for the size of the town. Bromsgrove had no court house, the Petty Sessions being held in the Town Hall where there was no accommodation for

Bromsgrove Police Station and Courthouse, built in 1889, designed by Henry Rowe the County Surveyor, and built by Tilt & Weaver. The Courthouse closed in 1997. Note gas lamp, flag pole and Triumph Herald car. WRO.

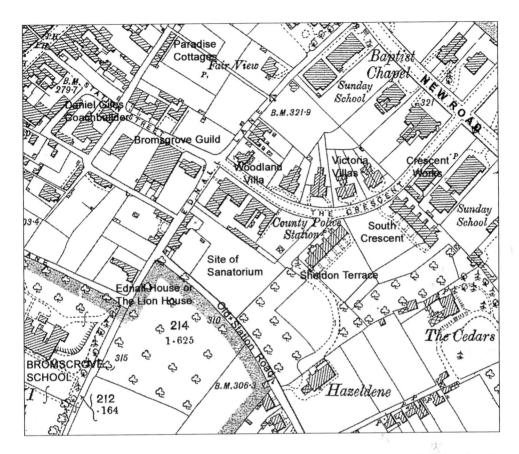

Map surveyed in 1901 showing the Crescent, Ednall Lane and Station Street. Note that there is not even a footway from the Crescent to Old Station Road, neither has Bromsgrove School built on the orchard field, nor built gates or lodge house. OS.

witnesses when not in court, very little accommodation for the public, and scanty accommodation for the Bench. Worcestershire County Council finally agreed in 1889 to purchase a plot of land on the Crescent to build a new Police Station and Court House combined. It was designed by the County Surveyor, Henry Rowe, and built by Tilt & Weaver, who produced between them a substantial and handsome building. The magistrates' court, built facing Ednall Lane, was simply styled, the ceiling panelled by moulded wood ribs, the walls having pilasters supporting a plaster architrave. The raised dais for the Bench was accessed from the Magistrates' Room behind, while there was a room for waiting witnesses and plenty of space in the court for the public. The Magistrates' Court was closed on 5 December 1997, its business transferred to Redditch, and the premises are now offices.

At the opening ceremony in November 1890 the Magistrates attending included Mr Smallwood of Rigby Hall, Mr Thomas White of the Newlands and Mr W.E. Everitt of Finstall Park, while public seating in the courtroom was packed with curious Bromsgrovians. Had they also been allowed to visit the police accommodation in the rest of the building, they would have been impressed. The grand archway entrance from the Crescent led on the left to the charge room and offices, with quarters for single policemen above – a dormitory for six. The superintendent's residence was on the far left of the entrance, with a private yard, while married quarters were in a range along Ednall Lane. A drying room was provided for the police to leave their sodden uniforms when necessary, and there was a corridor of six cells. There was a weights and measures room, and police horses were stabled at the back of the building, with harness room, trap house and manure dump. A charming garden was the finishing touch, with rose covered arches and box hedges which it is hoped was used by all the men rather than just Superintendent Jeffries and his family.

The police were as busy then as they are today, especially with the young. Just three examples of incidents that reached *The Messenger* around this time: in September 1899 the editor bemoaned the rising generation of 'Troublesome young Turks' who caused so much aggravation. Youths had been caught throwing stones in the Warwick Hall Estate up New Road, while girls were accused of climbing tombstones and playing games in St John's churchyard. A few weeks later a man was arrested at Bromsgrove Station for stabbing the guard with a pocket-knife – the guard was Henry Taylor of Aston Fields. A month or so on Ben Juggins, Walter Perrins and Alfred Hall, three lads from Aston Fields, were up before the magistrates for annoying residents in Factory Lane [Carlyle Road] by playing football with a paper ball. When the beak asked why they weren't in the recreation ground just along Stoke Road the boys said that children aged over 15 were banned from using it for football. They were let off, but ordered to pay 5s 6d (25½p) costs. Equally upsetting for law-abiding citizens was to find in 1895 that a number of the trees in New Road had been cut and mutilated. Do things ever change?

Behind the Police station was a patch of unused land that in 1923 was bought by Mr R.G. Routh and Mr Alec Mayall of Bromsgrove School for a sanatorium, built by Braziers. This was a sunny peaceful light building, ideal for the recuperation of little boys who were ill [demolished in the 1980s, now blocks of flats]. At this time there was no access from the Crescent to Old Station Road without going by Ednall Lane, for the footway running between the Police Station and Sheldon Terrace came to a full stop at the last cottage. The Headmaster of Bromsgrove School then made a deal with Bromsgrove Town Council, as follows.

Bromsgrove School Sanatorium built by Braziers in 1923 on Old Station Road opposite the school gates.

Kiteley's or Kiteless, a large field behind Bromsgrove School and Conway Road, was a traditional playground for the boys of Bromsgrove, who used it for cricket, football and all the other things that boys do when messing about. Footpaths led to it from Worcester Road, Worcester Street, Ednall Lane, and Charford Lane. In 1903 the field came up for auction, and was bought for the school by the Earl of Plymouth. In 1913 the new Headmaster, R.G. Routh, decided that this field was where he wanted to build – indeed it was necessary for the growth of the school that more classrooms, laboratories and new school hall and chapel be built on the campus – but the public footpaths were a major problem. The Council prevaricated; the closing of the footpaths would be very unpopular with Bromsgrove people, but on the other hand the Council needed the school to grow to flourish. In the end Routh made a proposal – that the school would vacate the swimming baths in Sanders' field across Worcester Street earlier than agreed in order that the Council could repair them for townspeople; that the school (or Routh) would purchase an acre of land by the swimming baths and Watt Close school and donate it to the town as a playground; that the footway from the Crescent would be continued to Old Station Road and made up by the school as a private road, just as Conway Road had been. The Council capitulated, and Routh got his

R.G. Routh, Headmaster of Bromsgrove School with his dog Thorn in 1925.

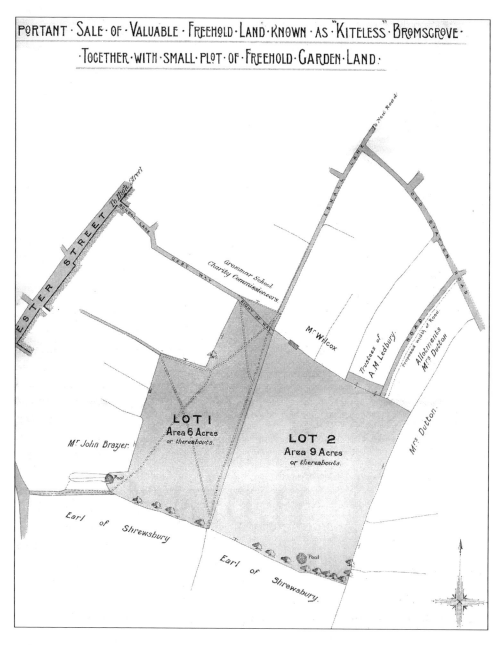

Sale plan of Kiteless field in 1903, bought for Bromsgrove School by the Earl of Plymouth. The public footpaths shown were a source of aggravation to the school, but it was not until about 1913 that R.G. Routh, Headmaster and also town councillor, managed to persuade the Urban District Council to close the paths. BC.

way. The footpaths were closed. Kyteless,[97] the new classroom block, was built in 1914, the Whitley Laboratories in 1921, and Routh Hall in 1926.

The promise of a road to join the Crescent with Old Station Road wasn't honoured until 1927 when C.E. Bateman's splendid gates were put up to guard the northern entrance to the school, where also a lodge house was built. At this point the old wall round School Green was demolished

Bromsgrove School gates designed by architect C.E. Bateman in 1925.

and the local path that ran from Ednall Lane along the Crocus Walk and between school buildings to cross the fields was moved to Conway Road, to go along the side of the playing fields down to Charford. The town was not happy, nor was George Bradfield:

> 'Here was a delightful field where we children were allowed to play freely, with footpaths from almost every point ... but now closed and absorbed, with the consent of the Bromsgrove Council, and without even a fight being put up by the people to whom the rights of way had been handed down by their forefathers, in trust for them to hand them on to their children. ... It was a shameful business.'[98]

C.E. Bateman, a well-known Birmingham architect, was also responsible for the house known as Thatcholme in Conway Road. This was not a school house, but built for Philip Brazier by the school builders, Braziers in 1929. Thatcholme was indeed thatched, until one November 5th a firework landed on the roof and it went

Thatcholme garden front with its original thatched roof. Thatcholme was designed by C.E. Bateman for Philip Brazier in 1929. R. Brazier.

The Dining Room of Thatcholme in Conway Road. Bateman designed the interior fittings of the house, some of which, like the Bromsgrove Guild plasterwork on the ceilings, were removed when the house became Bromsgrove School's Music Department. R. Brazier.

The Drawing Room of Thatcholme in Conway Road. R. Brazier.

up in flames. Despite alterations made to the house after it became Bromsgrove School's Music Department in the 1980s – the kitchen was moved to the garage, rooms were amalgamated to make larger spaces, the beautifully plastered ceilings were removed – it still showed its quality in architectural details, and it is good to know that the present Headmaster is living there.

However, other houses that did belong to the school were built along the southern side of Conway Road, to be lived in by masters and their families. Another house that later was useful to the school as a home for bachelor masters was Hazeldene. This was built in 1891 on his own land bordering Old Station Road for William Llewellin, whose family had for so long been living at Ednall House, though he had recently been living at his Blackmore Mill House. Now aged 61, Llewellin was a very wealthy man, having speculated in property with some success. He stayed at Hazeldene for only seven years until in 1898, feeling his age, he went off to Elmshurst on Stoney Hill, to live with his son Herbert Roland. In another three years, when he was 71, Llewellin went on holiday to Weston-super-mare as was his wont each summer, and died. He was regarded as a Bromsgrove worthy; he had been Court Leet Bailiff, a school manager, a member of the Workhouse Board and Churchwarden at both St John's church and All Saints.

Others who lived at Hazeldene were Samuel Adcock Ellis and Frank Holyoake, after whom Bromsgrove School bought it, using it for a number of years. Previous to this the bachelor masters lived in The Steps House next to the forty-eight steps to St John's church. Hazeldene was considered redundant in the 1970s, and so was demolished [a large number of houses in Kenyon Close now cover its gardens].

Sheldon Terrace had some longstanding tenants during the 1880s and 90s. For nine years Henry Stone Whitfield and his family lived here, while he built up his tailoring business in Worcester Street in the shop later owned by Vines. In 1893 the Whitfields moved up to Marlborough Avenue in order to be close to their new clothing factory in Aston Fields. Next door to the Whitfields lived the Powleslands, also in trade in town as drapers, who were here between 1891 and 1900. Also living here from 1889 was Mr John B. Tirbutt, Professor of Music and organist at St John's church. He, his wife and daughter moved into College Road in 1903.

Opposite the Police Station are two pairs of villas (Nos.12 & 14, 16 & 18 – 18 is called Ashdene – that were built in the 1890s, while Woodland Villa (No.20), was lived in in the 1880s by John Taylor, the wheelwright and blacksmith, followed by Daniel Giles whose wagon, carriage and lorry building works were down Station Street.

Hazeldene was built for William Llewellin in 1891. The house was later bought by Bromsgrove School as living accommodation for single masters, as in this 1967 photograph. The School sold the large plot of land for the building of Kenyon Close. Hazel Mosses.

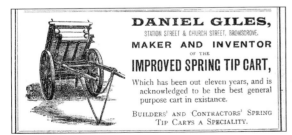

DANIEL GILES,
STATION STREET & CHURCH STREET, BROMSGROVE.
MAKER AND INVENTOR
OF THE
IMPROVED SPRING TIP CART,
Which has been out eleven years, and is acknowledged to be the best general purpose cart in existance.
BUILDERS' AND CONTRACTORS' SPRING TIP CARTS A SPECIALITY.

Left: Daniel Giles's Station Street carriage works was a large complex during the latter years of the nineteenth century and early twentieth, giving work to numerous blacksmiths and carpenters. The rural nature of the Bromsgrove area meant that wagons and carts were always in need of repair and replacement. Right: A glass plate photograph of Nos.12 and 14 The Crescent, built in the 1890s. HC.

After Mrs Elizabeth Llewellin's death in 1909 a plot of land on the corner of Station Street and Ednall Lane was divided into six Lots and put up for auction. The three Lots fronting Ednall Lane were bought by Arthur J. Amess, who built Hollymere and ran his building firm from the unbuilt plots to the side of the house. These plots, opposite the three little cottages, were then used as industrial units until a nasty fire in 2007. The Sale also included Paradise Row, and Melbourne Cottage, which at that time was divided into two dwellings.

Melbourne House, as the old Police Station became, was not in the sale. After the police went to the new Police Station in the Crescent the old courtroom was used for a year or so by the Art School. The School of Art, created in 1860, had previously occupied a glass-roofed room in the Institute premises in the old Crown Hotel in the High Street. This room later became the composing room of *The Bromsgrove Messenger*. Needing more space the School of Art had had to spread into other buildings, including Mr Lewis's manufactury in the Crescent for metalwork, and to Melbourne House in Station Street for more gentle art work. The School of Art eventually, in 1895, moved into the brand new building next to the Institute on New Road, and three years later Melbourne House became the centre of Bromsgrove's greatest artistic triumph, the Bromsgrove Guild.[99]

The Guild was to change the landscape of Bromsgrove by building two vast workshops on Station Street, dwarfing the cottages, inns and shop premises around

Aerial photograph of Station Street. On the far left are the Bromsgrove Guild workshops. Also on the left are the six cottages of Paradise Row. To the right of the Guild buildings is Waterloo Cottage, and to the right of that are the large premises of Daniel Giles, wheelwright and coachbuilder. The curved street at the bottom right is Worcester Street. BC.

them. They even made the large Bromsgrove School buildings look small. The Guild started off in November 1898 as a loosely organised group of artist craftsmen who worked in premises around Bromsgrove and Birmingham. Among them were Richard Tapp who ran the woodshop at Moat Mill, George Bankart (lead and plaster craftsman) and Henry Ludlow (plaster craftsman) both working at Puddle Wharf, and Benjamin Creswick (metal work) of Birmingham. They were brought together by Walter Gilbert who in February 1898 had been employed to run both the new Art School and the art department of Bromsgrove School. Gilbert quickly saw an opening for a commercial Guild such as the Century Guild of Artists, Ashbee's Guild of Handicraft, the Keswick School of Industrial Arts and the nearby the Birmingham Guild of Handicrafts.

In 1900 Walter Gilbert resigned from his post at the Art School, which then was passed to Amy Walford, who was Principal until 1905. Gilbert also stopped working for Bromsgrove School in 1901, so that he could concentrate on the Guild. Gilbert was commercially minded and realised there should be a larger pool of artists immediately to hand, so he advertised for more craftsmen to join locals such as Amy Walford (artist and designer) and Birmingham's Archibald J. Davies (stained glass). Among those attracted to Bromsgrove were Louis Weingartner (modeller and metal worker, in 1901), Celestino Pancheri (woodcarver, in 1905) and Leopold Weisz (Birmingham jewellery designer and sculptor, in 1905, who lost his life on the Titanic in 1912).

Bromsgrove Guild buildings dominated the skyline of the town between c1903 and 1996 when the earlier and taller of the two corrugated iron workshops was demolished, together with Melbourne House, to make way for flats. Melbourne House was built as the Police Station in 1840, was used as part of the School of Art, and finally became offices of the Bromsgrove Guild, which decorated the ground floor rooms with examples of plasterwork. This view looking up Station Street was taken in 1993.

A Bromsgrove Guild birdbath, owned by the same family for 80 years, made from castone, the Guild's cement based artificial stone. These and other figures were also cast in concrete from original Guild moulds in the late C20 by Bromsgrove Concrete Products of Puddlewharf.

Left: One of the mythical liver birds made to the design of Carl Bernard Bartels by the Bromsgrove Guild. Their wing span is 24 feet (7 metres), they are 18 ft tall and made of copper. Local legend holds that the birds face away from each other because if they were to mate and fly away, the city of Liverpool would cease to exist. Right: The Royal Liver Friendly Society's building on the Pier Head, Liverpool, architect W. Aubrey Thomas, 1911. The Bromsgrove Guild liver birds are on the two massive clock towers. The clock faces, 25 feet in diameter (7·62 metres) are larger than those of Big Ben.

The tall corrugated iron stained-glass workshop was built at the rear of Melbourne House about 1904, to be followed by a similar building designed by Ewen Harper & Brother, 1904-8, on the other side of the road. The first of these was demolished in 1996 for flats; the second is still in industrial use. Behind the east works, between Paradise Row and Ednall Lane, was a small area known as the statue garden, used to display garden furniture and statuary made from both lead and castone, the Guild's cement-based artificial stone.

The best known of the Guild's output are the Buckingham Palace gates with their Weingartner cherubs, the gilded 15ft (4.5m) Liver Birds in Liverpool and, for the very special little church at Dodford, wood carvings, plasterwork, weathercock and leadwork all made by Guild designers and craftsmen. However due to Gilbert's passionate evangelism and a growing reputation, their work was commissioned for many parts of the country, indeed of the world, including America, Canada and France. Metal work was made for the SS Moldavia in 1903, and in 1906 some 150 Bromsgrove men were producing plasterwork, stained glass, and a bronze and glass lift enclosure and staircase for the Lusitania. Also in 1906 they were doing work on its sister ship the Mauretania. The Guild work was not all on a large scale; individual items included lamp standards and railings, an ebony, silver and leather presentation box for Stanley Baldwin, commemorative trowels and keys, church pews and pulpits, garden statuary and stained glass windows. Among their regular products were plasterwork for the home, lead rainwater heads, domestic light fittings, and bronze and silver religious medallions and plaques.

During the Guild's heyday it became one of the town's larger employers, needing foundrymen, draughtsmen, french polishers, sand blasters, pattern makers, blacksmiths, glaziers, etc. Boys went to the Art

Commemorative gilded silver key, surmounted by a Bromsgrove boar, made by the Bromsgrove Guild for the opening of the new Market Hall in 1926. The Market Hall was opened by F.W.J. Coaker Esq. JP with great ceremony; J.N. Bryant JP was Chairman of the Urban District Council, Charles Crane Chairman of the Market Committee. WRO.

School for initial training, or became apprentices, and many spent their working lives in this stimulating environment. Thus the Guild achieved what so many Bromsgrove men had despaired of doing – finding a replacement for nail making.

During WWII the Guild was employed by the Ministry of Works making such items as bronze fitments for fire fighting equipment and metal components for tanks and torpedo boats. The Guild had already been affected by the slump of the 1930s, and the deaths of Walter Gilbert in 1946 and of the company chairman William McCandlish in 1947 added to the decline. George Whewell was asked to take over the company, and his careful policy of sub-contracting orders inevitably meant that the Bromsgrove workforce was reduced. Despite general austerity there was a demand for architectural metalwork for bomb damaged buildings, as well as for war memorials, but there was a shortage throughout the 1950s not only of materials but also of

An advertising postcard for one of the Guild leadworkers, Harry Hems, who lived in Central Road, Stoney Hill.

skilled craftsmen due to the attractions of the Austin motor company at Longbridge and of Garringtons at Newton. In 1966 the firm went into voluntary liquidation, leaving very few employees.

One of the Guild's last commissions was a pair of gates made for the District Council, which when it moved offices left them in situ at what is now St. John's Nursing Home. The other Guild gates from this period are at the Bromsgrove Rugby Ground, Finstall.

Chapter Seventeen

College Road – A New Road
for a New Century

Nearly all of the large field known as Pritchard's Field, and half of Gravel Pit Piece, were owned in the 1870s by George Dipple, a retired ironmonger and ale and wine seller, who was living at Fordhouse Farm. The fields abutted Stoney Hill on the east side, and Chapel Walk on the west up to the boundary of the Mount's field, the other half of Gravel Pit Piece which belonged to the Green family of The Mount [Wendron]. On George Dipple's death his surveyor son Alfred inherited the land. Gauging that the time was now ripe to sell, the two fields were put up for auction on 27 June 1893.

Dipple divided the land into 35 Lots, the fourteen facing onto Stoney Hill being rather smaller than those on College Road. The road itself had been pegged out, and Dipple promised it would be made up by Lady Day (25th March 1894), and he also agreed to widen the road on Stoney Hill [West Road] by 1st January 1895. A problem he had was to push his new road through the natural sandstone barrier at New Road. Supporting walls of engineering brick were therefore built against The Newlands and Holly Lodge land to prevent slippage; it seems this was not totally successful as buttresses were later built to give the walls more strength.

Properties to be built on College Road (Dipple had named the road himself) must, the Sale particulars say, cost £350 to build (this is £50 less than the requirement for houses on New Road in the Warwick Hall Estate), while a pair of semi-detached should cost £600. As with Warwick Hall Estate, no house could be used for retail of ale, beer, wines or spirits or other fermented liquors, nor any trade or manufacturing. Times had sufficiently changed for the words 'nail shops' not to be included in the list. He drew special attention to the 'healthy elevated position commanding views of the Lickey, Tardebigge … it is in the best part of the Town, and close to the Main Road to the Railway Station.' The seller also helpfully stated in the Sale particulars that 'One half of the Purchase Money of any Lot may remain on Mortgage at Four per Cent. Interest'.

Mr Samuel Saywell, whose College land was just the other side of the 'foot road' bordering the site [College Walk], purchased the first eight Lots, the last of which included a cottage facing Chapel Street, with stabling, cowhouse and other outbuildings, which he promptly named College Lodge. R.B. Brotherton, who collected so many of the Sale prospectuses and photographs used in this book, lived in this Chapel Street cottage for some years before he died. In 1903 Saywell built a house named Engleberg [demolished 2006, now Cypress Grange] on the corner against Chapel Walk and College Walk. His new unbuilt field continued to be a sports ground, used not only by his pupils at the College but also by other town teams.

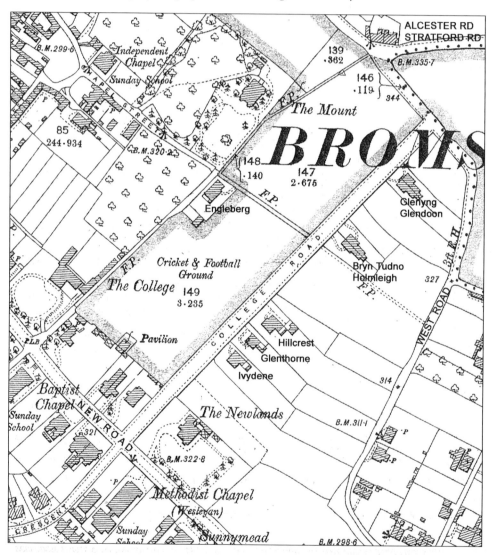

1901 survey of the College Road area. Stoney Hill's West Road is on the right. OS.

A Bromsgrove Guild interdepartmental football match on the College ground in 1909, the plasterers v. the metal shop. The houses behind are right to left: Mornacott (No.12), Redlands (No.14) and Hill Rise (No.16), Meldon (No.18) and Shirley (No.20), Bryn Tudno (No.22) and Holmleigh (No.24), The Georgian House (No.26). BR.

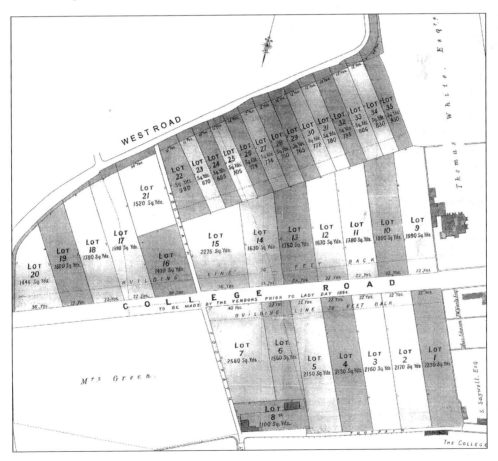

1893 Sale plan. Mrs Green was the owner of The Mount (now Wendron), S. Saywell Esq. was owner of The College. BC.

There is no record of other purchasers, though it would seem that the market was slow because only seven other plots were marked as sold when Dipple held another Sale on 29 May 1900. The properties already built shown on that plan were Ivydene (No.6), Hillcrest (No.10) and the pair called Bryn Tudno (No.22) and Holmleigh (No.24). The plots for Ivydene and Hillcrest, joined by Glenthorne (No.8) in 1901, had absorbed adjoining plots running down to Stoney Hill, making for very long slightly angled gardens.

Hillcrest (No.10), built in 1897 or '98, was the first College Road house, lived in for three years by Alfred Dipple himself, who moved up from Charford Lodge, until 1900 when Mr Herbert Ball, a timber merchant, rented it until 1904. The house was then lived in by Victor Drury of the Boot Factory, until he bought the Newlands in 1914, and Frank Holyoake was Dipple's tenant until at least 1919, continuing to live there until the 1940s. The 1919 Sale prospectus describes an 'Attractive Modern Freehold Residence' having a drawing room with 'handsome Mantel and Mirrored Overmantel', Dining Room, and 'Morning Room having Bookcases with glazed doors and Cupboards under', a 'large light Kitchen, with Parker and Winder's "City" Range'[100]. There were four bedrooms plus 'one Maid's bedroom, one Bath Room (h. and c.)' The garden had a tennis lawn and kitchen garden, 'Stabling for two with Loft over', a 'Coach-house or Garage, with inspection pit, Harness Room or Workshop' – a property that was moving with the times.

Bryn Tudno (No.22) and Holmleigh (No.24) were built by 1900 for Mr Dipple, and rented out to Mr William H. Weston (partner of J.B Wilson) and Mr Joseph Saywell, brother of Samuel Saywell of The College. Joseph was older than his brother, was also a schoolmaster, and for several years took an active part in the life of the town, dying in 1913, just a year before his brother. Miss Mary Dipple then briefly lived in Holmleigh, and Miss Tirbutt, a music teacher was next door (her father was organist and choirmaster at the Parish Church). These were four bedroomed houses, having bathroom with lavatory basin and airing cupboard, kitchen with 'Herald' range, and a scullery. Both houses were sold in 1919 from Albert Dipple's estate.

The builder Braziers' records state that they built three houses in 1898 on College Road land purchased by Mr Harrison,[101] most probably Hillcrest, Glenthorne and Ivydene. All three were inhabited when the Census was taken in 1901, despite Glenthorne's date stone saying 1902.

Glenthorne is a different style of build from those either side of it. Thomas Roper lived here first, and maybe its restrained style complemented his role as Accountant and Secretary to the Bromsgrove Gas-Light and Coke Company. He moved in 1914 to New Road, and seven years later Mr and Mrs W.J. Tilt came to Glenthorne where they lived for many years.

Left: Glenthorne (No.8) built in 1901 and lived in by Thomas Roper, Chief Accountant of the Gas-light and Coke Company. Right: Thomas Roper.

Ivydene (No.6) was lived in by John Valentine Burford, grocer and corn dealer of Worcester Street, from 1898 for at least forty years. This house, like Hillcrest, has a typically late Victorian feel, with big bay window and decorative porch entrance in white painted wood.

Two pairs of houses were put on Lots 6 & 7 by Tilts; Glenhyng and Glendoon in 1900, Sefton and Clifton in 1904. These matching houses were – still are – most attractive, very much of their period, with joint entrance porches, and still with their original window frames. From the beginning Mr Alfred Bird, manager of the Gas Works, lived at Sefton, staying there until the 1940s, and another long-time resident was Mr William Neale, who was at Glendoon until the 1940s. Later other members of the Neale family lived in the road – Frank at Shirley (No.20) from 1908, who in 1913 moved to Redlands (No.14) leaving the Misses Neale behind at Shirley.

Glenhyng in 1943 opened its doors as a private school, under the charge of Mrs Henderson, though shortly after she was joined or taken over by Mrs Ottilie Hild, an Austrian who came to England in 1936. She had set up a kindergarten in a single room overlooking Crown Close in Bromsgrove, before moving to College Road. This dynamic woman ran the young pupils with a rod of iron, and it soon became the best known private kindergarten in Bromsgrove. The youngsters were not only taught their three Rs, but also that good behaviour and thought for others was expected of them. One of the rituals she had for a while was for the whole school to be marched, in uniform, down to De Grey's for lunch. (De Grey's, in the

Postcard of Glenhyng (No.32) and Glendoon (34) built in 1901 by Joseph Tilt, builder of Birmingham Road. Glenhyng was later to become the well known preparatory school run by Ottilie Hild.

High Street, was a delightfully old-fashioned confectioner with tea room and restaurant upstairs, much loved by ladies in hats.) Mrs White, a gentle lady and a gifted teacher, took over when Mrs Hild retired, and she in turn retired in 1986.

The school was bought by Bromsgrove School who ran it in College Road before moving it in 2000 to Avoncroft College [now Avoncroft House, but previously The Grange] at Stoke Heath. Mrs Ottilie Hild died aged 83 in 1979. Glenyng and its pair Glendoon were refurbished and sold back into private ownership.

Engleberg (No.5), in the far corner of Saywell's playing fields, was lived in from 1903 by George F. Dixon, a coal merchant who moved from Alvechurch. In 1915 Dixon went bankrupt and left the house, and on 10 March there was a Sale of his furniture and

Engleberg (No.5) built 1903. It was bought from the Saywell estate by John N. Bryant, coachbuilder, in 1915. Photograph taken in 2006 just before demolition for Cypress Grange.

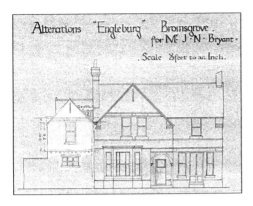 

Left: Engleberg was extended for John N. Bryant to these plans by Bromsgrove architect G.H. Gadd in 1920; further extensions were made at a later date. WRO. Right: Victor Drury (left) of the Boot Factory and The Newlands, New Road and J.N. Bryant of Bryant's Motor Engineers in the High Street, who lived at Engleberg.

chattels. The next inhabitant was John N. Bryant, whose father had opened a coach-building business in Alcester Road [Stratford Road] in 1854, moving to the High Street in 1865. Here he with his sons kept up with the times and by 1908 were 'motor builders'. The firm stayed in the High Street selling cars and petrol for many years, building an up-to-the-minute Art Deco shop front in the 1920s. John Bryant also updated and enlarged Engleberg in 1920, asking architect G.H. Gadd to do the plans. This very pleasing simple house was demolished in 2006 for a retirement home called Cypress Grange, as was the house next door, Penrhyn (No.3), which was taken down some ten years earlier for a retirement home called Westminster Court.

1903 brought Gervase R. Lee to College Road. He bought the plot of land between Ivydene and Thomas White's Newlands, together with the land behind reaching to Stoney Hill. Gervase Richard William Lee is something of a mystery; he was born in Birmingham, the son of a house decorator and painter and in 1881 was living with an uncle in Pershore Road, Birmingham as an architect's clerk. He managed to avoid being on the census of 1891, but is on that of 1901, visiting a jeweller William Taylor in Handsworth. He stated then that he was 'living on his own means', which usually meant that someone had inherited money or had income from rents. So this youngish man – aged 41 – appeared in Bromsgrove, built and presumably did the plans for The Rosary (No.4), where he lived until 1907, calling himself Richard Gervase Lee in the Directories. In 1904 Lee requested permission to build his second house, Woodcroft (No.2). Both of these houses are simple, well built and attractive in the then very fashionable Arts and Crafts style. The Rosary has a dominant half-timbered extended gable, while

Left: Garden front of Rosary (No.4) built in 1903 by architect R. Gervase Lee, where he lived for a few years. A later owner-inhabitant in the 1920s was Leslie Drury of the Boot Factory. Right: Woodcroft (No.2) built in 1904 alongside Rosary, to plans by R. Gervase Lee. J.B. Wilson lived here for many years, followed by Chaytor Pepper, his son-in-law. Pepper's son-in-law, David Parker, was the first to run a dental practice here.

the garden front has stone mullions and cills and unusual brick gables projecting well above the dormer roofs behind. Woodcroft has similar mullioned windows to the ground floor. Woodcroft became the home of John Broad Wilson Jnr in 1914, after his wife had rejected the idea of living at The Newlands, and was later followed by Mr A. Chaytor Pepper, his son-in-law. The house became a dentist's surgery for Chaytor Pepper's son-in-law, David Parker, and has remained one until today.

After Gervase Lee went off to pastures new, Mr James Trail moved into The Rosary, followed by Mr Alfred F. Genton. In 1924 Leslie Drury, son of Victor, bought the house; he lived there until 1941 when he rented it out to Mr F.H.Bullock, the Manager of East Worcestershire Waterworks Co. which had its offices in the Strand, the premises now occupied by Thomas Horton, Solicitors.

Mornacott (No.12) was built in 1904 for George Frayne, the retired draper of London House, High Street, then living at Inglewood in New Road. The architect he chose was Philip Green who worked from offices in New Road but lived at this time in Wellington Road. Although Green's houses in Wellington Road were Arts and Crafts in style (they were built later), Mornacott was more 'traditional' Edwardian – and none the worse for that. Mornacott, Ivydene and Hillcrest are all very pleasing houses, and continued to keep the standard for quality in the road. Following George Frayne came George Frayne Wilson, living there until at least the 1940s.

The next pair of houses built was Meldon (No.18) and Shirley (No.20) in 1906. For some years Frank Neale lived at Shirley, the Misses Neale taking over in 1914. The other half of the pair was Meldon, lived in by Mr William Dodd who in 1902

Left: Drawing of the south elevation of Mornacott (No.12) by Bromsgrove architect Philip Green, 1904. WRO. Right: Drawing of the west elevation of Mornacott (No.12) by Philip Green, for draper George Frayne in 1904. WRO.

had retired after forty years as Headmaster of the Church of England boys' school in Church Road. After his death Miss Dodd opened a preparatory school at Meldon for a few years in the 1940s. It is said that one of the pupils was young Winston Field of the drapery family, who emigrated to Rhodesia [now Zimbabwe] in 1921 to become a tobacco farmer. His involvement in the Rhodesian Front led to his election as Prime Minister of Southern Rhodesia between 1962 and 1964, to be succeeded by Ian Smith. Having been a pupil at Bromsgrove School Mr Winston Field was invited one year to be honoured guest at Commemoration (annual prize giving). To the Headmaster's mortification – and no doubt to the great pleasure of the listening boys – Mr Carey asked the audience to welcome to the platform Mr . . . . Aston Fields.

During the 1900 Sale the builder Alfred Tilt bought Lot 7, and after the Sale Lot 6, while Mr Harrison invested in Lots 5 and 8. The Georgian House (No.26), Lot 8, was not built until 1908, but it was worth the wait. Mr Harrison or Mr Tilt brought in the Birmingham architects Ewen Harper & Brothers to design both this and No.36 on the corner of College and North Roads. The Georgian House is in the then fashionable neo-Georgian manner, its date on the lead rainwater head, and described in the 2007 *Worcestershire* Pevsner as the 'best' house in the road.

The Georgian House (No.26) built in 1908, architects Ewen Harper & Brothers of Birmingham for the Tilt family of builders.

Postcard of College Road in 1911 showing the sports field fence on the left. Houses from right to left: Rosary (No.4), Ivydene (No.6).

Regular in style, it has a splendid stone porch and a pair of bay windows either side with curved lead-covered roofs. Ewen Harper & Brothers were also responsible for the Methodist Church at Headless Cross – the one with the openwork spire – and Birmingham's Methodist Central Hall in Corporation Street. The Georgian House was lived in by the Tilt family until the 1930s.

Redlands (No.14) and Hill Mount or Hill Rise (16) were the last of the houses built on the east side of College Road, neither appearing in the Directories until 1914. Redlands was the home of Frank Neale until well into the 1940s (he had moved from Shirley), and an equally long inhabitant was Mr J.A. Brighton, one of the last of Bromsgrove's nail manufacturers who was also Registrar of Marriages.

Samuel Saywell died in 1914, leaving his recently wedded widow to grieve and move out of their home into the smaller Sunnyside in New Road. The Sale of his properties was on 20 April 1915, when The College buildings were in the prospectus, together with Engleberg (which had been empty since the bankruptcy of Mr Dixon), College Lodge, two two-bedroomed houses in Chapel Street, a two-storey Warehouse in Windsor Street used by Messrs Jefferies Bros. the Grocers, and 'a fruit orchard on Chapel Street with 80 Pear, Apple and Plum trees'. This had hedges and 'iron protection hurdles and double unclimbable iron entrance gates', and the auctioneer suggested the orchard would be ideal for erection of bijou residences. The Lindens on New Road, previous home of Mrs Saywell, was also in the Sale in two Lots, the large garden being suggested as one of the best residential building sites in the district.

It was this 1915 Sale that opened up the western side of College Road for building. The sports field was truncated, and the land fronting College Road was divided into seven Lots, with the same restriction as in 1894 – that a detached residence should cost £350 to build, £600 for a pair. John Bryant at some point bought three Lots to add to his garden and extended Engleberg in 1920. There was little building movement on the land for many years, for war-time restrictions had their effect, and when it did the plots included the sports field and ran from College Road to College Walk. By 1926 but one house had been built, which was Penbryn (No.3) for Mr J.B. Smith [now Westminster Court], next door to Engleberg. No.1a, a bungalow built by Brazier for Mr Smith, was not built until 1960.

The Mount's field, then under the ownership of Mr J.B. Wilson was used as grazing for the wagon horses belonging to J.B. Wilson & Sons, as was the field running alongside Alcester Road [where the Library is today, on Stratford Road]. By the end of the 1940s all the plots on the Mount's field were built, including Mountfields, lived in by another Wilson, J.H.M., who was manager of Barclays Bank.

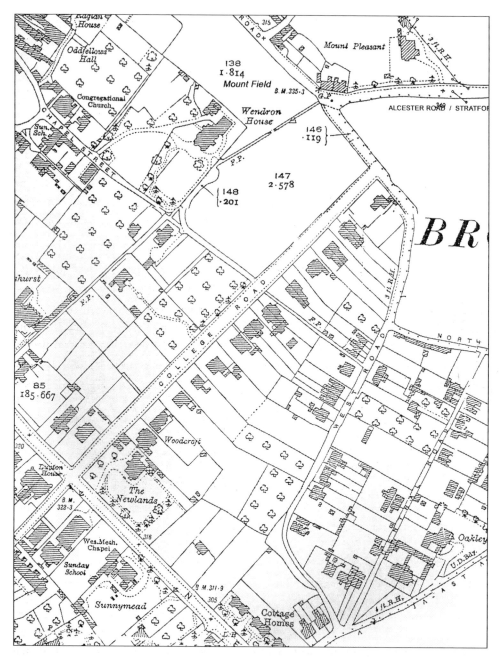

1926 survey map showing College Road and Stoney Hill. The Mount field (previously part of the Mount/Wendron land) was still pastureland, as was the field alongside that runs along Alcester (Stratford) Road to Windsor Street. OS.

Chapter Eighteen

The Closure of the Green Gap

The second swathe of building after the Victorian era was between the wars, in the 1920s and '30s. This was when the large houses were built on the Mount's field on College Road, council houses were put on New Road at Aston Fields, and detached houses, individually designed, were built on the east side of New Road and on Wellington Road and Marlborough Avenue.

Building along the southern side of Marlborough Avenue was facilitated in 1919 by the sale of over eleven acres of market garden land (worked by Edwin Dufty and Jimmy Evans the greengrocer) which reached down to Stoke Road. Included in the Sale was the Recreation Ground, which brought in rent of £20 p.a. from Stoke Prior Parish Council (this was bought by the Council). It wasn't until 1957 that market garden back-land on the other side of Marlborough Avenue was put up for sale by Miss Scott, thus opening up the opportunity to build Warwick Avenue, Brueton and Hampton Avenues. The houses along Marlborough Avenue, on both sides of the road, were nearly all individually planned though smaller than the earlier houses, making it one of the most attractive roads on the east of the town.

In 1945, concerned about the lack of sports facilities for the young, Major Llewellyn Ryland founded Bromsgrove Youth Organisation on Fordhouse farmland next to Cedar Terrace. BYO was well endowed, having an athletics track, playing field and pavilion which this enlightened man bequeathed under covenant for the use of the young people of Bromsgrove. Major Ryland, of the family paint firm Llewellyn Ryland in Birmingham, was a prominent and philanthropic figure in Bromsgrove for many years. He lived at Walnut Cottage, Finstall, moved to Devon in 1952, and died in 1972. There was worry that BYO would have to be wound up when Ryland left Bromsgrove, but fortunately the County Council took it over. The buildings were enlarged and used as an extension to the Technical College which at that time was based in the old School of Science & Art in New Road. The running track, originally cinder, was upgraded in 1995 as an all-weather 400m, six lane running track, and that and the other refurbished facilities are used not only by the resident youth club but by many local clubs and schools for sporting, gym and children's activities.

The closure of the Wagon Works was a great blow for the railway men. The years after WWII had been busy ones, catching up with some 175,000 wagon repairs that had built up during the war. But after this flurry the money-men were back in force and words like 'streamlining' and 'pruning unremunerative services' were to the

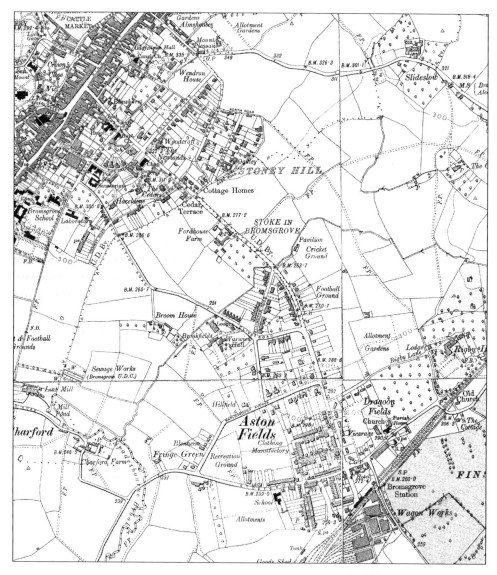

1926 map showing that even though New Road was being built up on the east and Aston Fields council housing was encroaching on fields, Fordhouse farmland was still a green stretch dividing Aston Fields from Bromsgrove town. OS.

fore. Freight wagon use was falling as use of road transport grew, and only 219 men were employed at the works when the inevitable happened; in 1962 British Railways announced that closure of Bromsgrove Wagon Works would be at the end of 1964. During the next two years equipment was removed. When the Wagon Works closed the banking engine shed also closed, the newer diesel engines sent to work from Gloucester. Modern diesels were much more powerful than the old steam engines, and need for banking declined in parallel with these improvements.

But the 1840 buildings got their revenge. When demolition was happening in 1980 even the most powerful ball crane had difficulty in knocking down Captain Moorsom's massive brick sheds and chimney. The housing estate on Wagon Works land does however pay homage to the railwaymen of the past in the names of the roads: Moorsom, Rutherford, Scaife, Clayton and McConnell.

It was in the early 1960s that Beeching's Report put many railway lines and stations under threat, but, to everyone's delight, not Bromsgrove. Relief did not last long. Down by the station a green notice suddenly appeared announcing that Bromsgrove had no future – the money-men, again, deciding that Droitwich, Bromsgrove, Redditch, Barnt Green and Alvechurch should all close. But hundreds of Bromsgrove people, incensed to find that their station was at risk, formed the 'Bromsgrove Passenger Action Committee' chaired by Ron Swift,[102] and pushed for a Public Hearing which they won. The service from Bromsgrove Station then hung by a whisker – only minimum commuter service was offered – two trains a day, one

up, one down. It took twenty years before the pressure group achieved its ends; thanks to them, today there are 40 trains calling on weekdays at Bromsgrove Station. During those twenty years the station buildings were demolished, the homely booking hall and the waiting room with a real coal fire on chilly days were lost, and today's passengers shiver in the cold wind even in the two small shelters. There is hope, however, that a new station will soon be built.

As was mentioned earlier, in 1927 the first tranche of council houses was built along New Road and Rigby Lane at Aston Fields, followed by 72 houses on Dragoon Fields, Corbett Close, Chaucer Road and Vicarage Gardens. However the housing that had the greatest effect on the town was the 12 acres

Beside the railway between 1970 and 1996 was the oil depot. This resulted in much traffic from heavy noisy oil tankers, and there were regular objections from people living in the neighbourhood. RS.

Left: Council houses built along a very narrow and rural looking Rigby Lane. Right: The first 100 houses of the Charford Council estate were built in the early 1950s, primarily to house workers for Garringtons. BC.

(4.8 hectares) estate built by Bromsgrove District Council at Charford. The need for this was to provide housing for employees at Garringtons, which had been opened on Newton Farm land. To enable this large estate to be built Little Charford Farmhouse and Charford Farm were demolished in 1950.

The Newton Works was established by the Deritend Stamping Company of Birmingham in 1940 as a Shadow Factory producing stampings for tanks and other military vehicles. The Shadow Factory scheme was instituted and funded by the Government for the construction of new factories to manufacture and assemble tanks,

Left: Garringtons' forging factory and offices built on Newton Farm land near to the railway. Right: From the 1954 map showing Garringtons, the Sewage Works at Sugarbrook, Newton Road running from Fringe Green, and the second group of Council houses off Rigby Lane. OS.

Left: One of Garringtons' early fleet of lorries. Right: Garringtons' John Fowler 4100013 diesel locomotive in use during the late 1940s, one of two. Garringtons built its own railway line connecting to the main line near the Newton signal box, which was worked until the mid 1970s. This locomotive was sold for preservation in 1982. Adrian Booth.

military vehicles, aero engines, aircraft and associated equipment. After the war the factory building was taken over by Messrs John Garrington & Sons Ltd of Darlaston who built a huge steel-framed glass-walled shop in 1948 to produce stampings for the automobile industry, and to make hand tools under the name of Flying Bird. At first skilled workers from the Black Country were bussed in daily, but it became obvious that a permanent solution was needed, and Garringtons' Housing Association was set up in co-operation with Bromsgrove Urban District Council. The first dwellings were 100 houses along Grafton Crescent and Austin Road, overlooking strawberry fields.

At its largest, Garringtons covered 75 acres, and employed 3,100 workers, filling the hole in Bromsgrove's economy left by the running-down of the Wagon Works

Below: Newton farmhouse which was demolished after Garringtons' arrival, a sports and social club built in its place. Note the milk churns on the left of the house. BC.

and its closure in 1964. The Garringtons sports and social club was built on the site of Newton Farmhouse. In the 1970s Garringtons was the biggest producer of engine connecting rods in Europe, with this country's largest forging press. During those years the quiet nights of numberless people were disturbed by the thump, thump of drop-forging at Garringtons, which rattled bedroom windows even as far as the top of Finstall. After some troubled years, and changes of ownership, the sad end of what had become UEF Garringtons came in 2002 when the gates were closed for the last time. The site is now a housing estate known as Breme Park.

Fordhouse Farm has not yet featured much in this book, primarily because its owners did not sell land for building. Fordhouse land was placed neatly between the Stoke Prior/Bromsgrove boundary and the brook running from Pikes Pool down to where it crosses Old Station Road and joins Sugar Brook. The farmhouse was interesting enough to appear in the 1968 *Worcestershire* Pevsner[103], described as 'brick, of three bays with a parapet sweeping up to a pediment in the middle. Below the pediment a lunette window. The other windows have moulded surrounds.'

In the 1830s the farm was part of John Ashmore's estate. The next notable owner was George Dipple, a retired ironmonger and ale and wine seller, who came in 1871 and stayed until 1876 when he went into liquidation. The Ford House itself then became a seminary for young ladies, run firstly by Miss Stokes and then from 1880 until 1887 by Mrs Eliza Milnes whose husband was a schoolmaster. John C.R. Gardner farmed between 1887 and 1891 when he died leaving a widow Elizabeth and three young children – their seven year old son also christened John C.R. In 1899 Henry Wheelock took a step nearer to Bromsgrove – having lived at

An aerial view of Fordhouse Farm, Fordhouse Cottage on the corner by the road. BC.

The Ford House, New Road, Bromsgrove.

BOARDING AND DAY SCHOOL FOR YOUNG LADIES.
PROSPECTUS ON APPLICATION.

An advertisement for the school in the Ford House during the 1880s. Pevsner thought the house was interesting enough to describe it for the Buildings of England series, but by the time the book was published in 1968 the house had already been demolished. BR.

the heart of Aston Fields, then The Lindens, then Slideslow Farm, and now Fordhouse where he settled down to life as a farmer, aided by his carter, Harry Brooks, who lived in Fordhouse Cottage. But being a farmer at Fordhouse lasted just two years, for in August 1901 Henry died, aged 55. Walter, his nephew, then farming at Caspidge, moved over to Fordhouse until 1904. After a few years with Mr T. Weaver running the farm there came Mr John Barnes.

Fordhouse Farm Cottage can be seen on the left of this postcard, and the houses on Stoney Hill's East Road – Elmshurst (Oakley House) to the far right.

225

1940s post card of New Road looking towards Bromsgrove, showing fields behind through the gap between the houses. A horse and cart was at that time still a normal form of transport for goods. Note the line of mature trees on the left.

Many older Bromsgrove men have happily reminisced about Jack Barnes and his farm and his cows, so I suspect he thoroughly enjoyed visits from the rapscallions who lived around the New Road area. Barnes sold his milk direct to customers, driving his pony and trap round the local roads, and filling jugs and cans with milk from his churns. The Barnes's were at the farm from about 1916; small pieces of land were sold off in the 1950s, and the property was finally sold for development in 1960.

So the 1960s were pivotal, when the eastern side of Bromsgrove suddenly changed its character from being genteely Victorian and Edwardian to become modern Twentieth Century. Small scale building became impractical, and changing attitudes and needs caused estates to be built by firms of developers, not by individuals or small local builders. Critically, the green gap between Bromsgrove town and Aston Fields began to close.

In the early 1950s the north of Stoney Hill – North Road – was built, and the east side of East Road also saw the builders, parallel to but lower than Stoney Hill's Terrace; this was on Fordhouse land – named in the 1840s as the Nine Acre Pasture and part of Fordrough Piece. Warwick Avenue, with its offshoots Stonehouse Road and Brueton and Hampton Avenues, was built in the early 1960s.

All these new and projected houses, full of young families, needed services, and in preparation for this the new High Schools were built to replace Bromsgrove's only

North Bromsgrove High School was built in School Drive in 1959; this photo shows it with additions in 1968. The new PFI school built to replace it was opened in autumn 2007.

High School at Parkside. North Bromsgrove High School came first in 1959 and in 1968 South Bromsgrove High School followed, an excellent building by Richard Sheppard, Robson & Partners, set in a most attractive spot on Charford Road on the site of Charford Mill; the truncated mill pool was an important feature of the site. (These schools were both replaced under Private Finance Initiatives [PFI] with new builds in 2007.)

Gardens of the East Road houses soon were backing onto the gardens of smaller houses along the new Fordhouse Road (built during the 1970s), its offshoots given locally known names: Oakalls and Hopgardens Avenues, Slideslow and Wendron Avenues. Bant Mill Road was built on the site of the old Fordhouse Farm, the houses extending over what was once Badgers Garden Piece and Carthorse Meadow.

The 1970s also brought the row of houses on Old Station Road opposite the Bromsgrove Lower School's playing fields; the field, known as Cherry Orchard, was part of the Broom House farm bought by Charles Whitley and given to Bromsgrove School. The school's trustees put this narrow strip up for auction in November 1959, with a vendor's restriction that only 25 houses be built costing no less than £4,250 each; it was sold on to Laings for £26,000. It was regarded then as the most

South Bromsgrove High School was built in 1968 on the site of Charford Lint Mill, its architects Richard Sheppard, Robson & Partners who included part of the old mill pool in their design. The pupils moved into a new PFI building next door in autumn 2007.

Peaceful countryside surrounding Hop Gardens Farm, which was demolished to build the Oakalls housing, and previous to that had the Redditch highway cut across its fields.

New houses were built along Old Station Road towards the end of the 1960s. This photograph from the Bromsgrove Lower School playing field in 1968 also shows some splendid elm trees (felled shortly afterwards), and behind can be seen (l to r) the Stoney Hill flats (replacing The Firs and The Ferns); Oakley House (previously called Elmshurst); the East Worcestershire Waterworks building (now New Road Surgery) and the houses built on Fordhouse Road. J.C. Page.

expensive building land in Bromsgrove. Slightly later Broom Park was built on the Broom House land that Bromsgrove School did not need, becoming Ragley Crescent, Harvington Road and Hanbury Close. The beautiful barn by the side of Broom House was carefully restored and is now a home.

The 1970s saw Harwood Park being built on the fields where the Cricket Club and Football Club had played. There you will now find a Hedges Way, named after Norman Hedges, and Davenport Drive, named for Eric Davenport, both fine cricketers and members of the Club.

The offices of the East Worcestershire Waterworks Company since 1899 had been in what is now Strand House [offices of Thomas Horton LLP], but outgrowing

In 1964 the East Worcestershire Waterworks Company built in New Road 'an ultra-modern office block set back from the road and surrounded by lawns and flowers beds' (from the Company's History, 1973). In 1994 this became the New Road Surgery. Severn Trent Water Co.

these premises under the leadership of Peter Lamont, Engineer Manager, a modern block of offices was built in 1964 on land next to the athletics field in New Road. Not very long after, being up-to-the-minute, a computerised accounting system was put in place. At the same time a new pumping station was built near the railway at Sugar Brook, on land south of the sewage works, with four deep boreholes which provided sufficient water – up to 3 million gallons a day. EWWC was absorbed by Severn Trent plc in 1993, and in 1994 the New Road doctors' practice moved from the Newlands surgery to this larger building which gave them room for expansion.

An indication of what was to come was confirmed in 1980, when for the first time the Ordnance Survey map showed a dotted line where the Eastern by-pass was to run.

The last big expansion of the built-up area came when the Oakalls house and farmland were sold for housing, to cover the green land between Harwood Park and the Redditch highway. As this is written the Oakalls is not quite finished, and we cross our fingers that the open space on Regent's Park Road will be left as amenity land.

The Oakalls, which stood surrounded by fields before being demolished at the turn of the century.

Chapter Nineteen

The March of Flats and the By-Pass

Whilst all the new housing estates were being built in the surrounding area New Road itself was changing quite dramatically. This was a period when large, elderly, often beautiful houses and public buildings were seized by developers and builders in order to put up flats or small estates as in Drayton Court and Sunnymead.

Lost houses, from south to north, include The Highlands (now Marlborough Court), The Lindens/Drayton (now Drayton Court), The Birches (the new buildings owned by the County Council), The Cedars (now Cedar Drive), Sunnymead (now Sunnymead road), Fernleigh (Fernleigh Court), Lupton (Lupton Court), and over the road Highfield House is now Alten Court. Sunningdale Court, on the corner of New Road and the Crescent, is on the Crescent Works land previously owned by Mr W.H. Lewis.

The demolition of the Methodist church provided a site for Raglan Court (named after a house that was behind the Oddfellows Hall, High Street, opposite the present fire station).

Elsewhere was similar: in Marlborough Avenue we lost Blenheim (now Springfield Avenue) and Hillfield (now Rutland Drive), while in College Road Penbryn is now Westminster Court, and Engleberg is Cypress Grange. Tucked away behind Warwick Hall was Brookfields; its drive is now Warwick Hall Gardens, and Warwick Avenue houses cover Brookfields' footprint. Hazeldene and its large garden on Old Station Road are now Kenyon Close.

Rigby Hall thankfully still exists, though its beautiful gardens are lost, while poor old Finstall Park was almost all lost to fire, and is surrounded by houses.

Saddest of all, the Cottage Hospital and the Institute & School of Science & Art, all buildings that Bromsgrove people had much affection for, were razed to the ground for the Nailers Court and Elgar Court flats.

The first mooting of a road to by-pass Bromsgrove was during the 1930s. Bromsgrove High Street, which was on the historic A38 between Plymouth and Derby, had long been cluttered by cars and lorries. Many will remember having to nip through the long line of lorries to cross Bromsgrove High Street, and it was quite impossible to chat to friends because of the noise. At last, to help the situation, in 1981 a road was opened up from St John Street across Crown Close to Stourbridge Road, parallel with the High Street – previously there was only a narrow way across the grassy space, leading to the back lane by the cattle market. This diversion did enable the High Street to become pedestrianised in 1982, but did not cure the congestion.

After some 45 years of talking (and a world war as well), Bromsgrove's eastern relief road did finally happen. In May 1980 the County Council accepted a tender for £2,781,737 from Wrekin Construction to build the road from Fringe Green to Townsend Mill. Gradually details were sorted out, and at last the great machinery arrived to cut a swathe across the small remaining fields. The road was opened with ceremony by Hal Miller, M.P. for Bromsgrove, on 18 May 1981.

With the opening of that new road we finish this story that started with the building of the railway. Those living in Bromsgrove in 1840 would be astonished not only by the wheeled vehicles moving at speed along the roads of today, but also by the hundreds of buildings that have appeared on the fields of orchard and grassland. Of the old farms and houses, only Broom House, Warwick Hall and Rigby Hall are still in some sort of existence; there are a couple of cottages at Aston Fields, and the pair at Fringe Green, that they might just recognise, while Ednall House (The Lion House), The Mount (Wendron) and the URC Chapel are the only familiar buildings close to the town centre.

In the 168 years between 1840 and when this book was written many houses and public buildings have been proudly built then later demolished. The close-knit communities that built up around the railway, the Wagon Works and Garringtons have now almost vanished, and instead of working within or close to the town, a large proportion of we newcomers commute to jobs nearer to Birmingham – or even in a few cases to London. The world is indeed a different place – though judging from tales about past Bromsgrovians appearing in this book, human nature is still much the same.

A jolly crowd of men from the Wagon Works in the early 1960s, not looking as though their jobs were under threat. Works Foreman Jack Howarth is in the front centre wearing a suit. Unknown photographer.

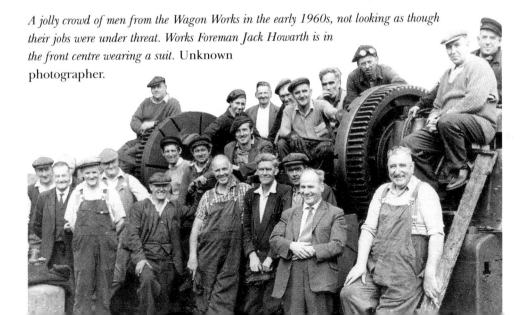

Appendix 1

Chronology

1815	Birmingham Worcester canal opened
1825	Gas arrived in Bromsgrove
1838	Rigby Hall built
1840	Birmingham & Gloucester Railway opened; skew bridge built under railway
1840	Police Station, Station Street
1842	Cricket Club formed
1848	National School opened in Aston Fields
1860	Stoney Hill opened for building
1864	Baptist Chapel, New Road
1865	The New Road opened
1866	The College [Elmshurst] built
1866	The Newlands built
1866	The Hop Pole rebuilt as Tudor House
1867	Reform Act: vote granted to working & middle class householders in towns
1867	Baptist Church built
1867	Conway Road opened
1868	Ecclesiastical parish split into Finstall and Stoke Prior
1869	The Cedars built
1869	St Godwalds [Primrose Hospice] built
1870	South Road, Aston Fields opened
1870s	The Crescent opened
1871	Carlyle & Middlefield Roads opened
1872	Bromsgrove Rugby Club formed
1875	Artisans Dwellings Act: all new houses must have lavatory and a tap
1876	Bromsgrove sewage works opened
1878	Avenue of trees planted in New Road
1878	1st Warwick Hall sale
1879	2nd Warwick Hall sale
1880	Aston Fields Post Office opened

1880	Aston Villas, Stoke Road, built
1880-81	1st Boer War
1881	Finstall Board School
1881	First houses built in Wellington Road
1882	Water piped to Bromsgrove
1883	St Godwald's Church built
1884	Reform Act: all male householders enfranchised
1884	Wesleyan Methodist Chapel, New Road
1885	Bromsgrove Rovers formed
1886	Water piped to Aston Fields
1886	Clothing factory opened, Carlyle Road
1886	Thomas White Almshouses
1888	Local Govt. Act created County Councils responsible for roads, drains, etc.
1888	Baptist Chapel schools, Ednall Lane
1889	First houses built in Clive Road
1889-02	Second Boer War
1889	Improvements to Railway Station
1890	Aston Fields Workman's Club
1890	Police Station, The Crescent
1891	Primitive Methodist Chapel [Salvation Army], Carlyle Road
1891	Cottage Hospital, New Road
1891	Third Warwick Hall Sale
1892	Gas in Aston Fields and New Road
1893	The Institute, New Road
1893	First houses built in Marlborough Ave.
1894	Finstall skew bridge built over railway
1894	College Road opened
1895	Bromsgrove Rural and Urban District Councils formed
1895	School of Science & Art, New Road
1897	Aston Fields sewage works opened
1897	St Godwald's parish hall
1898	Bromsgrove Guild established
1900	Rigby Hall Sale
1910	Broom House Estate sale
1914-18	World War I : Aston Fields war memorial lists 38 casualties
1915	Sale of The College [Elmshurst]
1917	The Cedars Sale
1918	Last Warwick Hall Sale

1924	Electricity brought to Bromsgrove
1927	First Council Houses, Aston Fields
1930	Dragoon Fields houses, Aston Fields
1930	Free County Library opened in Institute
1933	Aston Fields transferred to Bromsgrove Urban District
1939-45	World War II
1945	Garringtons at Newton Farm
1950s	Houses built on North Road, Stoney Hill
1960s	Warwick Avenue and its off-shoots
1961	N. Bromsgrove High School, School Drive
1964	Wagon Works closed
1968	S. Bromsgrove High School, Charford Road
1970s	Fordhouse Road and its off-shoots, Bant Mill Road, Broom Park, Harwood Park
1981	Market Street opened up as a relief road
1981	Eastern by-pass opened
1982	Pedestrianisation of the High Street
2002	UES Garringtons closed

Appendix 2

The Sewage System of Bromsgrove in 1876 – Mr Taylor's report

Report by Mr W.R. Taylor, Engineer to Bromsgrove Local Board as told to *The Messenger* on the opening of the new Bromsgrove Sewage Farm:

'The sewage is conveyed from the town by a pipe sewer a distance of half a mile, and at the out-fall it is conveyed into subsiding and filtering beds. From the out-fall it flows into a shallow tank, having an area of 200 feet. In this tank the heavy matter precipitates itself. The sewage then passes into a second deep subsiding tank, having a superficial area of 900 feet. At the end of this tank is a wall containing a number of pipes, through which the sewage passes, and when the tanks are full these pipes are below the water which prevents the floating matter passing beyond the wall. From this latter tank the sewage passes into a third subsiding tank 1600 feet in area, in which further subsidences takes place, and beyond this again is constructed a filter bed having an area of 600 feet, in which is fixed a perforated floor, covered with engine ashes. The sewage passes upward through the ashes and over a weir 30 feet wide, by which a very gentle motion is given to the water. Thence the now partially purified effluent passes into a fifth subsiding tank, having an area of 1500 feet, and beyond this is another filter, constructed somewhat similar to the last but being a "downward" filter, and having the larger area of 1200 feet.

The process thus far is complete, and the sewage passes thence into an open carrier which conveys it on to the land filter, which finally deodorises it and deprives it of the ammonia. Each of the subsiding tanks is built in brick work and paved with bricks, and made to slope to the centre, where is a funnel-shaped pit secured at the bottom with a large brass valve. Into these pits when the tanks are being cleansed the mud is swept passing through the valve into a mud drain leading to a well on the outside of the tanks eighteen feet deep. In the mud pit is fixed a strong chain pump, manufactured by J.T. James and Sons, Tivoli Works, Cheltenham. By this means the whole of the sludge is raised to the surface, and when dry it will be sold for manure.

The whole of the tanks, filters, mud wells, and pumps are in duplicate, so that one set can be cleansed while the other is at work. After undergoing this process of subsidence and filtration the sewage, as before remarked, passes on to the land filters. These are fifty in number, and are each about fifty feet square, and are formed by levelling the land of each bed. An embankment about fifteen inches high separates every bed. This land, which comprises about three acres, has been closely drained, three miles of pipes having been used for the purpose in the trenches. Over the pipes are placed layers of stone and gravel, previous to any earth being thrown in. The sewage passes from the open carrier through sluices into pipes, which carry the sewage on to each bed; every one being fitted with a valve at the inlet so as to regulate the supply. The land filters are divided into seven ranges of six and seven beds each, the soil being thrown into furrows. The sewage passes on the first range through the valves, and after a sufficient quantity has been allowed to run on to the first range, the water is diverted by closing the valves and opening the valves of the next range, and so on, until the whole seven ranges have been treated. In the meantime the sewage first turned on to the land has been gradually filtering through the prepared ground into the drains which empty their contents into a main drain which carries the filtered water, clear and bright, into the Spadesbourne. As giving an idea of the comparative purity of the water at its final outflow, it may be mentioned that several of the party drank of it, including the medical gentleman present, who declared it to be a fairly potable water, having only a slightly earthy impregnation, from passing through new soil. Arrangements are made for dealing with the storm water.'

The Bromsgrove Messenger, 2 December 1876

Appendix 3

Election Squibs

Mention has been made of John Cotton as architect and collector of local history. He was also known in Bromsgrove for his verses – nearly all rather bad ones – many of which were published (by himself). As a Liberal he took great delight in writing what he called Election Squibs against the Tories when they held election meetings. Here is a shortened version of 'A Review of the Bromsgrove Tories, East Worcestershire Parliamentary Election, 1880', from his *Election Squibs, Ballads & Broadsides*, 1898, included because he describes with an acid tongue a number of the men who have been mentioned in this book. Mr Burrows was innkeeper of the Golden Cross; the leader of the Tories at the time was Benjamin Disraeli, Lord Beaconsfield.

> Attend, ye Bromsgrove Liberals, and hear the story told,
> Of how the Tories came to town, and who were of the fold; [...]
> A grand palaver was proposed at the Golden Cross Hotel,
> And one who knows the 'burrows' there informed me what befel; [...]
>
> They praised the lapsing Government, and made a final stand
> On Beacon's (foul and fallow) field, that blot upon our land;
> The farmers cheered, but why they should I do not clearly see;
> What good they gain from Tory rule is a mystery to me.
>
> And now if you would like to know I'll tell you who were there –
> First Doctor Prosser heads the list, because he took the chair,
> A worthy man gone wrong, no doubt mislead by Tory notions;
> A few 'blue' pills would set him right, or his own drastic potions;
> Who knows, he yet may live to choose the road that leads to good,
> And join that convert to the truth, his brother, Dr. Wood.
>
> And there was Scott, the lawyer, with our estimable Vicar,
> Short-sighted both, or they would see through Ben the Tory tricker.
> Beside his partner Horton stood, suave-mannered 'midst the din,
> The marshal of the Tory ranks, and local whipper-in; [...]

And William Jefferies was there, whose shop stands at the corner,
He dotes on Beaconsfield and is of Liberal rule a scorner; [...]
From Smallwood's magisterial mouth mild approbation flowed –
He might have chose the better side who owns half the New Road.
And there was Sammy Saywell, who the sentiments encored,
And Green the grocer, who has learned to love a mortar board,
And Corbett too, the chemist, who laughs loud as a hyena,
Or some of Wagner's music from an operatic scena; [...]

His neighbour, Bown was there as well, the Tory ironmonger –
He sought for 'sops' to satisfy his impolitic hunger.
Will Frances, too, who changed his tools, the cleaver for the plough [...]
Bill Bolding next claims notice, with his gold chains, seals and all,
By 'Gin and Jingo' prompt to stand, and eke as like to fall;
And Walter Fawke, who tried to talk at a recent Lib'ral meeting,
When he received what he deserved – a most unwelcome greeting;
A soldier fond of flogging is a rarity at least,
Yet Fawke, although an army man, would lash one like a beast. [...]

And Fitch and Wilson, they were there, or Wilson, if not Fitch,
Since Wilson has a glass eye, why, an eye-glass would suit Fitch;
The visitors to their hotel would then know which was which.
A covey, too, of Partridges were fluttering round the table,
To pick up crumbs of comfort, but I don't think they were able;
Among them stood Will Holyoake, a man of merit rare,
I must confess my great surprise at seeing Holyoake there. [...]
Concerning others in the room I have no need to speak,
Their numbers, like their arguments, were limited and weak. [...]
So fight the fight and keep the faith, and ere the month be done,
Our men shall be at Westminster – the Liberal victory won.

However, an anonymous member of the Tory party retaliated equally libellously:

Come ye Bromsgrove Tories, and I will tell to thee,
The Liberal Committee, whose names ye cannot see! [...]

And next comes Jemmy Laughton, the *Liberal (?)* Nailmaster,
Up to his ears in politics, and bricks, and lath and plaster;
He builds a splendid mansion, for which poor nailers pay –

No 'Board of Arbitration' can there stand in his way.
Friend of the Working Men! He *works* his friends right well,
As many a sad sad story the last great strike can tell.

John Humphreys, the younger, the juvenile Radical swell,
Lieutenant of the Fire Brigade, who thinks he talks so well [...]
Next come the sons of Bunkum, the illustrious John and Will,
Two *bouncing*, restless mortals, who never can be still.
John often writes bad poetry, devoid of rhyme or reason,
And Will, I fear, he writes prose, and oft times prosy treason. [...]
In argument they get *worsted*, although they both are *Cotton* –
They argue from false premises, so all their views are rotten.

Great Wood next claims our notice, though a weak vessel he,
A 'Dr' called by courtesy – not a real 'M.D.' [...]

But what is all this shouting, and whence this clam'rous din?
The 'Party' seems elated when Millington comes in;
Of Bromsgrove School Head Master, though Bromsgrove he ignores
And gets his miscellaneous goods from the Civil Service Stores.
Alas! The times how changed they are, since Dr Collis good
Supplied the poor of Worcester Street with all the broken food
From the Grammar School's *Tory* table, which now, oh! Herbert fie!
Goes to feed the Chucky pigs in your own *Liberal sty!*

And Charlie Field, the draper – the young *Green Field* I mean,
With his fine open countenance in the front rank may be seen.
A nice young man is Charlie, whom all the girls adore,
Who sometimes struggles with his Pa upon the parlour floor.

Here's Barber Hill and Chattering Phil, and likewise Freddy Yates,
Altho' these all have noisy tongues they have but empty pates; [...]
And Tommy *White*, the indigo man, is of the party too [...]

So let us give three hearty cheers for England's Church and Queen
For a shadier lot than the Bromsgrove Rads I trow was never seen.

Notes to the Text

To avoid a rash of numerals on every page, information from *The Bromsgrove Messenger* and the Cotton Collection in Birmingham Central Library Archives have not normally been quoted as sources.

Chapter One

1   Having read Dr Fletcher's reminiscences (see Note 7 below), George Bradfield, who was born in Gas Square in 1858, wrote 'More Bromsgrove Reminiscences' for *The Bromsgrove Messenger* in June, July and August 1930. Bradfield, a nicely opinionated man, worked at the railway from 1870 before becoming an accountant, married a Gloucestershire woman, and lived in Cheltenham. It seems that he kept up with Bromsgrove matters through *The Messenger* which he received by post. The full text of both Fletcher's and Bradfield's reminiscences is conveniently found in John Cotton's scrapbook No.85 in the Cotton Collection, Birmingham Central Library.

2   A chapel of ease was an additional church, known as a chapelry, built for the convenience of parishioners living a distance from the parish church, in this case St Michael's at Stoke Prior. Chapelries sometimes later developed into parishes in their own right, as did Finstall.

3   In 1822 Ann Brettell, daughter of Richard Brettell and a woman of fortune, married Rev. Thomas Housman, later Vicar of Catshill. They were A.E. Housman's grandparents.

4   *An Autobiography*, Vol I, Herbert Spencer, Chapter XII, 1904.

5   Quotations from *The Victorian Railway Worker*, Trevor May, Shire Productions, 2003.

Chapter Two

6   This and other chapters on the railway are indebted to R.C. Swift and Neville Billington of Bromsgrove, and to publications listed in the bibliography.

7   Dr Fletcher's 'Reminiscences and Recollections', *The Bromsgrove Messenger* Dec.1929/Jan 1930. Dr George Fletcher was born in Bromsgrove in 1848, son of the respected Dr Fletcher Snr, living in the High Street. George Fletcher left Bromsgrove in 1872, aged 24, but in 1929/30 wrote for *The Messenger* his memories of the town.

8   *The Victorian Railway Worker*, Trevor May, Shire Books, 2003. The guard quoted worked for the Taff Vale Railway. Strong lobbying in Parliament by the railway companies meant that safety of railwaymen was not regulated by government with any strength until after World War I. By the 1890s the Railway Passengers' Assurance Company was advertising its insurance policies against railway accidents – their capital being £1,000,000, compensation paid £3,350,000; local agents in 1894 were Mr W. Gimson of Marlborough Avenue (recently retired Stationmaster) and Messrs Smith & Russon, High Street, Bromsgrove.

9   At the time of writing the District Council run Museum is closed for financial reasons.

Chapter Three

10   Dr Fletcher, Op.cit.

11   *Noake's Guide to Worcestershire*, J. Noake, 1868, Longman & Co.

12   Dr Fletcher, Op.cit.

13   *The Ancient Half-timbered Houses of England*, M. Habershon, John Weale, 1836.

14   *The Old Houses of Bromsgrove and Neighbourhood*, a very detailed paper read to the members of the Bromsgrove Institute by William A. Cotton, 1881, Charles Evans, Printer, High Street, Bromsgrove.

15   George Bradfield 'More Bromsgrove Reminiscences', *The Bromsgrove Messenger*, July 1930.

16   *Roads, Archaeology and Architecture* by Richard K Morriss, 2005, Tempus Publishing.

Chapter Four

17   Dr Fletcher, Op.cit.

18   *Glory Gone, the story of nailing in Bromsgrove*, Bill Kings and Margaret Cooper, 1989.

Chapter Five

19   Rev. Alan White's article in *The Bromsgrove Rousler*, No.19, December 2004 titled 'Bromsgrove College 1857-1915' gives a fuller history of the College and the Saywell family.

20   *Seventy Years at Bromsgrove School*, Jeremy Bourne, 1993.

21   Dr Fletcher, Op.cit.

22   *The Story of Bromsgrove*, William G. Leadbetter, 1946.

23   *Seventy Years at Bromsgrove School*, Op.cit.

24   'The Tale of a Bromsgrove Butcher', Robert Nokes and Thelma Lammas, *The Bromsgrove Rousler*, No.18, 2003.

Chapter Six

25   See Chapter Four for description of Bromsgrove, Stoke Prior and District Building Society.

26   From *St Godwald's: A Parish and its People*, Janet Grierson, 1984.

27   *The Bromsgrove Messenger*, 6 April 1861.

28   A letter to *The Bromsgrove Messenger*, from John Cotton's scrapbook; unfortunately undated and no signature.

29   Unseen deeds offered on Ebay, described as: "25 October 1805, Agreement for purchase at Finstall, Henry Ellins + Richard Williams".

30   Linen Sheets and a Bed of Nails, by John Parker, *The Bromsgrove Rousler* Vol XXI December 2006 – history of the Ellins family. Also Neville Billington generously shared his research on George Ellins, to be published in his work on William Creuze.

31   Both 1843 Sale catalogues from the collection of R.B. Brotherton.

32   Unseen deeds offered on Ebay, described as "20 March 1844, Surrender + admittance James Holyoak". A second sale of land in 3 Lots had been held on 8 August 1843, Lot 1, just over an acre on corner of Finstall Road and St Godwald's Road; Lot 2 was First, Second and Third Chapel Close immediately to the west of the railway bordering on St Godwald's Road; Lot 3 an unidentified meadow of 2 acres at Finstall surrounded by land owned by George Taylor, Richard Brettell and William Robeson.

33   Catalogue list of C & CA Edge, Birmingham Archives, Ms 1703.

34   In 1865 the rule that any pauper, no matter how long his or her residence in the parish, must be sent back to his or her parish of birth, was substituted by the Union Chargeability Act for a requirement of a twelve months residence as qualification for help from the local rates through the Guardians of the Poor.

Chapter Seven

35   Worcester Record Office, 899:1066 10809/1/i/1.

36   Sale of Rigby Hall estate, 1900 by Messrs Grimley & Son.

37   The list included: 'the corner of New Road to the Station; close to the railway bridge; 100
      yards (91m) up East Road four boulders; at Fringe Green one 5'6"x4'x2'4'
      (1.6m.x1.21m.x0.7m.); corner of Perry Hall (now Housman Hall); several round the Weighing
      Machine' – etc., etc. The boulders, they said, were Felspar Porphyrite, Compact Felstone,
      Felsphathic Ash or Felstone.

38   'A natural manure found in great abundance on some sea-coasts, esp. on the islands about
      Peru, consisting of the excrement of sea-fowl', *Shorter O.E.D.*, 1965. To be sold by surveyors and
      estate agents, massive profits could be made from importing guano, i.e. Mr William Gibbs
      whose fertiliser fortune paid for the wonderful Gothic Revival Tyntesfield House near Bristol.

39   Walter Fawke was not in the Charge of the Light Brigade, as is usually reported, according to
      records of the events in the Crimea.

40   *The Story of Bromsgrove Cottage Hospital*, J.T. Banks and C.E. Heydon, 1948.

41   Giuseppe Garibaldi was an Italian soldier who by conquering Sicily and Naples in a spectacular
      campaign in 1860, with an army of 1,000 Redshirts, played a central role in the unification of
      Italy. The imagination of people in this country was caught by this swashbuckling renegade,
      hence his name being used for many pubs and roadways.
      The railway men at Aston Fields were inspired to hold a meeting on 23 June 1860 'for the
      purpose of taking into consideration the propriety of expressing sympathy for the oppressed
      Sicilians by raising a subscription to aid Garibaldi and his patriotic army, in liberating them
      from Neapolitan despotism.' Denouncing the King of Naples for his oppression, the meeting
      'expressed a hope that the victorious Garibaldi would, ere long, break asunder the chain by
      which [the Sicilians] were enthralled'. A collection was taken and £1.5s.0d. was sent to the
      Editor of *The Birmingham Daily Post*.

Chapter Eight

42   Copyhold tenure went back to mediaeval times. Tenancy usually lasted for three generations of
      a family after which it could be renewed. The tenancy could be sublet, and even mortgaged or
      sold. Tenants were subject to payments, i.e. on a tenant's death a heriot was paid, and when a
      new tenant took over copyhold property he had to pay an entry fine. By the 1840s voluntary
      enfranchisement (turning copyhold into freehold) was allowed and in 1860 the Dean and
      Chapter of Worcester (the owners of Stoke Prior Manor) were, by Act of Parliament, allowed to
      sell their land through the Ecclesiastical Commissioners.

43   Janet Grierson in *St Godwald's: A Parish and its People*, 1984, says that these Sanders were related to
      Benjamin Sanders, Clerk to the Local Board and owner of the button factory in Willow Road.

44   Privately owned Deeds and Conveyances.

45   for Cotton's drawings see page 133, *John Cotton The Life of a Midlands Architect*, Jennie
      McGregor-Smith, Coombe Cottage Books, 2002.

46   for the full nailing story read *Glory Gone: the story of nailing in Bromsgrove*, Op.cit.

47   Ibid.

48   See *John Cotton The Life of a Midlands Architect*, Op.cit.

49   The name of the Oakalls is thought to relate to crops of flax (Linum usitatisimum) that were
      grown in the area, oakum being the fibres produced by passing a comb through the flax to
      clean and straighten them. In the 1770s 180 people in Bromsgrove were working in linen
      production, 140 employed in processing woollen goods and linsey, and as many as 960 were
      nailers. The wool trade lasted until 1840.

Chapter Nine

50   *Ancient Court Leet and Court Baron of the Manor of Bromsgrove*, R.B. Brotherton, 1985. This entry in the book, which is normally enormously helpful, is certainly incorrect in the first five lines as it mistakenly refers to W.F. Hobrough's life; thus could possibly refer to Hobrough in the remaining five lines.

51   See 'Two Notable Bromsgrovians' by Dr Douglas Bridgewater, *The Bromsgrove Rousler*, No.19, 2004.

52   The full story is told in full detail in *The Bromsgrove Messenger*, 28 June 1889 and 11 January 1890.

53   Most of the background on Mr Hobrough comes from *The Worcester and Birmingham Canal*, Revd. Alan White, 2005.

Chapter Ten

54   see *Bromsgrove Baptist Church Tercentenary*, 1966.

55   Charles Barber and his son Henry worked on the Baptist Chapel, neither of whom appear to have specialised in ecclesiastical decoration, for they advertised themselves in Hereford Kelly's Directories as plumbers, painters and glaziers.

56   David Banner describes his time in the old school during the 1940s in *Piano Row, Childhood Memories 1940s-1950s in Aston Fields and Finstall*, 1996.

57   see *Stained Glass Windows of Bromsgrove and Redditch, Worcestershire*, Roy Albutt, 2002.

58   A fuller history of the Wesleyan Methodists is found in *New Road Methodist Church, Bromsgrove: 100 years 1883-1983*, David Roberts 1983; also see *Stained Glass Windows of Bromsgrove and Redditch, Worcestershire*, Roy Albutt, 2002.

59   Henry Taylor of this firm lived at Leahyrst on Greenhill, Blackwell, and was responsible for the building of the Methodist Chapel next door to Leahyrst in 1882, see *Victorian Greenhill: Burcot to Blackwell*, Jennie McGregor-Smith, 2000.

60   The window can be seen from Stratford Road, and is also illustrated on page 101 of *The Bromsgrove Guild*, edited by Quintin Watt, 1999.

Chapter Eleven

61   *Terms for the Supply of Gas*, June 1835, Cotton Collection, Birmingham Central Library.

62   Midden: A dunghill, manure heap, refuse heap. (OED) A dumb-well was sunk into a porous stratum, to carry off surface water or drainage.

63   Times sometimes don't change: *The Bromsgrove Advertiser/Messenger* in September 2007 was reporting sewage smells in Stoke Heath.

64   *The East Worcestershire Water Act* of 1877. 'The limits of this Act for the supply of water shall be and include the borough of Droitwich and the towns of Bromsgrove, Redditch and the following parishes, townships and extra-parochial places that is to say Droitwich, Saint Andrew, Saint Nicholas, Saint Peter, Dodderhill, Dodderhill-in-Liberties, Hadzor, Hanbury, Upton Warren, Marlborough, Grafton Manor, Crutch, Ombersley, Elm Bridge, Elmley-Lovett, Chaddesley Corbett, Doverdale, Hampton-Lovett, Westwood Park, Bromsgrove, Catshill, Upper Catshill, Lower Catshill, Barnsley Hall, Lickey End, Rock End, Burcott, Vigo, Stoke Prior, Stoke Works, Stoke Wychbold, Rashwood, Tardebigge, Broad Green, Hewell, Holy Oakes Farm, Red Lane, Redditch, Crabbs Cross and Headless Cross and Ipsley in the County of Worcestershire'.

65   The mound over the now disused reservoir, shown clearly on maps, can still be seen from the road. It was covered with grass, and entered through iron flaps from above. Descent was down

an iron ladder. In recent years it has been used for storage. During the 1st World War in case of attack an amazing and complex alarm system was installed involving wires to detonators; it was never needed. There is a second reservoir, behind the 1924 Engine House, with a tunnel to the first.

66   For more on Burcot Waterworks see *Victorian Greenhill, Burcot to Blackwell*, Jennie McGregor-Smith, 2000.

67   This tank was superseded by a massive concrete water tower, though the unused brick one is still standing.

68   Initially the Company was in no position to supply all the districts included in the Act, and the following schedule gives an indication of the gradual spread of the Company's mains over the years.
     1882 Bromsgrove and Lickey; 1883 Redditch; 1884 Crabbs Cross, Barnt Green, Finstall and Bromsgrove Workhouse; 1886 Aston Fields and Webheath; 1892 Bentley and Droitwich Borough (supplied in bulk); 1894 Rednal (bulk) and Tardebigge; 1895 Stoke Prior; 1901 Alcester (bulk); 1902 Catshill and Bournheath; 1903 Studley (bulk); 1904 Astwood Bank (bulk); 1923 Alvechurch (bulk) and Beoley (bulk); 1924 Feckenham (bulk); 1928 Beoley and Alvechurch became part of the Company's statutory area.

69   East Worcestershire Water Company was absorbed by Severn Trent Water Limited on 1st September 1993.

70   *Bromsgrove Light Railways Order*, authorising the construction of Light Railways in the County of Worcester between Bromsgrove Town and Bromsgrove Railway Station Lickey End and Rock Hill, under the *Light Railways Act* of 1896.

Chapter Twelve

71   *Working Men's Social Clubs and Educational Institutes*, H. Solly, 1867, London

72   The tradition of pigeon racing continued well into the 1950s, the railway being a centre for sending birds off to be released for flights. David Banner in *Piano Row*, 1996, p.56, remembers at least fifteen pigeon lofts in the village.

73   *An Allotment Act* of 1887 directed local authorities to provide allotment gardens if there was a demand, which in 1907 was improved to insist that parish, urban district and borough councils made allotment provision. In recent times, after many years of decline, demand for home-grown vegetables has risen again – though, as happened at Aston Fields, there was great pressure to use allotments for building.

74   While speaking of vegetables, it was in 1894 that the Sewage Farm advertised for sale cauliflowers and carrots grown on their well-manured premises.

75   A relic of the Bromsgrove Loyal Association formed on Queen Victoria's accession when there were worries about the threat from France; a 'Loyal' dinner was held each year until 1908, attended by many of the great and good (gentlemen only) of the town.

76   *Bromsgrove Cricket Club – The First Hundred Years*, David W. Goodyear, 1992

77   Nasser al-Din Shah Qajar ruled from 1848 until his assassination in 1896. He was the first Persian monarch to encourage contact with Europe, wishing to benefit his country by introducing Western industry, politics and morals. To carry out improvements – and to enhance his own life-style – he wished to raise funds from granting foreign companies exclusive concessions over natural resources and Persian import and export commodities in exchange for cash payments; his country became a source of cheap raw materials and a market for industrial goods from Western countries. His three visits to England included investigation

into technological achievements that could be of use to his country, hence visits to factories in Birmingham. Having discovered photography he became an enthusiast, and also introduced into his country a modern postal system, train transport, a banking system and newspaper publishing. Earlier in his reign he attempted unsuccessfully to recover part of eastern Persia, Herat, that was under British control; Herat is today part of Afghanistan. He was forced to sign the Declaration of Paris granting Afghanistan supremacy over these former Persian territories.

78   Hewell Grange Estate Accounts 1897, Cardiff Record Office.

Chapter Thirteen

79   For information about the village shops up until the 1920s I am indebted not only to Palmer's Directories but also to Janet Grierson's *St Godwald's A Parish and its People*, which was written in 1984, twenty-four years ago, when memories pre-1920 were still available.

80   *Piano Row, Childhood Memories*, Op.cit.

81   *The Buildings of England Worcestershire*, Alan Brooks and Nikolaus Pevsner, 2007.

82   The journalist from *The Messenger* was clearly enjoying writing this piece, which appeared two days after the fire, 28 January 1888.

83   From *Christian Science Monitor*, Boston, USA, 24 June 1920, in Cotton Collection.

84   Dr Fletcher, Op.cit.

85   from *Christian Science Monitor*, Op.cit.

86   *St Godwald's A Parish and its People*, Op.cit.

87   A term used slightly incorrectly here because the roadway skews before and after the bridge, rather than the bridge itself; however it is always locally described as 'the skew bridge', probably because the original bridge was skew.

88   The official English Heritage Listing describes the archway thus: 'A heavy entablature with flat pediment with central raised part with shield, wide modillioned cornice, all supported on square piers with verniculated rustication and moulded capitals, between which is inset a semi-circular arch with rusticated voussoirs, keystone and moulded impost on rusticated pilasters.'

89   Dr Fletcher, Op.cit.

Chapter Fourteen

90   The following week others besides Mr White vocally objected at a parish meeting, crying 'No Popery' and 'No Jesuits wanted in Bromsgrove'.

91   Friendly societies were mutual aid organisations designed to help working-class people protect themselves against hardship. They were a solution to the problems people and their families knew they would face should they fall ill or die leaving their children or spouse with limited resources. The friendly societies movement grew as new towns and industries developed in the nineteenth century. Workers regarded friendly societies as a means of reducing their chances of ending their days in the Workhouse and each month contributed a small sum which provided payouts to those that needed them, the remainder being saved or invested.

92   The full history of the hospital to 1948 is *The Story of Bromsgrove Cottage Hospital* by J.T. Banks and C.E. Heydon, 1948, from which much of the detail has been drawn.

93   *John Cotton The Life of a Midlands Architect*, Op.cit., page 165.

94   A description of the splendid ceremony can be found on p.181 *John Cotton The Life of a Midlands Architect*, Op.cit. or in full in the *Bromsgrove Messenger's* special supplement of 4 August 1891.

95   Hospital Saturdays were part of a national movement founded in Birmingham in 1869. After 1948 and the creation of the National Health Service there was no need for such collections. The first collection in Bromsgrove in 1893 brought in £55; the highest sum realised was £3,661 in 1945.

96   *The Weekly Mail*, 26 February 1988.

Chapter Sixteen

97   It seems that R.G. Routh was responsible for the change of name from Kiteley's or Kiteless to Kyteless.

98   'More Bromsgrove Reminiscences', Op.cit.

99   The story of the Guild is told in detail in *The Bromsgrove Guild*, edited by Quintin Watt (1999).

Chapter Seventeen

100   Parker & Winder (later Parker, Winder & Achurch Ltd) were a Birmingham firm dealing with sanitary ware and domestic fittings, regarded as a 'quality' firm.

101   *Braziers Builders of Bromsgrove*, Alan Richards, 1996, p.149.

Chapter Eighteen

102   Others in the first days of the fight were Mike Abbott, Bill Jordan and Sam and Laurie Hardy.

103   *The Buildings of England Worcestershire*, Nikolaus Pevsner, 1968.

Bibliography

Much detail and background has been drawn from the following:

Bromsgrove, Redditch and Droitwich Weekly Messenger, 1860 onwards (on film in Bromsgrove Library)

Brotherton Collection: for house sale prospectuses and photographs (Private collection in Bromsgrove)

Census Returns, 1821-1901 (1841-1901 available on internet at http://www.national archives.gov.uk/census/)

Cotton Collection (Birmingham Central Library Archives)

Ordnance Survey maps (Worcestershire Record Office)

Palmer's and Kelly's Directories for Bromsgrove (Bromsgrove Library)

Worcestershire Record Office collections, especially for planning applications and deeds

Publications

Albutt, Roy, *Stained Glass Windows of Bromsgrove and Redditch Worcestershire*, R.Allbutt, Pershore, 2002

Banks, J.T. & C.E. Heydon, *The Story of Bromsgrove Cottage Hospital 1876-1948*, Messenger Co., 1948

Banner, David J., *Piano Row: Childhood Memories 1940s-1950s in Aston Fields & Finstall*, privately published, 1996

Billington, N., *Flint and Steel: The story of the birth of the Institution of Mechanical Engineers*, privately published, 1996

Bourne, Jeremy, *Seventy Years at Bromsgrove School*, Bromsgrove School, 1993

Bromsgrove Society Journals, *The Rousler*, 1986-2007

Brooks, Alan and Nikolaus Pevsner, *Worcestershire: The Buildings of England*, Yale University Press, 2007

Brotherton, R.B., *Ancient Court Leet and Court Baron of the Manor of Bromsgrove*, Bromsgrove Court Leet, 1985

Casserley, H.C., *The Lickey Incline*, Oakwood Press, 1976

Cooper, Margaret, *A Bromsgrove Carpenter's Tale*, Halfshire Books, 2001

Cotton, William A., *The Old Houses of Bromsgrove and Neighbourhood*, Charles Evans, 1881

Cotton, William A., *Bromsgrove Church: Its History and Antiquities*, Messenger Publishing Co., 1881

Crawford, Alan (Ed), *By Hammer and Hand: The Arts & Crafts Movement in Birmingham*, Birmingham Museums & Art Gallery, 1984

Duncan, David, *Life and Letters of Herbert Spencer*, Methuen, 1908

Foster, John (Ed), *Bygone Bromsgrove*, Bromsgrove Society, 1981

Grierson, Janet, *St Godwald's: A Parish and its People*, St Godwald's PCC, 1984

Hunt, Philip J., *The Black Horse and the Boar: The Story of Lloyds Bank in Bromsgrove*, privately published, 1988

Icely, H.E.M., *Bromsgrove School through Four Centuries*, Blackwell, 1953

Kings, Bill and Margaret Cooper, *Glory Gone: The story of nailing in Bromsgrove*, Halfshire Books, 1989

Leadbetter, William G, *The Story of Bromsgrove*, 1946

May, Trevor, *The Victorian Railway Worker*, Shire Publications, 2003

McGregor-Smith, Jennie, *John Cotton: The Life of a Midlands Architect 1844-1934*, Coombe Cottage Books, 2001

McGregor-Smith, Jennie, *Victorian Greenhill: Burcot to Blackwell*, Coombe Cottage Books, 2000

Morriss, Richard K., *Roads: Archaeology and Architecture*, Tempus, 2004

Noake's Guide to Worcestershire, Longman & Co., 1868

Nokes, B.C.G., *Finstall Parish Handbook*, privately published, 1958

Pevsner, Nikolaus, *The Buildings of England: Worcestershire*, Penguin, 1968 (for 2nd revised enlarged edition see Brooks above)

Richards, Alan, *Braziers Builders of Bromsgrove 1850-1990*, B&M Bromsgrove, 1996

Richards, Alan and Sheila, *Bromsgrove Now and Then*, Bromsgrove Society, 1988

Richards, Alan and Sheila, *The Bygone Bromsgrove Picture Book*, Bromsgrove Society, 1983

Spencer, Herbert, *An Autobiography*, Williams and Norgate, 1904

Watt, Quintin (Ed), *The Bromsgrove Guild: An illustrated history*, Bromsgrove Society, 1999

White, Revd. Alan, *The Worcester and Birmingham Canal: Chronicles of the Cut*, Brewin Books, 2005

Young, Michael H., *The Postal History of Bromsgrove & District*, privately published, 1994

Unpublished

John Lacey, *History of Bromsgrove*, 1776

Swift, R.C., MS relating to Bromsgrove Wagon Works

East Worcestershire Water Company, MS history, at Worcester Record Office, BA 11517.

Work in progress: The life and death of William Creuze, Warwick Sheffield and Neville Billington

To be published: expanded version of Billington, N., *Flint and Steel: The story of the birth of the Institution of Mechanical Engineer*

Index

Names of those appearing only once in the book have not been included.